A Faithful Sea

Islam and the West: Influences, Interactions, Intersections
Series Editor, Adnan A. Husain

This interdisciplinary series critically examines the historical
and constructed relationships between "Islam" and the "West". It
re-imagines them not as simply oppositional but as terms
through which to explore connected histories and experiences
from medieval to contemporary contexts.

Forthcoming titles

The Enlightenment Qur'an: Translation, Islam and Modernity,
by Ziad Elmarsafy

A Faithful Sea

The Religious Cultures of the Mediterranean, 1200–1700

Edited by
ADNAN A. HUSAIN
and
K. E. FLEMING

ONEWORLD
OXFORD

A FAITHFUL SEA

A Oneworld Book
Published by Oneworld Publications 2007
Copyright © Adnan A. Husain and K. E. Fleming 2007

ISBN-13:978–1–85168–496–0

Typeset by Jayvee, Trivandrum, India
Cover design by Transmission
Printed and bound by The Maple-Vail Book Manufacturing Group,
Braintree, MA, USA

Oneworld Publications
185 Banbury Road
Oxford OX2 7AR
England
www.oneworld-publications.com

Learn more about Oneworld. Join our mailing list to
find out about our latest titles and special offers at:

www.oneworld-publications.com

Readers (1993), *Les Relations entre les pays d'Islam et le monde latin du milieu du Xème siècle au milieu du XIIIème siècle* (2000), and *Saracens: Islam in the Medieval European Imagination* (2002). He is editor of *Medieval Christian Perceptions of Islam: A Collection of Essays* (1996 [New York], 2000 [London]), *Espaces d'échanges en Méditerranée antique et médiévale* (2006), and *Culture arabe et culture européenne: l'inconnu au turban dans l'album de famille* (2006). He is currently working on the history of Franciscan and Dominican missions in North Africa.

Steven M. Wasserstrom is the Moe and Izetta Tonkon Professor of Judaic Studies and the Humanities at Reed College in Portland, Oregon, where he has taught since 1987. His book, *Between Muslim and Jew: The Problem of Symbiosis under Early Islam* (1995) was given the Award for Excellence in Historical Studies from the American Academy of Religion. His most recent book, *"The Fullness of Time": Poems by Gershom Scholem*, which he selected, edited, and introduced, is the first edition of the poetry of the great kabbala scholar, Gershom Scholem.

INTRODUCTION

APPROACHING ISLAM AND THE RELIGIOUS CULTURES OF THE MEDIEVAL AND EARLY MODERN MEDITERRANEAN

Adnan A. Husain

In his famous posthumously published work entitled *Mahomet et Charlemagne*, Henri Pirenne declared that the unity of the Mediterranean that had existed in the ancient world under the Roman Empire had not been destroyed by the Germanic invasions, but rather had been broken later by the rise and expansion of Islam and the Arab conquests. Isolated from Byzantium in the western Mediterranean, the Carolingians created a fundamentally different, recognizably medieval social and political order. As he famously concluded:

> It is therefore strictly correct to say that without Mohammed Charlemagne would have been inconceivable. In the 7th century the ancient Roman Empire had actually become an Empire of the East; the Empire of Charles was an Empire of the West. In reality, each of the two Empires ignored the other. And in conformity with the direction followed by history, the centre of this Empire was in the North, to which the new centre of gravity of Europe had shifted. With the Frankish kingdom – but it was the Austrasian-Germanic Frankish kingdom – the Middle Ages had their beginning. After the period during which the Mediterranean unity subsisted – from the 5th to the 8th century – the rupture of that unity had displaced the axis of the world.[1]

While Pirenne's thesis, propounded here, was not new – in fact it had been articulated as early as 1922 in a series of publications that were

debated in their time and had even been conceived earlier during
World War I in 1916 while he was imprisoned in a German concen-
tration camp – it created scholarly controversy as the last historical
"testament" of the "foremost interpreter of the social and economic
development of Medieval Europe," as Peter Brown put it.[2]
Understanding it as a last testament helps explain its continuing after-
life in historiography on the origins of Europe and its relationship to
the Mediterranean, despite the fact that at many points the thesis has
been declared fundamentally refuted and the controversy over the
"Pirenne thesis" long resolved. It, nevertheless, persists in exerting
itself on the imagination and influencing subsequent historiography.[3]
This is partly because, by discussing the unity of the Mediterranean
and its rupture as fundamental to the origins of Europe, Pirenne constituted the Mediterranean as a problem for the trajectories of postclassical history. As he boldly asserted, "Islam had shattered the
Mediterranean unity which the Germanic invasions had left intact.
This was the most essential event of European history which had
occurred since the Punic Wars. It was the end of the classic tradition.
It was the beginning of the Middle Ages, and it happened at the very
moment when Europe was on the way to becoming Byzantinized."[4]
While controversy over the thesis and its conclusions has often taken
the form of a parochial, if spirited, battle among historians of
medieval Europe (and more narrowly among scholars of the early
medieval economy), nevertheless Pirenne helped inaugurate an idea
of the Mediterranean (and its unity) as a historical space that not only
has inspired the most ambitious works of "total history" but also has
proved an enduring conceptual frame for a recently flourishing field
of scholarship in a diverse array of disciplines and periods.

At issue in subsequent scholarship have been both the definition of
the Mediterranean as a region and the conceptions of it as a historical
space. Fernand Braudel in his monumental *The Mediterranean and
the Mediterranean World during the Age of Philip II* warned, "But what
of the Mediterranean of the historian? ... Woe betide the historian
who thinks that this preliminary interrogation is unnecessary, that the
Mediterranean as an entity needs no definition because it has long
been clearly defined, is instantly recognizable and can be described by
dividing general history along the lines of its geographical contours."[5]
While renowned for his dazzling and even poetically descriptive geographical and environmental account of the Mediterranean, Braudel
argued against those who would limit the scope of the Mediterranean

world to the sea and the societies on its immediate shores and coastlines. Instead he articulated a rather capacious definition of this "Mediterranean of the historian" distinguished from purely geographical terms, "from the northern limit of the olive tree to the northern limit of the palm tree," as he put it. Rather, for a Mediterranean of historical dimensions, in contrast to the short anomalous period of the Roman Empire, which he characterized as a closed system narrowly locking the Mediterranean apart from its surrounding regions, "the rule has been that Mediterranean civilization spreads far beyond its shores in great waves that are balanced by continual returns ... The circulation of man and of goods, both material and intangible, formed concentric rings round the Mediterranean. We should imagine a hundred frontiers, not one, some political, some economic, and some cultural."[6] This wider, flexible definition of the Mediterranean zone, thus, expands to embrace the contiguous cultures and political formations arrayed, even if extending distantly, about its shores.

The interplay between this more capacious understanding of the Mediterranean zone and the environmental and geographic definition of its boundaries dramatizes helpfully the, at times, contradictory tensions not only within Braudel's magisterial study but generally dividing the approach scholarship has taken, even recently, to conceptualizing the space of the Mediterranean in historical terms. Braudel himself self-consciously identified the methodological problem as partly a classic conflict of "structure and conjuncture" and more accurately, as he preferred to re-frame the question, a matter of distinguishing and assessing the importance of differing scales of historical temporalities. He, of course, famously expressed the priority of *la longue durée*.[7] The scholarly approaches resolve typically into two orientations. The first understands the Mediterranean fundamentally as the space in which interactions, encounters, contacts, and conflicts of various kinds have taken place among different peoples and their cultures and across the geographic, linguistic, ethnic, religious, and political boundaries that distinguish them. Consequently, the Mediterranean is characterized most critically by the distinctive diversity and heterogeneity of its space of encounter. When conceived in this fashion, its history most properly addresses itself to investigating these interconnections or interrelations and the multifarious forms they can take: trading networks and commercial exchange, military conquest and crusader discourses, travel and pilgrimage, intellectual transmission and cross-cultural flows, and the like. Such history concentrates on the mobile means and dynamic processes of interaction and so its stories are of the circulations of goods, peoples, knowledge and texts, of mutations, translations, and conversions.

The second major, albeit much rarer, approach to the Mediterranean has been to emphasize, and even insist upon, its profound unity. Most typically, conceiving of a Mediterranean unity, beyond the uniquely – if not essentially political – unity of the Roman Empire that could declare it *mare nostrum*, has meant engaging it broadly as a shared geographical space, ecology, environment, and, consequently, social economy. Despite the dizzying surface diversity, deeper structures and patterns account for the compatible rhythms of life built upon this shared environment. This approach, perhaps most closely associated with Braudel, argues that the shape of the Mediterranean when comprehensively studied reveals certain forms of society that are organically connected to a shared ecology and structural history.

Recently, Peregrine Horden and Nicholas Purcell in their celebrated *The Corrupting Sea: A Study of Mediterranean History* characterized the first mode of scholarship as "interactionist" and complained, perhaps echoing Braudel, that despite the proliferation of scholarship invoking the Mediterranean context much of it has been insufficiently grounded in the particularities of the geography and space of the Mediterranean. They contend that this body of work still depends on or takes meaningful shape within other historical categories, like "Europe" and "the Middle East" or "Christendom" and "Islam," and reflects uncritically and narrowly histories *in* rather than *of* the Mediterranean. Consequently, they argue that the field of Mediterranean history has yet to "achieve full articulacy and recognition."[8] However, they also reflect critically on the more purely "ecologizing" approach associated with Braudel, despite an obvious sympathy for the ambitions and results of his "total history." Recognizing an environmental and structural determinism of *la longue durée*, Horden and Purcell argue that Braudel underappreciated, despite his explicit avowals of their importance, the significance of mentalities, attitudes, beliefs, and symbols.[9] We can amplify their concerns by adding that, above all, religion, religious change and conflict, and the discourses that sustain and articulate the various kinds of identities receive often uncritically perfunctory attention. To these two basic orientations, the "interactionist" and the "ecologizing," they optimistic romance with medieval Judeo-Islamic ideals of "perfection" in sobering and poignant contrast to both Goitein's own belief in the turn for the worse in religious relations at the end of the thirteenth century and contemporary discourses and anxieties about the status of the Mediterranean as a contested space of cooperation and confrontation. Sobering as well, however, is what Wasserstrom calls, and regards with ambivalence, Goitein's "old-fashioned, straightforward, head-held-high Orientalism," evident no less in his descriptions of the training and experiences that he believed to have assisted his understanding of the Geniza people and their medieval world than in the conclusions and assumptions that occasionally inform his less nuanced and sophisticated portrait of the broader Islamic culture and Muslim society. In the preface to volume two, Goitein comfortably credited with "throwing light into many a dark corner of the Geniza world" his ethnographic and linguistic studies of Yemeni Jews, "those most Jewish and most Arab of all Jews," who came to Israel as refugees. He also attributed his understanding of "communal texts" and "traditional Oriental education" to his experiences as a colonial officer, more precisely the senior education officer in the British Mandatory Government of Palestine charged with administering the schools of "Oriental Jews."[32] Although a colleague's preface to the posthumously published fifth volume asserts that Goitein read widely in sociology and anthropology, a serious engagement with the modern debates and methods of these disciplines does not make itself strongly evident.[33] Instead, Goitein's epilogue to this volume provides a résumé of his philological training in Oriental studies and his nineteenth- and early twentieth-century historiographical exemplars, like Jacob Burkhardt and Michael Rostovtzeff. Simultaneously, it confessed an apparent disinterest in the historiographical legacy of the Pirenne thesis (this despite his own assertion of the unity of the Mediterranean in the period of his study, 950–1250), revealed a late and perfunctory encounter with the project and approach of Braudel, and generally confirmed a relatively limited engagement with many contemporary and relevant developments in historiography on medieval Europe.[34] The intense focus of decades working with the unedited and often fragmentary Judeo-Arabic manuscript documents of the Geniza and the "sociographic" description of their world (a world hardly known in any real depth before, it must be emphasized), along with the endemic conditions of Orientalist scholarship, worked to limit the interpretive scope and analytical range of his monumental five-volume study.

Some have explained the relative neglect of *A Mediterranean Society* outside the small circles of medieval Jewish and Islamic studies partly in these terms, describing it as not properly Mediterranean in conception and scope.[35] But this might not be so surprising in some way, since this can generally be said of these disciplines as a whole, a testimony to the isolation of historiographical traditions relevant to premodern Mediterranean history. Horden and Purcell, while acknowledging the value of Goitein's study, surmise that the limited reception of the work among other scholars is simply "because it lacks a geographical setting other than the one incidentally provided by its documents."[36] This would seem to acknowledge partly that because it concentrated on the Arabic–Islamicate cultural spheres of the Mediterranean the study has not been as readily engaged by scholars in temporally and geographically neighboring fields, more an illustration of the problem than an explanation of it. While it might qualify more easily as history *in* the Mediterranean than *of*, in Horden and Purcell's terms, Goitein's portrait of the diasporic Jewish community reveals a network across the Mediterranean (and beyond) of contacts, communications, and commerce, of the movement of people, their texts, and ideas. Although *A Mediterranean Society* focuses on the vantage the Jews of the Islamic world provided from a major node in this network, that of Cairo's community and its Geniza repository, the numerous examples of migration to Byzantium and of refugees from the western and northern shores fleeing oppressive conditions and suffering expulsions demonstrate, in just one respect, the interconnections of the diaspora across a number of different political, linguistic, and ethnic boundaries throughout the Mediterranean world. Moreover, although he did not elaborate much on the designation of this society as "Mediterranean," Goitein was conscious of his purpose in doing so, writing at the very outset, "This study is called *A Mediterranean Society* because the people described in it are to a certain extent representative of their class in the Mediterranean world in general, and its Arabic section in particular."[37] He argued that the Jews of the Geniza records revealed exemplary aspects of the economic, social, and religious life of bourgeois traders of the High Middle Ages which were typical of and relevant to the wider Mediterranean, and, indeed, gave insight to humanity at large about its past.[38]

One of the major questions posed not only by Goitein's study, but also for so many treatments of the Mediterranean, has been the critical role of trade (and especially long-distance trade) in conceptualizing the region's unity historically. In the context of elaborating a history of religious culture the question of trade and its role for cross-cultural and inter-religious relationships assumes major importance; many of the presumptions that have patterned such study will require a critical assessment. For Pirenne, as for many others, the presence of long-distance trade and shipping lines connecting different parts of the Mediterranean into an economic unity had been decisive. Consequently, much of the criticism of his thesis has been on the basis of the economic analysis of the presence, or lack, of long-distance trade. His vision of trade almost seemed to require some sort of religious or cultural compatibility to enable it, since he posited so radical a rupture with the advent of the Arabs and Islam that he could only imagine trade happening through Jewish intermediaries. More commonly, these notions about trade have assumed a liberal tenor, familiar to us today, that posits it as an integrating force for the peoples of different religions and cultures. Such studies highlight the way economic relations and commercial exchange could create secular relations among diverse peoples despite conflicting identities. What has often been assumed but unproven are the consequences of such commercial relations for other forms of interchange across the boundaries of religion, whether intellectual, cultural, or even religious exchange and engagement itself. Goitein argued that the ease of commercial cooperation between Jews and Muslims in the Islamic world allowed members of these communities to overcome some aspects of narrow and bigoted notions of one's own religious superiority. Typically, economic partnerships and relations were facilitated socially by connections among coreligionists, which he documented thoroughly through the rich sources of the Geniza. However, the numerous examples of Muslim business partners, he argued, allowed them to recognize and experience that there were good, worthy, and responsible human beings in the other communities one traded and worked with through mercantile or commercial contact.[39] However, what is needed is to demonstrate other sorts of possible interchange at a deeper cultural level and elaborate the consequences of the history of commercial and trading interactions on the shaping of religious culture. Such a project requires integrating other kinds of sources that allow us to perceive these movements and connections, for to investigate the unity of the Mediterranean only through trade as the mode of encounter is to radically narrow the circulations across confessional boundaries and the changing forms of hybridity, syncretism, and heterogeneity that rendered religious identity and tradition (as well as other forms of culture and social practice connected to it) a living part of Mediterranean historical experience.

Several of the contributions to this volume engage with aspects of this and other related questions. Molly Greene's historical portrait of the Greek diaspora in the Mediterranean details the conditions that allowed for what she has identified as the "sixteenth-century moment," consciously compared to the increase in wealth and social influence during the same period experienced by the Jewish diaspora of the Mediterranean. As in Fleming's study of Jewish perceptions of confessional identity in an unfolding salvation history and the parallel motifs in Greek responses to the conquest of Constantinople, conditions of the sixteenth century had far-reaching consequences on the Mediterranean economy and religious culture. Greene notes that competition for Greek skilled labor in industries of war and trade reflected the conflicts between expanding Ottoman power and Italian, especially Venetian, attempts to preserve their Mediterranean empire. Ottoman favoritism toward Greek commerce and labor, which aided the recruitment of Greeks, was connected to the confessional system in which Ottomans favored the Orthodox Church of its many Greek subjects. Yet, as Greene shows, this competition for Greek diasporic commercial and maritime skills allowed Greeks to cooperate and trade lucratively across the boundaries between Ottomans and Venetians. Ultimately, these conditions meant the community in Venice was able to establish a confraternity and thus free themselves from the control of Latin clergy, choose their own priests, and assert their own Orthodox liturgy, practice, and identity.

Such struggles by a small foreign merchant community to preserve and assert religious identity and autonomy recall the earlier episode of the Latin Christian community of Tunis discussed by John Tolan in this volume. An interesting picture of the dynamics of medieval religious identity in the context of Muslim–Christian interaction emerges in his examination of this community as perceived through the concerned eyes of the friars charged with their pastoral care. Unlike what is often presumed, the friars' chief concerns were, in this context, generally unrelated to the impractical dreams of missionary conversion of Muslims. While Ramon Marti, Dominican polemicist and Orientalist, later in the thirteenth century would reportedly be in Tunis to preach before the Sultan, his predecessors in North Africa principally engaged the difficulties of ministering the sacraments in a foreign context and guarding – at times unsuccessfully – the orthodox Catholic identity of the merchants, and others in the Latin community, like mercenaries and captives. The source for these social and religious challenges takes the form of answers based on interpreting canon law given to the questions posed by the Dominican Prior and Franciscan Minister in Tunis seeking to adjudicate practical concerns arising from social experience in a non-Christian society. Tolan demonstrates that this legal source was not divorced from social reality as a theoretical exercise in prescription but a practical attempt to apply canon law to exceptional circumstances and give guidance on diverse matters of ritual and spiritual sanction. The articles deal, for example, with the reversion of converts to Islam who had Muslim wives and children; merchants and mercenaries illicitly supplying the Saracens with provisions, articles, and manpower for war; and rich Christians pawning Christian subordinates to Muslims when in debt. New challenges inspired new solutions in the traditions of canon law, as Tolan demonstrates, leading to the drawing of new boundaries between mortal sin and excommunication which relied on analogies to the canon law for heresy. In this way, the interpretation of canon law by Raymond de Penyafort, the author of the epistolary tract, resembles the techniques of the two "religions of the law" in the form of Jewish rabbinical *responsa* or fatwa literature of Muslim jurists on similar questions of inter-religious encounter in social life. In fact, a broader comparative perspective might reveal even greater convergences in approach, if not actual decisions, among the scholastic traditions of Muslims, Christians, and Jews in the theaters of contact created by trade and broadly in the heterogeneous societies of the Mediterranean. In the Venice observed by Greene, as well, the challenge was the autonomy of the religious community, in some sense the effort to acquire a sort of *dhimmi* status held from Muslim authorities, bolstered by the growing power of the community. Greene's account suggests perhaps that such conditions of competition from an attentive social and political regime compelled Venice almost to Ottomanize their religious and trading policies, at the metropole and in the threatened colonies. In this case, economic strength developed through a flourishing interconfessional "Mediterranean" trade allowed the reassertion of a public Orthodox religious identity within Catholic Venice.

Margaret Pappano examines the other side of the coin, as it were, namely the complex and textured consequences of expanding Ottoman power and Italian political and commercial relations with it on the religious culture of Florence and its literary expression in the hagiography and confraternal drama dedicated to the cult of a local saint, Rosana, whose complex story seems to have begun with a character in an earlier medieval popular romance. Pappano investigates the truly Mediterranean career of the pan-vernacular romance, dramatizing inter-religious social and political relations between a converting Saracen prince and his virginal Catholic beloved, *Fleur et Blancheflor*, as the precursor to the Florentine devotional literature on the story of Rosana in the fifteenth century. She provides a subtle reading of the transformations among the various versions of setting, plot, and character. The interpretation of the play and hagiography contrasts them as reflections of the complex Florentine relationship with the Ottomans, built on privileged commercial trade, cultural exchange, and rumored political alliance. Interestingly, anxieties about this lucrative trade and such close economic and political relations produce a new narrative and imagery of the virginal heroine's body, miraculously preserved from the carnal and mercantile lusts of the Saracen Sultan of Babylon to mark the integrity of Christian identity despite the polluting threats of trade in the inter-religious environment of the Mediterranean. Consequently, the literary texts of Rosana's cult support both the discourses of crusade and revenge in an imperial vision of the Mediterranean with Rome as center of Christendom and a counter-discourse of accommodation with the Turk through the fantasy of the forcible Christianization of Muslim lands through the virgin Rosana's conversion of an Anatolian sovereign and ally against the Muslim Mamluk Sultan of Egypt. This motif recalls perhaps a greater and equally enduring Mediterranean fiction or dream of Latin Christendom since at least the thirteenth century which made its way through the hagiographies of Francis to those of St. Louis and beyond – the conversion of the Muslim sovereign to Christianity and the success thereby of universal mission. The early Ottoman sultans, it seems, represented the latest candidates. Such redeployed motifs converge with the responses of other religious communities to the spectacular emergence of Ottoman power; as Fleming notes in her comparisons between and within Orthodox and Jewish perceptions, even as they differ in some ways in their imagined scenarios or interpretations of history, these discourses nevertheless also connected these communities and their traditions to a broader religious culture of the early modern Mediterranean. Likewise, such attentive investigations, in this case through popular devotional literature, reveal the dynamics of religious culture, shaped through interconfessional encounter, and the counter-currents that emerge within prevailing discourses in the historical negotiation of religious identity.

Anne McClanan builds upon the picture of the importance of trade and commerce as a feature of inter-religious contact by examining the traffic in special commodities which also conditioned developments in Tuscan devotional culture, in this case in its visual expression. Her close analysis of Bulgarini's fourteenth-century *Assumption of the Virgin* in Siena affirms the cultural impact of Byzantine religious artifacts and their circulation in the artistic and spiritual economy of the wealthy Italian centers of Mediterranean trade through purchase and plunder. Like several other essays included here, this work emphasizes the importance of political or economic rivalry for shaping religious culture through the reception of broader Mediterranean forces into local contexts. In this case, the pan-Mediterranean plague and the weakening of Byzantium and its broader economic and cultural consequences, ever since the devastations of the Fourth Crusade and Latin interregnum, helped create a reformulation of motifs of devotional art. The essay examines this specifically through the novel depiction of the Apostle Thomas holding the belt of the Virgin, advertising the recently acquired relic and engaging Byzantine visual ideas.

While connections between the Eastern and Western churches might persist through ecclesiastical memories and occasionally expressed ideals and plans for reunification (particularly in the geostrategic discourses of crusade proposals envisioning a restored unity under Papal hegemony), a shared late antique history was being exploited by a contemporary imbalance in wealth and power to enrich the urban landscape of sacral art, giving cultural ground for the concerns about and antipathetic attitudes toward the Latin Church later expressed in the Orthodox historical sources discussed by Fleming. This investigation, mentioned earlier, treats Jewish perceptions of history in the contrast between a refugee Sephardic rabbi of Salonika and a Romaniote rabbi of Crete in their treatments of the Ottomans and their increasing dominance in the Mediterranean. Fleming, illustrating the diversity within these religious traditions and communities, suggests the difference to be one between an Ottoman Jew and a Jew under Latin domination imagining a salvation through an eschatologically significant Ottoman sultan as Messiah. The correspondences and juxtapositions with Orthodox writers, also attempting to divine the significance of Ottoman conquest in a theologized history designed to sustain their communal and religious identity in an inter-religious world and specifically against Latin Christianity, complete a picture of shared interconfessional discourses about a shared history *in* the Mediterranean which shaped religious identity, reno-vated religious traditions, and patterned religious cultures *of* the Mediterranean.

Finally, Wasserstrom's attention to Goitein's conviction that the thirteenth century marked a significant change in the experience of the Jewish minority in both the *dar al-Islam* and Christendom raises the important historiographical theme, engaged in a number of this collection's contributions, of the experience of minorities in the medieval and early modern religious cultures of the Mediterranean, whether as trading diasporas, conquered but uncon-verted enclaves, or expelled refugees. Often these communities serve the role of litmus test for the changing conditions of religious identity and its social and political consequences in a heterogeneous Mediterranean. They inform the larger judgments, whether compar-ative or not, in historiographical discussions about premodern "tolerance" and "intolerance." Increasingly, the treatment of religious minorities has provided the counter-narrative to that of "renais-sance," the symbolic marker of an incipient enlightened or humanis-tic modernity distinct from a preceding medieval barbarism. Whether it is the expulsions of 1492 or the pogroms of later medieval Europe, violence against minorities as a measure of intolerance has forcefully rewritten the historiographies of progress. Even the medieval "renaissance of the twelfth century" has earned a dark counter-history. R. I. Moore's *The Formation of a Persecuting Society*, for example, drew on and inspired a burgeoning literature and debate by arguing that the genealogies of modern intolerance and violence against religious minorities, heretics, and other social marginals had discursive precursors in the proto-national state formation of twelfth- and thirteenth-century medieval kingdoms. Subsequent studies of the social role of violence in the multiconfessional environ-ment of medieval Spain have challenged the sort of analysis that con-nected medieval persecution with modern genocides. The notion of crucial or decisive "turning points" remains a compellingly seductive trope of historiography on questions of both the unity of the Mediterranean, *à la Pirenne*, and the roots of intolerance, and some-times both together.[40]

In this volume, Karla Mallette captures the tragic ironies of the history of the Muslims of Lucera from their rebellious origins in the hybrid island culture of Sicily to their forcible removal by Emperor Frederick II over the next several decades to an isolated enclave of Islamic urban society above the plain of Apulia, where they served as dependent, loyal imperial troops until their eventual massacre and collective destruction in 1300 by Charles II of Anjou. By examining literary references, particularly in commentaries to the *Divine Comedy*'s elliptical allusions to political figures and internecine wars on the Italian peninsula in the thirteenth century, Mallette weaves literature and history to navigate between and challenge popular narratives of Christian–Muslim relations from Huntington's "Clash of Civilizations" to Richard Bulliet's characterization of an "Islamo-Christian Civilization."[41] Instead, she posits the thirteenth-century history of Muslim Lucera as an example of an intermediate and conflicted period of engagement between hostile identities and shared political cultures, which she characterizes as a "culture of memorialization." Contrary conditions frame the situation: the increasing economic and military strength of Latin Christian powers evident in the Iberian peninsula after Las Navas de Tolosa in 1212, the Norman conquest of Sicily in the twelfth century, the persistence of a Latin Christian enclave in the Levant through persistent if intermittent crusader invasions until 1291, the Latin control in the thirteenth century of numerous eastern Mediterranean islands and coastal zones, and diasporic communities of Italian and Catalan merchants controlling commercial shipping, one of which John Tolan's study discusses. Nevertheless, as Mallette observes, the prestige of Arabo-Islamic culture persisted and complemented the imperial ideals of cosmopolitan display to make symbolically valuable subjected Arabs and Muslims beyond their simple economic and demographic utility. This resonates with the different meanings and, thereby, different politics of confessional identity in the imperial Ottoman Mediterranean, whose consequences are discussed in several other essays in this volume, notably those of Ariel Salzmann, Katherine Fleming, and Molly Greene.

Ariel Salzmann's in particular perceives a shifting role of the Inquisition. She suggests that the medieval institutions developed to combat heresy and monitor the orthodoxy of the forcibly converted had transformed later into a forerunner of an immigration service, policing those who transgressed religious boundaries through conversion, a metaphor of and analogue to actual crossings of borders. In some sense, Salzmann suggests that by the seventeenth century geographical place had come to be mapped more thoroughly by confessional and political identities. Or at least that the conditions for Christians to exist in Muslim Egypt were carefully circumscribed by status and function in the microcosm of expatriate communities, perhaps the outcomes of the anxious work of the friars Tolan studies in a much earlier period. Salzmann amplifies the engaging story of the Maltese priest by imaginatively invoking the contexts in which he moved and the elusive motives of his trangressions through space and across confessional boundaries. The islands of Mallette's definition of "insularity" – exposure to hybridity – have become charged with the pressures of uniforming political and confessional identity, turning Cyprus into less a cosmopolitan node of the movement and circulation of heterogeneous groups through the Mediterranean and more an early offshore Ellis Island, a buffer for reincorporation. This could be called a secularization of the Inquisition that is tantamount to the elaboration of a political and cultural division of the Mediterranean from a space of hybrid encounter and inter-religious contact into the plane of Europe versus Turk as a forerunner to a world of nation-states.

Mallette provocatively suggests in fact that only when their symbolic value to their political sovereigns declined could the extermination of these Muslim minorities be imagined. But perhaps this implies less that the Muslims of Sicily ultimately preserved their religious identity longer as a consequence of their displacement from a hybrid Mediterranean island to the "continent" as the Emperor's Muslims (a status that reminds us of the "King's Jews") than that Muslim religious identity took a different form under these circumstances. For that matter, so too did Christian self-consciousness in response to Muslim presence in rural, inland Apulia as an alien, almost mercenary, force for a line of imperial dynasts tainted by charges of heresy in their political rivalry with the popes and their allies.

Taken together, though, the studies in this volume suggest that there is a *longue durée* of intercultural relations. Each of the great Mediterranean historians attempted to define the unity of their Mediterranean while asserting its demise. Goitein, for example, reflected this through the lens of the treatment of minorities and the breakdown of the tolerance he elaborated on by studying the experience of the Jewish trading diaspora of the Mediterranean. Pirenne imagined the region's unity ending through the early Islamic conquests. Braudel asserted its persistence as late as the sixteenth century. Even Horden and Purcell have identified our present age as a post-Mediterranean one, after its unity has waned slowly in the modern world. Similary, decisive turning points have been identified for the genealogies of violence and genocide against a persistent feature of the Mediterranean world, its diversity and heterogenity. The benefit of such a collection that crosses the boundaries of the premodern, from medieval to early modern, may come in recognizing and illustrating the way the *longue durée* of cross-cultural contact and inter-confessional encounter has had irreducible consequences for the religious cultures of the Mediterranean. By recognizing the region as both a space of encounter and a cultural unity forged in different ways at different times with eventful consequences, an alternative sort of history of the Mediterranean is possible, the urgency of which is clear. If we are to re-imagine the Mediterranean, we must engage the features that perhaps most uniquely define it – its religious cultures and their shared histories – while inventing the historiographical narratives to represent these histories. Doing this will not mean erasing the differences of traditions or identities or submerging conflicts. Rather one must recognize that this common history was forged out of conflicting universalisms that have nevertheless patterned and shaped one another in particular social and theological encounter. The fact of a complex history with many periods and trajectories of conflict does not occlude a complementary history also of periods of cooperation, interchange, connection, synthesis, and symbiosis. These episodes and counter-discourses can and need to be incorporated into a re-imagined history. Nevertheless, history has always been in some measure about conflict, whether on the basis of class, politics, or gender. But that nonetheless has not precluded the possibility of community.

NOTES

1. Henri Pirenne, *Mohammed and Charlemagne*, trans. Bernard Miall (London: Allen & Unwin, 1954), p. 234.
2. Most notably Henri Pirenne, "Mahomet et Charlemagne," *Revue Belge de Philologie et l'Histoire*, 1, 1922, pp. 77–86; see Anna Riising, "The Fate of Henri Pirenne's Theses on the Consequences of the Islamic Expansion," *Classica et Medievalia*, 13, 1952, pp. 87–130, which provides a thorough bibliography and review of the scholarship; Peter Brown, "*Mohammed and Charlemagne* by Henri

Pirenne," in *Society and the Holy in Late Antiquity* (Berkeley: University of California Press, 1982), p. 63.

3. As recently as the 1980s, new archeological evidence inspired a revisiting of the thesis and subsequent scholarly interest and debate. See Richard Hodges and David Whitehouse, *Mohammed, Charlemagne and the Origins of Europe* (Ithaca, N.Y.: Cornell University Press, 1983).

4. Pirenne, *Mohammed and Charlemagne*, p. 164.

5. Fernand Braudel, *The Mediterranean and the Mediterranean World in the Age of Philip II*, trans. Sian Reynolds (New York: Harper & Row, 1972), pp. 17–18.

6. Braudel, *The Mediterranean*, pp. 168–170.

7. Braudel, *The Mediterranean*, pp. 16, 17–22. It would, of course, unduly burden this discussion to do more than refer to his briefest remark on this subject in the prefaces to the first and second editions of the work. I must omit reference, here, to the rich historiographical debate his work has occasioned for generations of historians.

8. Peregrine Horden and Nicholas Purcell, *The Corrupting Sea: A Study of Mediterranean History* (London: Blackwell, 2000), pp. 10–15; Braudel, *The Mediterranean*, p. 18.

9. Horden and Purcell, *The Corrupting Sea*, p. 42.

10. Ibid., p. 45; see also the interesting remarks in W. V. Harris, "The Mediterranean and Ancient History," in *Rethinking the Mediterranean*, ed. W. V. Harris (Oxford: Oxford University Press, 2005), pp. 1–40, esp. pp. 20–29.

11. See, for example, most recently David Abulafia, "Mediterraneans," in *Rethinking the Mediterranean*, pp. 64–93; also, for "the Mediterranean" as a concept applicable to other regions and particularly Southeast Asia, see the collection, *From the Mediterranean to the China Sea: Miscellaneous Notes*, ed. C. Guillot, D. Lombard, and R. Ptak (Wiesbaden: Harrassowitz, 1998); for the greater Indian Ocean region, see Sanjay Subrahmanyam, *Explorations in Connected History: From Tagus to the Ganges* (Oxford: Oxford University Press, 2005).

12. A novel and illuminating example of the dynamics of this process between Jews and Muslims, Judaism and Islam, from late antiquity to the thirteenth century is Steven M. Wasserstrom, *Between Muslim and Jew: The Problem of Symbiosis under Early Islam* (Princeton, N.J.: Princeton University Press, 1995).

13. It hardly bears referencing the influence here of Samuel Huntington, *The Clash of Civilizations and the Remaking of World Order* (New York: Simon & Schuster, 1996) and the whole trajectory of the last several decades of published work of Bernard Lewis, but most relevantly *What Went Wrong? Western Impact and Middle East Response* (New York: Oxford University Press, 2002). Marshall Hodgson's reflective use and definition of the concept of "civilization" avoids in his inveterately comparative and world-historical framing a narrow sense of the isolation often implied in the term "civilization," and his articulation of the "Islamicate" as the cultural style divorced from religious belief is highly salutory. Nevertheless, the focus of his account is not self-consciously "the Mediterranean," and medieval interchange after the "formative" period of Islam receives substantially less attention. See his *The Venture of Islam*, vol. 1, *The Classical Age of Islam*, and vol. 2, *The Expansion of Islam in the Middle Periods* (Chicago: University of Chicago Press, 1974).

14. They treat these topics in chapter 10, "Territories of Grace," of Horden and Purcell, *The Corrupting Sea*, pp. 403–460.

15. As one approving review, perhaps cued by this vocabulary, described, "Like cyberspace, the sea is inherently unpoliceable. It is a huge gaping hole in the centre – a no man's land into which restless and shifty characters can disappear and pop up again. This is the image of the 'corrupting sea' – the hole that gives the doughnut its shape and character." James Fentress and Elizabeth Fentress, "The Hole in the Doughnut," *Past and Present*, 173, 2001, p. 204. Horden and Purcell engage with the problem of metaphor, again both seriously and amusingly, as well as a number of other issues in "Four Years of Corruption: A Response to Critics," in *Rethinking the Mediterranean*, pp. 348–376.

16. Pirenne, *Mahomet et Charlemagne*, pp. 89–108.

17. "For more than three thousand years after civilizations first emerged, the contacts among them were, with some exceptions, either nonexistent or limited or intermittent and intense." See Huntington, *The Clash of Civilizations*, pp. 21, 48; note Edward Said's response on this point in "The Clash of Definitions: On Samuel Huntington," in *Reflections on Exile and Other Essays* (Cambridge, Mass.: Harvard University Press, 2000), pp. 569–592.

18. The notable early exception is Daniel C. Dennett, Jr., "Pirenne and Muhammad," *Speculum*, 23, 1948, pp. 165–190.

19. See for example, John V. Tolan, *Saracens: Islam in the Medieval European Imagination* (New York: Columbia University Press, 2002); and, of course, Edward Said, *Orientalism* (New York: Pantheon, 1979).

20. Brown, "*Mohammed and Charlemagne* by Henri Pirenne," p. 68.

21. Ibid., p. 69; Horden and Purcell, *The Corrupting Sea*, p. 24; and see Kate Fleet's trenchant criticism of the book on these grounds, "The Mediterranean," *Journal of Early Modern History*, 6, 2002, pp. 62–73.

22. Braudel, *The Mediterranean*, p. 13.

23. Ibid., p. 14.

24. Ibid., *The Mediterranean*, pp. 171–188. Note, p. 180, "But the conflict between the Mediterranean and the neighbouring desert is something more than plough versus flock. It is the clash between two economies, civilizations, societies, and arts of living." Also, p. 187, "For 'Islam is the desert', declares the essayist Essad Bey, it is the emptiness, the ascetic rigour, the inherent mysticism, the devotion to the implacable sun, unifying principle on which myths are founded, and the thousand consequences of this human vacuum."

25. Ibid., pp. 171–188, 757–775.

26. Ibid., pp. 758–760.

27. See M. E. Yapp, "Europe in the Turkish Mirror," *Past and Present*, 137, 1992, pp. 134–155, which argues that the use of the term "Europe" in writings involved in marking a difference with the Ottomans, meant to distinguish Europe from the Mediterranean, in contrast to use of "Christendom."

28. Hodgson, *The Venture of Islam*, vol. 1, pp. 110–132.

29. Garth Fowden, *Empire to Commonwealth: the Consequences of Monotheism in Late Antiquity* (Princeton, N.J.: Princeton University Press, 1994), esp. pp. 80–168.

30. Dmitri Gutas, *Greek Thought, Arabic Culture: The Graeco-Arabic Translation Movement in Baghdad and Early 'Abbasid Society* (London: Routledge, 1998), pp. 84–87.

31. Cornell Fleischer, "The Lawgiver as Messiah," in *Soliman le Magnifique et son temps*, ed. Gilles Veinstein (Paris: Documentation francaise, 1992), pp. 159–177.

32. S. D. Goitein, *A Mediterranean Society: The Jewish Communities of the Arab World as Portrayed in the Documents of the Cairo Geniza*, 6 vols. (Berkeley: University of California, 1967–1993), vol. 2, p. 8; see also his epilogue to vol. 5, p. 498, where he refers to the Yemeni Jews as "unedited texts" in comparison with the documents of the Geniza, linguistically and, as he put it earlier, "psychologically."

33. Ibid., vol. 5, p. xvii.

34. Ibid., pp. 496–502. The principal exceptions seem to be David Herlihy's social history of the family in medieval Italy and some engagement with the question of "individuality" through John Benton's work on Guibert of Nogent.

35. Harris, "The Mediterranean and Ancient History," pp. 38–45, cited also by Wasserstrom.

36. Horden and Purcell, *The Corrupting Sea*, pp. 35–36.

37. Goitein, *A Mediterranean Society*, vol. 1, p. viii.

38. Ibid., vol. 5, p. 502. Noting that the history of this community "brings us into contact with humanity at large," he movingly observed, "Every happening of the past is a nonrecurrent single episode; yet it has relevance to the general experience of mankind. This relevance is manifested in the tales of the narrators. It is the privilege of the historian to conceive the accidental past as ever-present life."

39. Ibid., vol. 2, pp. 275ff.

40. See, for example, R. I. Moore, *The Formation of a Persecuting Society: Power and Deviance in Western Europe (950–1250)* (New York: Blackwell, 1987); see the different picture offered in David Nirenberg, *Communities of Violence: Persecution of Minorities in the Middle Ages* (Princeton, N.J.: Princeton University Press, 1996). The relevant literature is enormous, particularly for the experience of Jews in medieval and early modern Europe. Goitein seems to have associated the Mediterranean unity he perceives with this ostensibly liberal period of free trade and flourishing of the Jewish community of the Geniza, which together end in the thirteenth century.

41. Richard Bulliet, *The Case for Islamo-Christian Civilization* (New York: Columbia University Press, 2004).

1

INSULARITY

A LITERARY HISTORY OF MUSLIM LUCERA

Karla Mallette

The English adjective "insular" possesses undeniably negative connotations. According to the *Oxford English Dictionary* (O.E.D.), the word
signifies first "Pertaining to islanders; esp. having the characteristic
traits of the inhabitants of an island (e.g. of Great Britain)."[1] Apart
from the somewhat eccentric decision to introduce the self-reflective
element – is the parenthetical gloss on the meaning of the word
"island" strictly necessary? – the definition yields no surprises: value
neutral, it betrays no connotations either negative or positive.
However, the entry veers south in the next clause: "cut off from intercourse with other nations, isolated; self-contained; narrow or prejudiced in feelings, ideas, or manners." The word, in modern usage,
connotes willful singularity, resistance to alterity. What is more, it regularly carries the political resonance alluded to in the O.E.D. definition: "cut off from intercourse *with other nations.*" People may *isolate*
themselves, but so may nations; and an *insular* nation bodes ill to itself
and to those foreign powers it ignores and resists. The O.E.D. cites an
early (1800) appearance to a cognate adjective, "isolated": "The
affected, frenchified, and unnecessary word *isolated* is not English,
and we trust never will be." The sentence is delicious, of course,
because it expresses the very quality to which the word refers, and
illustrates its xenophobic nuances in the process.
    It may seem odd to describe an 1800 use of the word "isolated" as
early. Clearly, "isolated," like "insular," derives from a Latinate root.
The earliest use of the adjective "insular" (to mean "of or pertaining to

an island," as, for instance, "insular vegetation") dates to 1611. But the earliest appearance of the word with the expanded semantic range discussed above – "cut off … self-contained … narrow or prejudiced" – dates to 1775. And the word did not become common in this usage until after the beginning of the nineteenth century. The adjective "isolated" was a borrowing from the French *isolé* (itself a borrowing from the Italian *isolato*); the O.E.D. entry on "isolated" begins by citing English authors using the French *isolé*. And English authors continued to use the French original for some time after the English language had created its own cognate. Thus the English "isolated" (formed, like the Italian *isolato*, on a Latinate verb model) was first attested in 1763. But as late as 1788 Boswell quoted Johnson as saying, "This Hanoverian family is *isolée* here. They have no friends."

A similar pattern is attested in the Romance languages. The earliest cited use of the Italian verb *isolare* listed in the *Grande dizionario della lingua italiana*, dating to the sixteenth century, does not convey negative connotations. Indeed the Italian definition allows the word a *positive* connotation. One may isolate a spot for the purposes of successful defense; one may isolate an element (of a landscape, a structure, a construction) in order to cast it in brighter relief. The first citation of the verb with negative political connotations (the full definition reads, "to exclude a State partially or totally from diplomatic, political, economic, and cultural relations with other States") comes from Mazzini (1805–72).[2] During the nineteenth century *isolare/isolato* also came to signify social or psychological estrangement.[3] The word traveled a parallel path in French, where it had by the beginning of the nineteenth century acquired the meaning of separation from similar (or, in the case of human referents, like-minded) entities. Petrarch – who wrote with such conviction of separation and solitude – did so without recourse to the words *isolare* or *isolato*, neither of which existed in Italian before the mid-sixteenth century.

The vicissitudes of Mediterranean history shed an intriguing light on the shifting lexical range of the word "insular" and its related English and Romance cognates. "Insularity" began to acquire its negative connotations – and the *political* dimension of that negativity in particular began to be prominent – around the midpoint of the eighteenth century. The history of Great Britain, of course, had a significant impact on the evolution of the word. Indeed Napoleon's Continental System, instituted in 1806 and intended to *isolate* Great Britain and to consolidate the power of the European states, constitutes a significant point of reference for this lexical history. In return Britain – in order to secure a trade route to her colonies, Egypt and in particular India, accessed after the opening of the Suez Canal in 1869 by means of the Mediterranean shipping lanes – would occupy first Sicily and then Malta. During the early modern period the Mediterranean islands were significant predominately as means for northern European empires to consolidate and administer their colonial holdings. The same, of course, was not true during the Middle Ages. Certainly, mainland kingdoms administered the Mediterranean islands as colonial states throughout much of the Middle Ages. However, the islands were desirable not only from a strategic point of view, but also because of their agricultural and cultural productivity. That is, they might serve as the jewels – to cite a relevant metaphor – in the crown of particularly ambitious monarchs, rather than mere stepping stones between continental states and continental colonies.

Indeed, the connotations of cultural *isolation* born by the word "insular" have little relevance to the Mediterranean islands during the Middle Ages. On the contrary the affliction of the Mediterranean islands tended to be the opposite: an inability to protect themselves from a too promiscuous connectivity. The Mediterranean islands functioned as way stations for merchants and armies; the competing cultural traditions of the medieval world washed their shores; in an era that predated policies of cultural protectionism, they had little capacity to insulate themselves from cultural influence and cultural conquest. "Poor Mexico!" commented Porfirio Diaz, in an epigraph that has since become famous. "So far from God, and so close to the United States!" One might imagine a similar lament for Sicily, Malta, Cyprus, Majorca, Corsica, Sardinia during an earlier era: "So far from God, and so close to everyone else!" Of course, the intense cultural connectivity experienced by the Mediterranean islands might at times be viewed as a blessing (at least by historians), since it made the islands depositories of the cultural riches of the Middle Ages.

No island illustrates these truisms of Mediterranean history with greater conviction than Sicily. Sicily – the largest of the Mediterranean islands, located smack in the center of the sea – presented an irresistible temptation to all states with imperial ambitions in the Mediterranean from antiquity until the nineteenth century. ("Sicily," Cicero wrote in the opening lines of the Verrine Orations, was "the first of the provinces; Sicily first taught our ancestors how glorious it could be to rule other peoples.") The growing dominance of the Atlantic economy and Turkish control of the Mediterranean would contribute to Sicily's economic and cultural marginalization from the fifteenth century on. However, during the Middle Ages in general, and for a two-hundred-year period in particular, Sicily remained culturally vibrant and economically dynamic. Like most of the Mediterranean islands Sicily swung back and forth between the Islamic and Christian cultural orbits, like a gauge registering the relative power of the competing monotheisms in the Mediterranean basin. And for two hundred years the state embodied an extraordinary cultural ambiguity. After a spell of Byzantine rule, Sicily fell under Muslim control for roughly two centuries; the Islamic conquest of the island began in 827, and the Norman conquest in 1038. Under the Normans, though Sicily functioned as a Christian state, it witnessed the birth of an extraordinary culture of fusion. During the Norman era Sicilian poetry was written in Arabic; palatine architecture followed Islamic models; a Christian king commissioned the writing of the greatest geographical treatise of the Middle Ages (by al-Idrisi) in Arabic; and Christian monarchs surrounded themselves with Arab functionaries.

In this essay, I will use the history of a Muslim colony created by the Sicilian king almost two centuries after the opening of the Norman conquest of the island – the city of Lucera, on the Italian mainland – to illustrate a pivotal moment in the history of relations between Muslims and Christians on Italian soil. Most social and economic historians know little about Lucera; literary historians are not likely to have heard of the city at all. Yet Lucera stands as a clear signal of the shift in the balance of power that occurred in the northern Mediterranean during the late Middle Ages. More than that, it represents an important tendency, amply attested in the northern Mediterranean in general: the reluctance of Christian conquerors to purge conquered territories of their Muslim residents. Not expulsion but rather a limited integration followed by containment and isolation typified the policies of the first Latin Christian rulers of southern Italy toward conquered Muslim populations. In recent years social and economic historians have produced masterful studies detailing the Christian state's accommodation of its Muslim residents in Sicily. It remains – not only for social and economic historians but also for literary historians like myself – to ask *why* Christian rulers responded to their Muslim subjects as they did. What did domination of a Muslim population signify in the new Christian states of southern Europe?

The period of Norman rule in Sicily came to a close with the death of Frederick II, the son of a Norman mother and a Hohenstaufen father, in 1250. Frederick – notorious among his contemporaries for his philo-Muslim tendencies; more than one pope accused him of being a Saracen himself – possessed a robust appetite for the Islamic sciences, and communicated amiably with Muslim leaders and philosophers during his career as monarch. But he had a cooler and more pragmatic attitude toward the Muslims of his own state. Though the island had been in Christian hands for almost two centuries when his reign began, Muslim settlements remained. And these settlements continued to be a source of unrest. In an episode attested by Muslim historians (though not by Christians), the daughter of a prominent Muslim resistance leader barricaded herself, following her father's assassination by Frederick's functionaries, in Entella, a mountaintop city to the south of Palermo. Ibn 'Abd al-Mun'im al-Himyari's geographical dictionary recorded the negotiations between the unnamed daughter and Frederick. She tricks him into sending troops into the city, whom her followers massacre. Frederick admires her tactical savvy; he challenges her to surrender, become his wife, and bear his children. She throws his words back in his face: "I am master of you more than you are master of me, and I have injured you more than you have injured me. Behold: I have prostrated you with the chains of my guile."[4] The Emperor's troops besiege the city and the heroine's resistance finally ends, when she recognizes the hopelessness of her position, with her suicide. The event (which begs an operatic treatment) may well be fanciful. But the heroine's father (Ibn 'Abbad) was a historical figure, a rebel who resisted Christian rule and struck independent coinage in his name from his hilltop stronghold.

In response to continued Muslim unrest and tension between Muslim and Christian populations on the island, beginning in 1222 or 1223,[5] Frederick ordered the relocation of all Muslims to a city on the mainland: Lucera, located in Puglia near the city of Foggia. Frederick's choice for the location of the Muslim colony is intriguing. The city is of considerable strategic importance. Situated on an elevation in the middle of the largest plain in southern Italy, the city commands a view as far as the Adriatic (fifty kilometers distant) on a clear day. Along with Castel del Monte, also placed on a hilltop, Lucera played a crucial role in Frederick's defensive network, making it impossible for troops to move through the plains of Puglia without being sighted. The city's residents provided a standing army for his ceaseless battles. It seems likely that Frederick chose the location of the city in part for tactical reasons, in order to keep troops handy for speedy deployment.

Frederick – to the much iterated consternation of the Christian hierarchy, including two successive popes – spent a considerable amount of time in Lucera. He maintained a castle there, furnished (reputedly) with a harem. He saw to it that the material needs of the city's residents were met and guaranteed their religious freedom. As temporal ruler of the city, Frederick had an obligation to promote the conversion of the residents to Christianity. Yet Innocent IV complained that Frederick ignored his responsibility for his subjects' fate in the next life, that the priests sent to convert the residents were denied access to the city. The accusation clearly served as munitions in the war of words between Frederick and the Pope. However, Frederick had good motives for resisting the conversion of the Muslims. His Arab warriors, one reasons, might lose their legendary fierceness were they to convert to Christianity. Frederick's meticulous maintenance of Lucera and his proclivity for spending time there are typical of the behavior that gained him his reputation as a fellow traveler to his Muslim subjects despite his heavy-handed treatment of them.

Lucera remained Muslim after Frederick's death in 1250. An Arab source records that an envoy of the Sultan of Egypt visited Manfredi, Frederick's natural son, in Puglia. Although the envoy did not visit Lucera, he learned about the city during his visit. "Its inhabitants," he wrote, "are all Sicilian Muslims. Here public prayer is observed on Friday; Islamic rites are practiced publicly."[6] And Manfredi, like his father, called on the residents of Lucera to serve as his troops. Arab warriors stood with him in his battles against the Pope's pick for monarch of Sicily, Charles II of Anjou. Manfredi rode out to the battle in which he died, at Benevento, from Lucera, and his wife returned following the battle to take refuge at Lucera. Following Manfredi's death the Angevin kings of Sicily administered Lucera. They protected the city's religious independence, a policy that generally found guarded papal support. The Pope might single out the city as an object of his wrath – as Clement IV did, for instance, during the Muslim rebellion of 1266–69, when he authorized the preaching of a crusade against Lucera.[7] And Charles levied taxes on the city which reached extortionate levels, provoking the flight of residents from Lucera. But the city was maintained and its infrastructure in general guaranteed by both secular and religious powers in southern Italy. Under less chaotic conditions than the uprising of 1266–69, another pope – Innocent IV – received the overtures of a Muslim resident of Lucera, known as Giovanni Moro.[8] And following the uprising, Charles chose not to exile the Muslims; he elected rather to tax them at rates even more ruinous than before.[9] The administrative powers of southern Italy seem to have accepted an accommodation with the existence of a city of Muslims in their midst. And the city itself seems to have functioned as a refuge of last resort, underscoring its status as a protectorate of sorts. Not only Manfredi and his wife but also the Jews of southern Italy, during one of Charles's pogroms, sought refuge in Lucera.[10]

In 1300 Muslim Lucera was destroyed. Two months earlier Charles had exhorted the residents to convert in order to escape taxation. In August, with no other warning, he ordered that the Muslims of the city be taken prisoner in order to be sold into slavery. Although Charles made it abundantly clear that he expected to see a profit on the depopulation of the Muslim city, those in charge of executing his orders did not follow them to the letter. The evacuation of the city's residents became a wholesale slaughter, a fact that suggests that the residents of the region had not (unlike the temporal and spiritual authorities of the kingdom) made their peace with the Muslim community in their midst.[11] A cloud of rhetoric, not unexpectedly, obscures the monarch's motives for the annihilation of the Muslim colony. His intention to sell the residents into slavery indicates that Charles anticipated a monetary gain from his action, and the War of the Sicilian Vespers currently underway gave him a clear incentive for seeking revenue. However, historians do not rule out religious motivations. Charles also drove Jews out of his kingdom. And the destruction of Muslim Lucera was of a piece with the spirit of the age: the growth of intolerance in Christian communities which reflects an increasing emphasis on religious orthodoxy, and a resistance to and repression of heterodoxies.

The history of Muslim Lucera is largely unknown to social, economic, and political historians. Literary historians know even less about the city, for a simple reason: it has left virtually no trace in the literary record. The author of the definitive recent study on Lucera, Julie Taylor, cites a political poem written in Provençal by a Genoese merchant, Calega Panzano, that disparages the Sicilian monarch's support of the "can descrezen de Nucheria" ("the miscreant dogs of Lucera").[12]

Beyond this unsavory mention, the only acknowledgements of the city in the late medieval Italian literary record that I am aware of can be found in the medieval commentaries on Dante's *Commedia*. Dante did not mention the city in his work. However, the early commentators mention the city at two moments in particular when Lucera seems to bear a particular relevance to the material that Dante treats: *Inferno* X and *Inferno* XXVIII. In the tenth canto of the *Inferno* Dante listed the name of Frederick II among those damned for Epicureanism, disbelief in the immortality of the soul. Here the commentators cite the creation of a city of Muslims on the Italian mainland as evidence demonstrating that the Sicilian monarch has eminently earned his damnation. Their adornment of the historical record suggests the power the city held in the medieval Italian imagination. Thus Boccaccio's comments on *Inferno* X, 119, where Frederick's name appears:

> And out of contempt for the Church [Frederick] sent to Tunisia for a great quantity of Saracens, and he gave them by decree a city long since dismantled, called Lucera (or in the common language Nocera), practically in the center of the Pugliese plain; and he built for himself a wondrous and beautiful and strong castle, in one section of the city that lay a bit higher than the other, which still stands. The Saracens made their houses within the dismantled city, each as well as he could; and since the countryside was fruitful they lived there willingly, and they multiplied to such a quantity that they had the run of all of Puglia, whenever they had the desire.[13]

Boccaccio's description of the city is accurate in some details. Lucera was known as either Lucera or Nocera; built in the center of a plain, it included (as it had since antiquity) a fortified section and a separate residential quarter, the center of the modern town as it was of the medieval. More fancifully, Boccaccio maintains that Frederick imported residents for Lucera from Tunisia (a notion repeated by Cristoforo Landino, a late fifteenth-century commentator whose comments here are modeled on Boccaccio's[14]). And tellingly Boccaccio represents the Muslim city as a patent offense to the Christian residents of Puglia.

However, the bulk of the references to Lucera occur in commentary on *Inferno* XXVIII, in which the pilgrim enters the realm of those damned for "sowing discord," the schismatics. The canto is among the starkest and most gruesome in the *Inferno*; the punishment of the damned consists of a bodily mutilation to answer the mutilation of the community of believers they inflicted in life. The first sinner Dante encounters is Muhammad, his body split from neck to crotch. Divine justice has sundered the head of Ali, Muhammad's companion in damnation, from the chin to the forehead; together, the two of them represent the incalculable damage wrought by the prophet of Islam on the Christian community. Before we meet the sinners, however, Dante prepares us for the grotesque disfigurement of the damned we will encounter in this region of hell by describing the war fields of Puglia. He lists a series of particularly bloody battles fought in Puglia in order to evoke the carnage he is about to describe. The early commentaries bring up Lucera for one of two reasons when elucidating these introductory verses of canto XXVIII. Some of the commentators mention Lucera in connection with a skirmish at Benevento cited by Dante: the battle in which Manfredi, the natural son of Frederick II, lost his life. Thus L'Anonimo Fiorentino records a memorable challenge from Charles spoken on the battlefield: "Go, now, tell the Sultan of Lucera that either I will send him to hell, or he will send me to paradise."[15] Another of the battles that Dante lists occurred between Charles of Anjou and Conradin, grandson of Frederick II, in 1268. This battle coincided with the Muslim uprising of 1266–69: the Muslims had taken up arms when they heard that Conradin had entered Italy, in the hopes that he would liberate them from the Angevin yoke. The reference to the battle in *Inferno* XXVIII is fleeting: "And there near Tagliacozzo, where old Alardo [a military adviser] won without arms" (*Inferno* XXVIII, 17–18). The commentators Jacopo della Lana, L'Ottimo Commento, Francesco da Buti, and Benvenuto da Imola mention the Muslim uprising when glossing this line. Clearly, the rebellion at Lucera does not constitute a prerequisite for understanding Dante's brief allusion to a battle at Tagliacozzo, or for that matter to the battle at Benevento. In fact, after Guiniforto delli Bargigi's 1440 commentary, the commentators no longer find it necessary to mention Lucera in order to elucidate either of the two battles mentioned in canto XXVIII. However, the early commentators think it expedient to inform the student of the *Commedia* about the Muslim uprising. And most of them specify in addition that Lucera was "a city in Puglia which King Manfredi made; and he caused it to be inhabited by his Saracen soldiers in order to put the knife to the throat of those Pugliesi who did not want to live under his rule."[16]

The references to Lucera in the early commentators' glosses on these lines seem to be informed not by the explicit relevance of the material but rather by a dense network of associations. *Inferno* XXVIII is, after all, the canto in which we meet Muhammad. Muhammad's followers populated the city of Lucera. Sermons preaching crusade against the Muslims of Lucera accompanied the uprising of 1266–69 to which Dante refers. Although these sermons would have been preached at least sixty years before the commentators wrote, they may well have contributed to the city's repute as an object of horrified titillation, and more specifically in the popular imagination may have linked the Muslim uprising to Conradin's attempt to claim the throne of Sicily. Dante cites, in rapid succession, two battles fought between Charles of Anjou and Frederick II's descendents – Manfredi and Conradin. Public opinion perceived all the men of the Sicilian ruling family, Frederick and Manfredi in particular, as crypto-Muslims and identified them closely with their Muslim residents. Furthermore, Lucera enjoyed a reputation as the origin of the fierce warriors who won so many battles for Frederick (although their win–loss record during Manfredi's and Conradin's lives was less impressive). For such associational reasons, it seems, Lucera bubbled to the surface of the commentators' consciousness. When the city's fame subsided in the popular imagination the commentaries ceased mentioning it in connection with the canto.

The comments on Lucera, however, serve as a useful record from another point of view. Contentious though they may be, they constitute (to my knowledge) the most compendious record we possess – composed, admittedly, at some distance from the fact, and by observers not from the Kingdom of Sicily but from central and northern Italy – of popular response to the city of Muslims in Puglia. They make it clear that near-contemporaries linked the colony closely to the figure of the Sicilian monarch. Boccaccio attributes agency for the creation of the city to Frederick II; Jacopo della Lana, L'Ottimo Commento, and Francesco da Buti make Manfredi the city's mastermind. But all of the commentators see the city as an outrage imposed on the Christians of Puglia by the Sicilian king. Thus the comments on Lucera perceive the city as further evidence of the identification of the Sicilian king with his Muslim subjects. The battlefield challenge directed at Manfredi by Charles of Anjou – certainly too exquisite to be true – states the case unequivocally: a monarch who may be a foreigner but is certainly a Christian faces down a pretender to the throne who may have been born on the Italian peninsula but whose confessional pedigree is rather more ambivalent. History records to whom God chose to grant victory.

The remaining references to Lucera in commentary on the *Commedia* fall into two categories. One of the early commentators, Benvenuto da Imola, seems to have an immoderate interest in the city, and brings it up whenever he finds (or can create) an opportunity.[17] And a number of commentators mention the city in connection with a reference to a city called Nocera in a passage introducing Francis of Assisi (*Paradiso* XI, 48).[18] In fact Dante refers in this passage to a small and obscure Umbrian village also called Nocera. Transferring the city to Puglia makes hash of Dante's geographic allusion. But because the Umbrian Nocera was unknown whereas the Pugliese Lucera/Nocera possessed a certain notoriety, the commentators displace Francis's Lucera almost three hundred kilometers to the south. It is tempting to believe that once again an implicit back story drew the commentators' attention to Lucera, despite its irrelevance to the passage under consideration. Dante mentions a "heavy yoke" that lies upon Nocera. His reference is oblique; to the present day, commentators do not agree on his meaning. But the year 1300 – in which Dante the pilgrim embarked upon his journey to the afterworld – is also the year in which Charles ordered the destruction of Muslim Lucera. It is tempting, though not intellectually defensible, to suggest that Dante alluded in these lines either to the "yoke" of Muslim occupancy or to the "yoke" of the massacre of the Muslims of Lucera in 1300. But it is equally tempting, and somewhat more defensible, to speculate that these associations caused the early commentators to link Dante's Nocera (so clearly identified, in the *Commedia*, with Umbria) to the Pugliese Lucera. At any rate the Muslim city and its extermination represent a striking omission in Dante's encyclopedic compendium of his Italy.

Historians have proposed a number of competing models to describe the competitions and communications between Muslims and Christians from the Middle Ages to the present day. Often these models are generated in order to characterize Mediterranean history in particular. Pirenne's narrative – in which the expansion of Islam across the Mediterranean forces Christians into seclusion in northern Europe – served as a useful foil for more fully elaborated descriptions of social and economic history. Braudel and, fifty years later, Horden and Purcell did not explicitly discuss the dynamics of Muslim–Christian relations. But they modeled a sophisticated methodology to describe the evolution of social, economic, technological, and cultural systems across the Mediterranean basin. As a result they integrated Islamic and Christian history, to a certain extent, into a more organic vision of regional history. The most successful contemporary metaphor for imagining Muslim–Christian cultural relations (though its creator did not intend specifically to describe Mediterranean history) was produced, of course, by Samuel Huntington. Most serious historians disagree with Huntington's polemical summary of the history of relations between the Islamic world and the Christian West, characterized by the sonorous catchphrase "Clash of Civilizations." Few of us, however, have done as much about our dissatisfaction as Richard Bulliet, who wrote an essay in which he proposed an alternative metaphor to describe relations between Muslims and Christians during fifteen hundred years of shared history. The very notion that the world we live in can be divided into separate "Muslim" and "Christian" spheres becomes problematic if one considers the historical record of cohabitation and cultural and economic trade. Bulliet argues that Islamic and Christian civilizational configurations in fact overlap for much of their history. They are "sibling societies," he writes, that go through parallel developmental stages at parallel moments in their history, only to experience decisive separation toward the end of a millennium and a half of shared history. One cannot have a "clash" of civilizations if one is speaking about a symbiotic "Islamo-Christian civilization." It is, he writes, the transformations of modernity which produced variant responses from Muslims and Christians, and provoked a pronounced separation between the two civilizations. They part ways with increasing frequency and intensity during the years between 1500 and 1900: "the siblings that had for so long trodden the same developmental path parted company."[19]

Bulliet's narrative is much more promising than Huntington's as a model for characterizing a vast sweep – geographical and chronological – of human history. Both original and tantalizingly simple, it (like a good scientific theory) invites contributions from other historians who might flesh out the bare-bones sketch Bulliet offered in his brief essay. Historians of culture in general and of literature in particular might prefer to think of the Christian and Muslim cultural spheres not precisely as "siblings in step," and might prefer to finesse the "parallel" relationship that Bulliet posits between the two civilizations.[20] We may agree that during the near-millennial history that stretched between the seventh and sixteenth centuries Islam and Christianity evolved in tandem, that "Latin Christians and Middle

East Muslims experienced common challenges in parallel time frames."[21] However, we may choose to emphasize the imbalances between the two civilizations at key moments in this stretch of history, imbalances that might serve as an engine of progress in one or both of the communities. During the dynamic period of expansion that followed the revelation of Islam, while the Christian world remained relatively dormant, Muslims inherited from the Greek speakers of their conquered lands the philosophical traditions that had fallen into disrepair under the Christian watch. Muslim philosophers translated the works of the Greeks into Arabic and elaborated them with commentaries. Half a millennium later Christians began to retranslate this philosophical tradition from Arabic into Latin. These translations had an incalculably important impact on the Christian philosophy of the twelfth and thirteenth centuries precisely because of the disparity between the two communities. Christian Europe lacked a sophisticated philosophical tradition; Muslim Europe introduced it to one. The Christian response to Islamic philosophy suggests a perception of identity between the two communities: both upheld monotheistic scriptural traditions in a region that had previously been unified by Roman and Greek intellectual traditions. At the same time a decisive disproportion between the communities functioned as a spur to progress, both during the era of Arab acquisition of Greek thought and during the subsequent period when Christian philosophers Latinized those Arabic translations and commentaries. Finally, Christian-European emancipation from Islamic influence through an unmediated access to Greek texts began toward the end of the fifteenth century (when Bulliet dates the beginning of a sharper divide between the two civilizations), when Christian appetite for rationalistic thought also began to increase.[22] Literary historians and intellectual historians may indeed see the relationship between the Muslim and Christian worlds on the sibling model. But they may emphasize the existence of a healthy dose of sibling rivalry between the two civilizations.

The history of Lucera must be seen in the light of the increasing competition between the two communities during the late Middle Ages. The creation of Lucera in the 1220s predated the stark divide between the Islamic and Christian spheres enunciated across the Mediterranean during the fifteenth century. However, the twelfth and thirteenth centuries saw the emergence of a distinct difference in the balance of power between the Muslim and Christian worlds. The creation of Lucera was contemporary with the crusades in both the eastern and northern Mediterranean. It coincided, that is, with an increasingly belligerent stance from the Christian population of Europe: an increasing willingness to make territorial claims in the Holy Land and (more successfully) in southern Europe, and an increasing technological capacity to forward such claims convincingly. But, alongside this hunger for land, Christian intellectuals articulated a hunger for knowledge. And the chief source for this knowledge was precisely the Muslims whose states Christian militia were overthrowing. Thus the translation movement and territorial aggressions of the twelfth and thirteenth centuries constitute two expressions of the same urge: a movement toward a more marked distinction between the Muslim and Christian communities of southern Europe, and a more marked cultural self-consciousness on the part of the Christians of the Mediterranean in particular.

That is, the intellectual history of the period between roughly 1100–1350 – from the First Crusade until the advent of the plague – introduces subtle but decisive glosses to the social and economic history of the same period. The culture of translation demonstrates unequivocally the faultiness of Huntington's "Clash of Civilizations" model; but the social and economic history of the same region during the same period will bring us to the same conclusion. The intellectual record demonstrates, however, a motivation not only for continued communication between the Christian and Islamic cultural spheres. It suggests an incentive also for the sustenance of Muslim communities on terrain recently occupied by Christians: Islamic culture functioned still as a prestige culture, albeit a prestige culture now in Christian hands. Thus the intellectual record both supports and deepens Bulliet's description of an "Islamo-Christian civilization." It suggests that, while the Muslim and Christian cultural spheres share a scriptural and a socio-economic foundation and evolve in parallel stages, at the same time the *discrepancies* between them serve as provocations that stimulate evolution.

In particular, intellectual history can render visible and intelligible the *culture of memorialization* that evolved in the Muslim–Christian borderlands of southern Europe.[23] During the Norman era in Sicily, Sicilian poets wrote panegyrics for the Christian kings in Arabic. Palatine architecture imitated contemporary Islamic models. The Norman monarch Roger II commissioned the greatest geographical treatise of the Middle Ages. Written by al-Idrisi in Arabic, it was never translated into Latin for the benefit of Christian Europe. Norman Sicilian coinage bore inscriptions in Arabic; after Arabic literacy was lost in Sicily, during the reign of Frederick II, the coinage continued to bear Pseudo-Kufic inscriptions. Social and economic history can explain these phenomena to a certain extent. The Norman monarchs "performed" Arab culture in order to communicate with the Arab states that were the greatest maritime powers at the time. However, social and economic history does not exhaust the significance of these events – particularly in light of the fact that the monarchs staged these performances for a predominately Christian audience, long after their pragmatic efficacy was exhausted. In Sicily during the twelfth and thirteenth centuries, Christian monarchs artificially extended the bureaucratic and, to a more limited extent, cultural life of the Arabic language even after their harsh economic policies and the hostility of the Christian residents of their realm had effectively exterminated the Arab population of the kingdom.

Recent work in social history – in particular, the scholarship of Jeremy Johns and Alex Metcalfe – has demonstrated the importance of imported Arab bureaucratic practices in the Norman state in Sicily. In his study of the use of language in Norman Sicily, Metcalfe draws the conclusion that "language was a measure of identity and ... Romance dialects had a prestige status over Greek and Arabic."[24] At the same time, the social historians' research articulates the power that Arab bureaucratic culture in general and the Arabic language in particular held over the popular imagination. Official documents were redacted in Arabic, according to Johns, with little regard for the capacity of the public to read Arabic. Rather they functioned as "symbols of royal power."[25] That is, the efficacy of Arab bureaucratic culture only partially justified its use in Norman Sicily. The imported Arab functionaries and the language and bureaucratic forms they brought with them also served – even in the relatively pragmatic theater of domestic politics – an incantatory function.

In the domain of intellectual production, of course, pragmatic efficacy may in effect count for little; perceived value gains in relative power. The Christian ruler of a state recently won from Muslims might use the Arabic language and imported Arab bureaucratic practices for a variety of reasons, pragmatic and not. He might display Muslim culture as spoils of war, as emblems of the victor's power. Or he might manipulate the language of the conquered because it is a more effective instrument, at least in certain portions of his conquered territory, for communicating with the population. Again he might adopt the Arabic language in frank tribute to the achievement of the Arabs, still – despite the Christian advances of the twelfth and thirteenth centuries – the dominant culture and the dominant military power in the Mediterranean. Or he might use the Arabic language when none of the bureaucratic or literary languages of the Christians seemed equal to the task. Certainly pragmatic motivations cannot sufficiently explain al-Idrisi's geography, written in Arabic under the supervision of Norman monarch Roger II, or the Arabic panegyric by al-Atrabanishi which uses Qur'anic imagery to celebrate Roger's power and the wealth, beauty, and (ironically) tranquility of his kingdom.[26]

The city of Lucera, too, seems to have functioned in part as a memorial to Sicily's Arab past. The city constituted first a means to resolve a demographic problem and to generate revenue for the crown. However, while fulfilling these purposes it simultaneously served others. It allowed the monarchs of Sicily to maintain a manageable Arab population, to contain Sicily's Arab population without exterminating it. It furnished Frederick with a harem and Manfredi with a refuge; it provided troops for both of them. Charles of Anjou seems not to have enjoyed parallel fringe benefits, but rather to have used Lucera strictly as a source of revenue. And his destruction of the city in 1300 suggests that when the ruler of Sicily could extract *only* economic value from Lucera – when the city no longer served as refuge or resort; when the monarch no longer wished to project an image of himself as administrator of Muslim citizens as well as Christians – its extinction could be imagined. The references to Lucera in the literary record make no mention of the economic significance of the city. Rather they perceive it as an outrage perpetrated on the Christian communities of Puglia by Frederick and Manfredi. Thus Calega Panzano's citation of Lucera in the context of vituperation of the Sicilian monarchs; thus the presentation of the city in the lists of evidence against Frederick and Manfredi in commentary on the *Inferno*. (Interestingly, no commentator mentions Lucera when elucidating *Purgatorio* III – the canto in which Dante presents a *redeemed* Manfredi – before the American poet Longfellow, who records that Manfredi's wife took refuge in the city after his death in battle.[27]) Lucera does not play a pragmatic role in the medieval literary record – it does not represent a solution to a set of demographic and economic problems – but rather a symbolic one. The city

symbolizes for the literary witnesses the transfer of a Muslim population to Italian soil, and a civic administration's protection and perpet-
uation of that population. And both the creation and the sustenance
of the city constitute, in the popular imagination as witnessed by the
literary record, a scandal.

The Sicilian Muslims' exodus from Sicily to the Italian mainland –
while it may not have taken them appreciably farther from God
than they found themselves at the outset – certainly carried them
away from the Mediterranean. That is, their "continentalization"
effectively *isolated* them from the connectivity of a medieval
Mediterranean island, from the social, economic, and cultural cross-
currents that they knew and that sustained them in Sicily. It seems
evident that Sicily's Muslim community was moribund before
Frederick's extradition policy began. The transfers may not have
shortened the history of Muslim Sicily. On the contrary, the creation
of a Muslim ghetto city on the mainland may have lengthened the life
of Sicily's Muslim community by concentrating it in a single location
and guaranteeing that (up to a labile point, determined by contemporary exigencies and sensibilities) the residents' rights would be protected and their needs would be met. By relocating the Muslims of
Sicily, Frederick clearly meant to reduce a source of civil unrest and
generate a source of revenue. However, at the same time he created a
Muslim preserve that perpetuated the life of the Muslim community
of Sicily far longer than would otherwise have been the case.

Historians have not yet adequately explored the motives for the
continuation of a Muslim community under Christian rule in Sicily.
Or, rather, historians have limited their search for motive to the
spheres of social and economic history, which, while they explain
much, do not exhaust the significance of the creation and sustenance
of a Muslim colony on the Italian mainland. During the late Middle
Ages, Christian communities in the northern Mediterranean began to
differentiate themselves in an increasingly decisive way from the
Muslim communities with whom they had for centuries shared
terrain as well as cultural, social, and economic institutions. What
we historians – literary as well as social and economic – must yet
account for is the extent to which Christian communities kept
their Muslim neighbors within their sights during this period of self-
differentiation. As the two communities began to outgrow the sibling
relationship described by Bulliet, before European Christians constituted Islamic civilization as Saidian *other*, in an intermediary stage the

Muslim and Christian communities of the Mediterranean held each other at arm's length, in a position to comprehend both the identities and the differences between their civilizational formations.[28] A volatile tension between emulation and resistance, between preservation and extermination, seems to characterize this period; and we historians have not yet developed a vocabulary to describe it.

NOTES

1. *OED Online* (<http://dictionary.oed.com>), s.v. "insularity" (accessed 1 August 2005).
2. Salvatore Battaglia and Giorgio Bàrberi Squarotti, *Grande dizionario della lingua italiana* (Turin: Unione tipografico-editrice torinese, 1961), s.v. "isolare."
3. The earliest citation with this meaning comes from Melchiorre Gioja, *Del merito e delle ricompense: trattato storico e filosofico* (Lugano: Tip. della Svizzera italiana, 1848).
4. Karla Mallette, *The Kingdom of Sicily 1100–1250: A Literary History* (Philadelphia: University of Pennsylvania Press, 2005), p. 153. For a translated version of this text see, pp. 151–153; for the Arabic text, see Évariste Lévi-Provençal, "Une héroïne de la resistance musulmane en Sicile au début du XIIIe siècle," *Oriente moderno*, 34, 1954, pp. 283–288. On Ibn 'Abbad and the episode involving his daughter and Frederick II, see Julie Taylor, *Muslims in Medieval Italy: The Colony at Lucera* (Lanham, Md.: Lexington Books, 2003), pp. 8–11; and Mallette, *The Kingdom of Sicily*, pp. 108–109.
5. Taylor, *Muslims in Medieval Italy*, p. 11. I rely for the substance of the discussion of Lucera that follows on Julie Taylor's masterful recent study, based on an exhaustive survey of the documentary sources.
6. Pietro Egidi, *La colonia saracena di Lucera e la sua distruzione* (Naples: Pierro, 1915), p. 32.
7. Taylor, *Muslims in Medieval Italy*, pp. 143–144; see also Maier's discussion of the crusade, which includes the edited text of the extant sermons: Christopher T. Maier, "Crusade and Rhetoric against the Muslim Colony of Lucera: Eudes of Châteauroux's *Sermones de Rebellione Sarracenorum Lucherie in Apulia*," *Journal of Medieval History*, 21, 1995, pp. 343–385.
8. Taylor, *Muslims in Medieval Italy*, pp. 129–130.
9. Ibid., pp. 148–149.
10. Ibid., pp. 173–174
11. Ibid., pp. 177–178.
12. Ibid., p. 141.
13. "E per dispetto della Chiesa mandò a Tunisi per una gran quantità di Saracini e diede loro per istanza una città stata lungamente disfatta, chiamata Lucera, come che i volgari la chiamino Nocera, nel mezzo quasi di Puglia piana; ed egli per sé dall'una delle parti, la quale è alquanto più rilevata che l'altra, vi fece un mirabile e bello e forte castello, il quale ancora è in piè. I Saracini nel compreso della terra disfatta fecero le lor case, come ciascun poté meglio; ed essendo il paese ubertoso, volentieri vi dimorarono, e multiplicarono in tanta quantità

che essi correvano tutta la Puglia, quando voglia ne venia loro." Boccaccio, commentary on *Inferno* X, 119. My source for all commentary on Dante cited in this article is the Dartmouth Dante Database (<http://dartmouth.dante.edu>), accessed during August 2005.

14. "[Federico] tornò adunque in Italia. Et racquistò el regno: et in contumelia del papa mandò in Tunizi per molti saraceni: et concesse loro ad habitare Lucera hoggi decta Nocera: la quale è in Puglia piana: et mosse guerra al papa: et molta crudeltà usò contro a' prelati." ("Frederick then returned to Italy and reconquered the kingdom. And in contempt for the Pope he sent to Tunisia for many Saracens. He conceded to them as a home Lucera, today called Nocera, which is in the plain of Puglia.") Cristoforo Landino's commentary on *Inferno* X, 109–120.

15. "Ales dit mo alle sultayn de Nocere oge metray lui en enferne, o el metra moy a paradisis." L'Anonimo Fiorentino, commentary on *Inferno* XXVIII, 15–17. In addition, Guiniforto delli Bargigi in his comments on this passage tells us that many Saracens from Lucera died alongside Manfredi.

16. I translate from Jacopo della Lana (on *Inferno* XXVIII, 17–18: "Fu quella Nocera una città in Puglia, la quale fe' lo re Manfredo, e fella abitare a saracini suoi soldati per tener lo forcato nella gola a quelli pugliesi, che sotto suo signorìa non vuolseno essere"); L'Ottimo Commento (*Inferno* XXVIII, 17–18) and Francesco da Buti (*Inferno* XXVIII, 7–21) say essentially the same thing. Benvenuto da Imola informs us, curiously, that Conradin was besieged at Lucera (*Inferno* XXVIII, 15–18).

17. In addition to the remarks in connection with *Inferno* XXVIII, Benvenuto brings it up when discussing *Purgatorio* XVI, 115–120 (where Dante makes reference to Frederick II); *Paradiso* III, 97–102 (where Dante mentions Frederick's mother, Constance), and finally in his comments on *Paradiso* XI, 43–48 (where Dante refers to a Nocera in Umbria).

18. Thus Francesco da Buti: "This is a city in Puglia which was much burdened by those from the house of France who at Dante's time ruled it" ("questa ène una città di Puglia, la quale era molto gravata da quelli della casa di Francia che al tempo dell'autore la signoreggiavano;" *Paradiso* 11, 43–54). The connection between the Nocera mentioned in this passage and the Pugliese Lucera is also made by Jacopo della Lana (*Paradiso* XI, 43–51) and L'Anonimo Fiorentino (*Paradiso* XI, 46–48).

19. Richard Bulliet, *The Case for Islamo-Christian Civilization* (New York: Columbia University Press, 2004), p. 43.

20. Ibid., pp. 16, 15.

21. Ibid., p. 15.

22. See Bulliet, however, on the traditional view that during the Enlightenment "the European Christians, unlike the Muslims, were spectacularly open to new ideas and in the process of achieving, in the Enlightenment, a transcendent, post-scriptural understanding of the world that many Muslims are still reluctant to embrace ... This historical construction, too, is open to query." Bulliet points out that the continued growth of the world Muslim population during this period opened Muslims to a number of new languages, customs, and cultural institutions; in contrast, "the new ideas that the Europeans were open to were their own, not those of their imperial subjects. When Europe was comparatively weak in the middle centuries, cultural borrowing from Muslim neighbors made good

sense. But with empire came a conviction of superiority that closed most west-ern minds" (pp. 42–43). That is, historians may overemphasize both Europeans' omnivorous intellectual appetite during the early modern period and the rela-tively lean intellectual diet of the Muslim world.

23. Particularly interesting in this light is Caroline Bruzelius's discussion of the architectural use of *spolia* in the Angevin Kingdom of Sicily. Bruzelius highlights the reuse of ancient Roman and medieval Christian traces in churches con-structed under Charles II in his Sicilian territories. And she sees this tendency as evidence of Charles's awareness of his role as "renovator and supporter of the church": Caroline Bruzelius, "Charles I, Charles II, and the Development of an Angevin Style in the Kingdom of Sicily," in *L'État Angevin: Pouvoir, culture et société entre XIIIe et XIVe siècle* (Rome: École Française de Rome, Palais Farnèse, 1998), p. 114. In the context of the current discussion, we might read Charles's use of *spolia* as an assertion of historical pedigree meant to counter the earlier Sicilian monarchs' rather more cavalier attitude toward their state's lineage, and in particular their eagerness to memorialize the Arab past and pedigree of their territories. For further discussion of the containment and memorialization of Arab culture in Norman Sicily, see Mallette, *Kingdom of Sicily*, pp. 47–64.
24. Alex Metcalfe, *Muslims and Christians in Norman Sicily: Arabic Speakers and the End of Islam* (London: Routledge, 2003), p. 178.
25. Jeremy Johns, *Arabic Administration in Norman Sicily: The Royal Diwan* (Cambridge, England: Cambridge University Press, 2002), p. 298.
26. For the text of the poem by al-Atrabanishi see Ihsan 'Abbas, *A Biographical Dictionary of Sicilian Learned Men and Poets* (Beirut: Dar al-Gharb al-Islami, 1994), pp. 54–55; for a translation see Mallette, *Kingdom of Sicily*, pp. 139–140 (and discussion, pp. 25–27). For a modern edition of al-Idrisi's text see al-Idrisi, *Opus Geographicum*, ed. E. Cerulli (Leiden, The Netherlands: Brill, 1970); the text has been translated into Italian as *L'Italia descritta nel "Libro del re Ruggero,"* ed. M. Amari and C. Schiaparelli (Rome: Salviucci, 1883).
27. See his comments on *Purgatorio* III, 112. Commentators who mention Lucera in particular, or Manfredi's associations with Saracens in general, when discussing this canto – none earlier than Longfellow's 1867 commentary – include Ernesto Trucchi on *Purgatorio* III, 94–102 and 115–117; John Carroll on *Purgatorio* III, 103–123; Charles Singleton on *Purgatorio* III, 112; Giuseppe Campi on *Purgatorio* III, 121–123; and Giovanni Fallani on *Purgatorio* III, 145.
28. On the emergence of Saidian Orientalism toward the end of the Middle Ages, see Suzanne Akbari's elegant reading of the cartographic record: Suzanne Akbari, "From Due East to True North: Orientalism and Orientation," in *The Postcolonial Middle Ages*, ed. Jeffrey Jerome Cohen (New York: St. Martin's Press, 2000), pp. 19–34.

2

TAKING GRATIAN TO AFRICA

RAYMOND DE PENYAFORT'S LEGAL ADVICE TO THE DOMINICANS AND FRANCISCANS IN TUNIS (1234)[1]

John Tolan

On 19 January 1234, Raymond of Penyafort, major penitentiary (*paenitentiarius*) to Pope Gregory IX, wrote a letter to the Dominican Prior and the Franciscan Minister "in the kingdom of Tunis." These two friars had written to the Pope with forty quite specific questions concerning problems that they faced in serving the Christian community of Tunis; the response was written by Raymond at the Pope's behest:

> You ask to be instructed by the Holy See what you should do in regard to the following items. Your questions [lit., articles], which are transcribed below, were read before the Lord Pope. His responses, which he emitted after deliberation concerning each item, I faithfully disposed, in accord with his special mandate, [are] binding, so that in the confessional [*foro paenitentiali*] you may intrepidly judge according to their tenor.

What follows is a series of forty short articles, the *Responsiones ad dubitabilia circa communicationem christianorum cum sarracenis.*[2] Each article contains, first, a question that the Dominican Prior and the Franciscan Minister in Tunis had posed to the Pope, then the Pope's response, as transcribed by Raymond. The questions involved concern the sinfulness (or not) of everything from selling iron nails to Muslims to surreptitiously baptizing their children.

This text offers a unique glimpse of the workings of the Latin Christian community in Tunis and of papal responses to the problems posed by Christians living in Muslim lands. In the first place, it provides documentation of trade practices of European (principally Italian and Catalan) merchants in Ifriqiya (roughly what is now Tunisia). In this it complements other important documentation: the treaties (in Latin and Arabic) between European and Maghrebi rulers; and the great number of trade documents (primarily contracts) in the archives of Pisa, Genoa, Venice, Barcelona, and other cities. What is particularly intriguing about this document is that it places these issues clearly in the framework of papal interdictions against certain kinds of trade with Muslims: one sees some merchants openly flouting these prohibitions, others trying to respect them or making excuses for not respecting them.

Moreover, the *Responsiones* give us a unique glimpse at the richness and complexity of the European Catholic community in Tunis that the friars seek to serve: not only the Italian and Catalan merchants, but also mercenaries, crusaders, fugitives, captives, or pilgrims on their way to Jerusalem. We find, in particular, a number of marginal persons whose existence is seldom registered in other contemporary documents, in Arab or Latin: renegades, slaves, converts, mixed couples.

The *Responsiones* are also an important document in the early history of the Dominican and Franciscan orders, in two ways: they show the increasing presence of those orders beyond the borders of Catholic Europe, and also the role that these orders play in the papacy's effort to more forcefully and effectively exercise its authority. Before becoming Pope Gregory IX, Cardinal Hugolino knew both Dominic and Francis and was cardinal protector of their two orders. As pope, he had both men canonized and took an active interest in the consolidation and expansion of both orders. The document provides testimony of the attempts of the papacy and the mendicants to extend their reach into new realms; here as elsewhere (e.g. the University of Paris at the same time), the mendicants drew resistance from secular clergy who did not want to see their prerogatives encroached upon.

This document shows a clear and close collaboration between the Pope and his penitentiary Raymond of Penyafort (1175–1275), one of the premier canon lawyers of his day. A Catalan trained in law first in Barcelona and then in Bologna, Raymond entered the Dominican order in 1222. Pope Gregory IX called Raymond to Rome in 1230 and made him the architect of the *Decretals*, the great compilation of papal decrees that was to become one of the pillars of canon law. Gregory had ordered him to compile the *Decretals* in 1230; in 1234, when Raymond wrote the *Responsiones*, he was still working on them. They would be officially promulgated in the Bull "Rex pacificus" of 5 September 1234.[3] In the *Responsiones*, we see Raymond struggling to apply the basics of canon law (as outlined notably in Gratian's *Decretum*) to the very particular circumstances in Tunis, in the *dar al-Islam*, where the traditional threats of excommunication and interdict carry little weight and over whose Muslim rulers the Pope obviously has no authority.

ECCLESIASTICAL ATTEMPTS TO LIMIT ILLICIT TRADE BEFORE 1234

The *Responsiones* mention merchants of different provenance active in Tunis: Genoans, Pisans, and "Hispani" (probably Catalans from Barcelona and perhaps Majorca, based on what we know of their trade in the region).[4] The Emir of Tunis was Abū Zakarīyā (1228–49), first independent sovereign of the Hafsid dynasty: members of his family had earlier been appointed governors of Ifriqiya by the Almohad caliphs of Marrakech, but, with the decreasing power and increasing unpopularity of the Almohads, Abū Zakarīyā refused to recognize their authority over him. In his relations with Christian maritime states, the Emir continued the policies of his predecessors, opening the port of Tunis to traders from the Italian maritime cities and from Barcelona.[5]

Abū Zakarīyā made agreements with various European maritime cities, granting privileges to their merchants. In addition to access to markets and preferential tariff rates, a mercantile city often obtained a *funduq*, an establishment that combined lodging for the merchants, storage space for their goods, and often such other facilities as a chapel, bakery, and tavern.[6] In addition, the Emir granted the city the right to appoint a consul, who ruled over the expatriate community and acted as the merchants' representative when dealing with the sultan or his officials (particularly the *sāhib al-diwān* or customs master). Documents mention that the Genoese had a *funduq* in Tunis in 1233, the Catalans in 1250. In the same way, we learn that the Venetians had a consul in Tunis in 1231, the Pisans in 1234, the Sicilians in 1239, the Genoese in 1250, the Catalans in 1258. The establishment of these *funduqs* and consuls was probably in many cases several years before their first mention in the documents. The *funduqs* were placed at the lower, eastern edge of the Medina, just west of the port and the customs. The increasing presence of European traders led to the development of industries geared to export: ceramics, metal-working, tanning, etc. It also created a variety of jobs: boat captains who transported goods from deep-water ships to quay, long-shoremen, translators, etc. The diversification and growing complexity of Tunisian urban society are reflected in the number of legal texts, particularly fatwas, which, starting in the thirteenth century, deal with urban professions of merchants and artisans. The impact of this trade is seen on the local written Arabic of the period, which borrowed from the Romance languages such terms as *qubtan* (captain) and *murqad* (market).[7]

The *Responsiones* mention many products that were exchanged, though the list that one can glean here was by no means meant to be representative of trade practices; rather, the friars mention those items which were or might be thought to be banned from trade with Muslims. These restrictions originated in the efforts by various popes and church councils to prohibit the selling of arms to enemies of the crusaders. The various Italian maritime republics were closely involved with transporting and supplying the crusaders and the Latin East. They also carried on lucrative trading with Muslim states in the region: the Fatimids and subsequently Ayyubids in Egypt, in particular. Ibn Tuwayr, a Fatimid functionary, describes stockpiles of arms in the caliphal palace "made by Frankish hands." In an 1154 treaty between the Fatimid Vizier al-Abbās and the Pisans, the Vizier reserves the right to buy any iron, pitch, or lumber that the Pisans bring to Egypt, at prices set by the state; the Pisans are free to sell other goods at market prices. This shows to what extent the Fatimids counted on their Italian trading partners for strategic materials: iron for manufacturing arms, pitch and lumber for ships. Two years later, when King Baldwin III of Jerusalem accords commercial privileges to the Pisans, he stipulates that in return they are not to provide Egypt with wood or iron.[8] Rulers of the region were quite aware of the dangers of their allies selling arms to their enemies: an example from a Muslim perspective is related by the chronicler Maqrīzī, who tells of a Mamluk vizier condemned by his sultan for selling arms to the Franks.[9]

It was at the Third Lateran Council (1179) that the Roman Church first attempted to establish a ban on such trade. The council proclaimed:

Cruel avarice has so seized the hearts of some that, though they glory in the Christian name, they provide Saracens with arms and wood for ships, and become their equals or even their superiors in wickedness, supplying them with arms and all they need to attack Christians. There are even some who in their cupidity act as captains or skippers in Saracen galleys or pirate vessels. Therefore we declare that such persons should be cut off from the communion of the church and be excommunicated for their wickedness, that catholic princes and civil magistrates should confiscate their possessions, and that if they are captured they should become the slaves of their captors. We order that throughout the churches of maritime cities frequent and solemn excommunication should be pronounced against them.[10]

Selling arms to the enemy has long been a lucrative practice; attempts to ban such trade, in the Middle Ages as today, meet with limited success. Here, selling arms or wood to "the Saracens" is prohibited, as is serving "as captains or pilots" on Saracen ships. The punishments inflicted are of two types: spiritual (excommunication) and physical – lay powers are exhorted to confiscate the possessions of these illicit traders and reduce them to slavery. The council orders that this sentence be reiterated regularly in the churches of "maritime cities" – which suggests both the seriousness of purpose and perhaps a certain sense of futility, a sense that without such constant reiteration neither the traders nor the lay powers are likely to take the canon seriously.

The problem is clearly as pressing in 1215, in the mind of Pope Innocent III and of the prelates assembled for the Fourth Lateran Council, which proclaims (in canon 71, immediately after provisions for launching a new crusade):

We excommunicate and anathematize those false and impious Christians who, in opposition to Christ and the Christian people, convey arms to the Saracens and iron and timber for their galleys. We decree that those who sell them galleys or ships, and those who act as pilots in pirate Saracen ships, or give them any advice or help by way of machines or anything else, to the detriment of the holy Land, are to be punished with deprivation of their possessions and are to become the slaves of those who capture them. We order this sentence to be renewed on Sundays and feast-days in all maritime towns; and the bosom of the church is not to be opened to such persons unless they send in aid of the Holy Land the whole of the damnable wealth which they received and the same amount of their own, so that they are punished in proportion to their offence. If perchance they do not pay,

they are to be punished in other ways in order that through their punishment others may be deterred from venturing upon similar rash
actions. In addition, we prohibit and on pain of anathema forbid all
Christians, for four years, to send or take their ships across to the
lands of the Saracens who dwell in the east, so that by this a greater
supply of shipping may be made ready for those wanting to cross over
to help the Holy Land, and so that the aforesaid Saracens may be
deprived of the not inconsiderable help which they have been accus-
tomed to receiving from this.[11]

The council has deemed it necessary to reiterate, strengthen, and
clarify the measures taken in 1179. The prohibited trade items are
ships, arms, and timber (as in the earlier council), but also iron.
Prohibited activities include, as earlier, captaining Saracen ships, but
also more generally giving "any advice or help" to Muslims. For the
next four years, in preparation for the crusades, shipping to the lands
of "the Saracens who dwell in the east" is prohibited, in order to use
the resources of the maritime cities in the interest of the coming
crusade. While these clauses broaden the scope of the prohibitions,
others narrow that scope: it is specifically those actions done "to the
detriment of the Holy Land" that are prohibited, and trade specifically
with "the Saracens who dwell in the east" – not, in other words, with
those of the Maghrib. One can almost sense the presence of Genoese
and Pisan lobbyists in the papal court, salvaging their lucrative trade
with the Maghribi ports, in which they benefit from the advantageous
tariff rates accorded to them by the Almohads.[12]

As for the punishments inflicted on illicit traders, the council reit-
erates the 1179 provisions: excommunication, confiscation of goods,
and slavery. It also adds another option, as penance in order to achieve
absolution: devote the double of one's ill-gained profits to the succor
of the Holy Land. Those who refuse to pay, the council threatens
vaguely, are to be punished "in other ways."

ILLICIT TRADE IN TUNIS IN 1234

When Raymond wrote to the friars of Tunis in 1234 (nineteen years
after the Fourth Lateran Council), the problem was still perceived to
be real. Jerusalem was in Christian hands, though precariously, thanks
to the Treaty of Jaffa between Emperor Frederick II and Egyptian
Sultan al-Kâmil in 1229. Some of the measures taken by the Fourth

Lateran Council were clearly meant to be in effect for four years only – the time needed to mount a new crusade. Lateran III had no such restrictions, and some of the prohibitions in Lateran IV were no doubt meant to be permanent. The friars in Tunis have to deal with these issues in a number of ways: at times, it seems, they receive anxious traders who want to be reassured that their trade practices are licit; at other times, they actively condemn the trade practices of merchants who refuse to heed them or to recognize their authority. The friars clearly cannot rely on the help of lay authorities: both church councils obliged kings and other secular authorities to enforce these rules and to punish offenders (prelates often threatened and cajoled in vain to get European rulers to heed these injunctions). In Tunis, the only punishment the friars can use is spiritual: excommunication. In the responses given to the friars' specific question, Raymond and the Pope try to draw clear and coherent distinctions between three types of trade: practices that incur excommunication; those which are illicit but do not incur excommunication; and those which are licit.

Some types of trade are clearly prohibited and punished by excommunication. Merchants who sell ships, lumber, arms, or iron to Muslims are to be excommunicated, the *Responsiones* declare (¶1), specifically citing the two Lateran councils: those who sell to the detriment of the Holy Land are excommunicated by Lateran IV; those who do so in order to fight Christians by the "first" council (meaning Lateran III). Those who were unaware of these prohibitions are still excommunicated; they can, however, be absolved and are given lighter penance than those who were conscious of the prohibitions (¶33, 37). The friars (¶5) also ask about those who take swords, knives, or other weapons into "lands of Saracens" without intent to sell (but only for their own self-defense) and who subsequently sell them to Saracens. They too are excommunicated, as are hired hands on ships of traders involved in illicit commerce, though the latter can be given lighter penance, at the discretion of the confessors (¶40).

Yet large grey areas remain; some items are prohibited only if and when they will be used or risk being used for military action against Christians. The friars report (¶2) that "Spaniards give or sell spurs, bridles and saddles, concerning which we wonder whether they should be considered arms." Trade in these items was not specifically prohibited by any council; yet clearly if Catalan merchants were equipping Arab cavalry, this could present a military threat to Christians. The Pope responds, "if they do this in time of war, they are excommunicated."

This principle, that peacetime trade of non-military items is licit but wartime sale to enemies of Christians incurs excommunication, inspires the decisions on a number of other trade items. This is true, for example, of food (¶3). The friars provide a long list of different food items (everything from goats to chestnuts) sold to "Saracens" by Catalans, Genoans, and Pisans. The Italians seem to specialize in grain, wine, and legumes, the Catalans in livestock. The question is whether such trade incurs the sentence of excommunication. The response: if traders are supplying Saracens who are fighting against Christians, they are excommunicated. This same principle applies to Christian merchants hired to transport victuals from one "Saracen" port to another (¶4), to those who carry iron from one Saracen port to another (¶23), and to those who transport armed Saracens (¶24). These concessions were important to the merchants (particularly Pisans and Genoese) who dominated the long-haul traffic in the Mediterranean and who regularly transported goods and passengers between Muslim ports. One thinks of the numerous Muslim pilgrims to Mecca, such as Ibn Jubayr who took a Genoese ship to Alexandria on the first leg of his trip in the 1180s;[13] many of these travelers would have been armed.

Other passages of the *Responsiones* deal with exceptions made to the prohibition of trade of certain items. Selling wood and metal to Saracens was prohibited according to the two councils, but the friars asked if it was licit to sell "ligna parvicula" (tiny pieces of wood [¶25]). They asked the same questions about hemp, pitch, and flax, materials essential for building and equipping ships (¶26). Iron and weapons were banned, but what about "cultellos parvissimos et clavos minutissimos" (tiny knives and teensy-weensy nails [¶27])? Here we imagine the traders communicating their concerns to their confessors; the friars, inclined towards leniency, in turn seek reassurance from Rome. In each of these cases, the response is the same: peacetime trade for non-military purposes is permitted; supplying those at war with Christians is prohibited.

Other illicit trade practices were not specifically prohibited by the councils; they therefore do not incur excommunication. The friars mention Christian merchants who sell other Christians, as slaves, to Muslims (¶6). The Pope rules that such slave-traders are not excommunicated, but "they sin mortally." The slave-trade was booming throughout the Mediterranean. While it was illegal for Christians to own Christian slaves (Gregory IX would relax these prohibitions in the case of non-Christian slaves who converted to Christianity – they remained slaves; Raymond of Penyafort came to the same conclusion in his *De casibus*[14]), here we see Christian merchants selling Christian slaves to Muslims. Yet other Christian merchants captured Jews or Muslims (especially women) and sold them in Muslim lands (¶7). To be able to do so, they passed them off as Christians. What shocks the two friars, and for them perhaps merits the excommunication of these Christian slave-traders, is "iniuriam quam faciunt nomini christiano in huiusmodi venditione" (the insult they proffer to the Christian name through this type of sale). The capture and sale of these women, and the deception involved, posed less of a problem than the insult involved in calling these Jews and Muslims Christian. Here too the Pope concludes that this behavior involves mortal sin, but does not merit excommunication. In these two instances, it is clear that Raymond and Gregory are attempting to interpret and apply existing canon law, rather than to make new legislation. If these practices do not incur excommunication, it is because no previous council or papal decree specifically imposed excommunication on them.

Other stipulations deal with the legality of more mundane aspects of trade. The friars speak of clerics practicing trade, and of the scandal that this caused. Raymond exhorts the friars to restrain such clerics through ecclesiastical censure, or through other canonical punishments (¶32). Other questions deal with usury and related commercial practices. Gregory (¶14) refers the friars to his own decretal *Naviganti*,[15] where he declared that a merchant who receive more money than that which he has loaned is considered a usurer. However, one who buys grain, oil, or other merchandise and then resells it for profit is not deemed to be a usurer, since the price of these items fluctuates according to time and location. If usury is illicit, what about theft of such usurious profits? When the thief comes to confess, should he be required to return the ill-earned gains to those from whom he stole them? Yes, says Raymond (¶22), just as, in a similar vein (¶21), he orders the restitution to Muslim authorities in the case of theft of *decimas sarracenis*, taxes paid to the Saracens (probably the *jizya*).

The document is in some ways as interesting for what it does not say as for what it does. Only perfunctory attention is paid to usury, routinely condemned by popes and church councils and as routinely practiced by merchants, often under the flimsiest of disguises. The two friars (and presumably their confessants) seem largely undisturbed by these practices, focusing principally on two elements: those practices which involve direct or indirect military aid to Muslims at war with Christians; and practices that could oblige or encourage Christians to apostatize.

THE DIVERSITY AND COMPLEXITY OF THE LATIN COMMUNITY OF TUNIS

The commercial practices of European merchants in Tunis provided grist for many of the questions that the friars of Tunis sent to Pope Gregory. But the Latin Christian community that these friars served was not merely composed of merchants. One of the principal points of interest of the *Responsiones* is the grand diversity of the Europeans with whom the friars came into contact: converts from Christianity to Islam, mixed Muslim–Christian families, crusaders, mercenaries, captives, slaves, and even "mortgaged" Christians.

We know from local Arabic documents that many of the Christians who came to Tunis ended up marrying Muslims and converting to Islam. Various Hafsid sultans had European concubines, bought in the slave markets or received as gifts; while it was permissible for such women to remain Christian, in general the path to higher social status involved providing the sultan with a son and converting to Islam. We also know that while many European mercenaries remained Christian, others converted to Islam and adopted Arabic honorific names (*laqab*) that highlighted their military prowess.[16] It may well be that many of the translators were Europeans who prolonged their stay in Tunis, learned Arabic, and may or may not have converted to Islam.[17]

In their eighth question, the friars observe disapprovingly that some Christians "obligant vel impignorant viros vel feminas de familiis suis saracenis, necessitate compulsi." The words *obligare* and *impignorare* both have legal meanings of "pawn" or "mortgage," so this passage could be translated as "they pawn or mortgage to Saracens men or women from among their servants." What seems to be happening here is that Christians – especially, but not exclusively, knights (*milites*) – in debt (*necessitate compulsi*) are handing over to Muslims Christian men and women from among their *familiis* (servants) as guarantees for their debts or other legal (perhaps military) obligations. What bothers the friars is not the pawning of humans, but the spiritual risk involved in handing over Christians to

Muslims for indefinite periods of time (one imagines that these persons became permanent possessions of their new lords in the event of default on the debtor's obligations). Many of them, particularly the young (*pueri vel puellae*), ended up converting to Islam: "fiunt postmodum sarraceni." The Pope's response (as in ¶6–7) is that such practice is mortal sin, but does not incur excommunication.

The mention of *milites* most probably refers to mercenaries in the hire of the Tunisian emir. We know from other documents that Catalans, in particular, sold their military services to Tunis.[18] Perhaps more surprisingly, the friars (¶15) mention the presence of crusaders (*crucesignati*) who apparently have set off to fight the Saracens, gotten as far as Tunis, and for one reason or another not fulfilled their vows. Some of them are afraid of the Saracens; some have married without telling their new wives that they are *crucesignati*. The Pope responds that the friars should let those who cannot fulfill their vows – on account of illness, indigence, or other reasons – perform alternative penance; but that those who are able to go should be compelled to do so as soon as they can. It is difficult to know from this fleeing mention who these crusaders are, what they are doing in Tunis, and who the women they have married are.

Some of the friars' questions have to do with the practical problems of performing sacraments in a Muslim-ruled country with few clergy. Is it permissible to celebrate mass without wearing consecrated vestments, if necessary? No, responds the Pope (¶18). Is it permissible to perform extreme unction or to anoint catechumens with only one or two priests? The response is that the bishop and only he may do so (¶19). In these passages, one catches glimpses of the friars attempting to efficiently and discreetly perform their sacramental duties for the Christian community in the face of difficulties: lack of personnel, lack of consecrated vestments, etc.

The friars also ask (¶16) if it is permissible to celebrate mass before dawn "on account of the fear" of some of the Christians. In other words, some Christians in Tunis were afraid to practice their religion openly, and wished to do so in clandestine night-time services. Who were these fearful Christians? Certainly not the Italian merchants or the Catalan mercenaries, whose religious rights were in general assured by the Emir – often guaranteed through written treaties. These might be nominal Muslims, Christians who had converted to Islam but who continued to consider themselves Christians. They might be dependants or slaves of Muslims, who had converted in order to better their lot. For these people to openly return to Christianity would be tantamount to apostasy and would be in theory punishable by death. Gregory and Raymond respond that, yes, pre-dawn mass may be held on account of "fear of Saracens," but otherwise not, except for midnight mass at Christmas.

A further set of problems was posed by conversions of Christians to Islam. One of the friars' questions (¶10) involves those who were Christian and subsequently converted to Islam, "postmodum facti sunt sarraceni." Some converted when they were young, some when they were adult; some slave, some free: many of them converted, say the friars, largely because they were ignorant about the articles of the faith. Such apostasy, in Christian Europe, was illegal – potentially a capital crime. But of course in Muslim Tunis there was no question of punishing them, since they were beyond the reach of Christian princes and indeed of spiritual penalties such as excommunication (because they had voluntarily removed themselves from communion with the Church, according to Gratian's *Decretum*).[19] The concern here is for their relatives who have remained Christian. According to canon law, Christians ought to shun the company of heretics;[20] exceptions are allowed for those who seek to bring them back to the Catholic fold. Yet the friars realize that if they try to prohibit Christians in Tunis from maintaining contact with their Muslim relatives, they will have little luck, and will most likely only push them to apostatize as well. "It seems to us that they cannot easily abstain from frequenting the above-mentioned people, either because they love them according to the flesh, as their children, or because they receive food from them." The Pope answers that they may frequent these Muslim "causa correctionis vel necessitatis" – in other words, either in order to try to bring them back into the Christian fold or for material necessity. By applying Gratian's legislation concerning heretics to Muslims, Raymond and Gregory place Islam – in legal and practical terms – in the category of heresy. This is in line with much contemporary theological reflection on Islam, particularly the work of Latin Christian polemists against Islam in the twelfth and thirteenth centuries.[21]

The following section (¶11) deals with the problem of mixed marriages. While it was not legal for a Christian to marry a non-Christian, the question here is what happens when one member of a married Christian couple "labatur in haeresim," slides into heresy – in other words (in this context) converts to Islam (here again Islam is treated as heresy). Gratian echoes earlier church legislation in strictly prohibiting marriage between Christians and non-Christians. Yet exceptions are made in cases of conversion: Causa 28 of the *Decretum* deals with the case of a married *infidelis* who converts to Christianity and whose spouse remains *infidelis*. Gratian affirms that it is permitted for the new Christian to separate from his non-Christian wife, but also that he may remain married to her if he chooses to do so. The key distinction here is to know whether the now Christian member of the couple can remain married to his spouse without *contumelia creatoris* (insult to the creator.) This is a direct reference to *Decretum* c28 q2 c2: when the non-Christian spouse hates Christianity, and is guilty of insult to the creator, the Christian spouse may not only separate from the infidel, but may marry anew. The Bible prohibits divorce; separation or annulment is allowed on specific grounds, including consanguinity and adultery. The *Decretum* affirms that *contumelia creatoris* is a sort of spiritual adultery, far worse than the mere physical kind, and that it is therefore grounds for separation and annulment of marriage. Raymond and the Pope apply Gratian's ruling concerning conversion of the marriage of a convert to Christianity to the case of mixed couples where a Christian has converted to Islam.

In general, of course, conversion in Muslim Tunis is envisioned in only one direction: to Islam. While I have suggested that some of the Christians who in "fear of the Saracens" participate in secret nighttime services may be nominal Muslims who have surreptitiously returned to Christianity, only one passage (¶9) deals with the actual baptism of Muslims. Some Christian servants or slaves of Muslims took care of Muslim children. They asked the friars whether they could and should secretly baptize these children: if the children then died before the age of discretion, they would be saved. The Pope responds that they should be baptized. We may presume, then, that a number of Muslim children of thirteenth-century Tunis were secretly baptized by their Christian nannies.

POWER STRUGGLES BETWEEN MENDICANTS AND SECULAR CLERGY

One further dimension of this text merits consideration. The friars are not the only Christian clergy present in Tunis. They at times come into conflict with priests who resent their presence and who refuse to recognize their authority. The friars ask the Pope how they should proceed in the case of certain married *fratres spirituales* (¶12) present in Tunis *before* the arrival of the friars. Such marriage was in clear violation of the principles of the so-called "Gregorian Reform" of the eleventh century. This is the same sort of problem as was faced in the wake of the crusades (particularly the Fourth Crusade), which brought Latin clerics into contact with married clergy of the Eastern churches. The response here is that such men should be separated from their wives if possible, but otherwise they may remain married; in no case should new marriages of clerics be contracted.

Another fundamental issue of the reform movement was the immunity of clerics from lay justice and punishment. The friars mention the case of "some people" who seize "clericos latrones" (thieves who are clerics) and whip them (¶28). The question is whether those people are to be excommunicated and whether the friars can absolve them. The Pope responds that, yes, they are to be excommunicated, and, yes, the friars can absolve them. Hence the principle of clerical immunity is affirmed, but those laymen who have punished errant clerics can receive absolution.

Other questions involve the Pope's delegation of powers to the friars. Pope Honorius III had conferred upon them the power to grant absolution to excommunicates in cases where the persons could not easily (*commode*) come to Rome to receive absolution directly from the Pope (¶20). The friars ask, What does *commode* mean? In response, Gregory confirms the powers granted by his predecessor and defines what *commode* means here: the friars may absolve excommunicates who are prevented from traveling to Rome by illness, old age, or poverty. Others should go to Rome to receive absolution from the Pope. In a similar vein, the friars have received the power of according absolution *in extremis* (¶31). They ask what that means: does a fever or dysentery qualify? The Pope answers that a person should be considered *in extremis* only if there is real danger of death.

In the above situations the friars have a clear power to absolve excommunicates in specific cases, a power conferred by Honorius III and confirmed here by Gregory IX. Their other powers over clerics in Tunis are less clear, and were actively disputed by those clerics. We have seen that the Pope exhorts the friars to use ecclesiastical censure against clerics who practice trade (¶32); this suggests that the friars have jurisdiction over clerics in Tunis – at least in some circumstances. The friars also ask (¶30) "who should be considered residents" (*qui intellegantur commorantes*)? Someone who has been in Tunis a year? Six months? The response is that anyone who intends to stay there, in particular if he has been there one year, should be considered a resident. The suggestion seems to be that the friars have some spiritual authority over these *commorantes*, although it is far from clear exactly what that authority is; whether, for example, it entails the right to collect tithes or other ecclesiastical taxes or fines. In an interesting parallel, at about the same time Egyptian *ʿulamā* ruled that a Christian merchant who spent over one year in Egypt should be considered a resident *dhimmi*, and should be made to pay the *jizya* (the annual poll tax paid by *dhimmis*).[22]

One of the friars' questions deals with a conflict of authority involving Genoese priests. As we have seen, the friars mention that the Genoese were selling ships to the Saracens, in clear violation of papal and conciliar directives (¶1). Yet the Genoese merchants claimed that *their* prelates did not prohibit such trade. The implication is that the Genoese, whose economic interest is clearly in braving these prohibitions, have priests who look the other way. The Genoese do not recognize any authority of the mendicants in Tunis to pronounce their excommunication: that authority would presumably reside in their own priests, their archbishop, and ultimately the Pope. Since there is no Christian bishop in Tunis, the Genoese insist that they owe obedience only to their own clergy. In the response, the Pope sidesteps this difficult issue of authority, simply insisting that the Genoese merchants are excommunicated by the authority of two church councils: the Third Lateran Council pronounced the excommunication of those who sold arms to those fighting Christians, while the Fourth Lateran Council excommunicated those who carried on trade "at the expense of the holy Land." Gregory had recently confirmed the appointment of the Franciscan Agnello as bishop of Fez, to serve the Latin Christian community of Almohad, Morocco; the establishment of a bishop eliminated (at least in theory) the jurisdictional problems so evident in Tunis.[23] The following year (1235) the Pope sent, as emissary to the "King of Tunis" Abū Zakarīyā, John, "minister of the Order of the Minors in Barbary."[24] It is not clear if this John was the same Franciscan minister who (with his Dominican counterpart) sent the forty questions to Gregory. What is clear is that Gregory was in close contact with the Franciscans in Tunis and was employing them to further his

62 *A Faithful Sea*

own interests in Tunis and to act as privileged intermediaries with the Emir.

The *Responsiones* provide a fascinating glimpse at the European "expatriate" communities of Tunis, in all their complexity and diversity. This text also shows how Pope Gregory IX and his Dominican penitentiary Ramon Penyafort pragmatically adapted church legislation to the situation on the ground, aware of their limits at the same time as they attempted to affirm the authority of the papacy. The Franciscan and Dominican orders were key players in this, throughout Europe and, here, beyond Europe's borders.

NOTES

1. Earlier versions of this article were presented to the Medieval Studies Seminar of the University of California—Berkeley and to the meeting of the Medieval Ethnicities Research Group at the University of Lancaster. My thanks to the organizers of those events, in particular Maureen Miller, Sarah Barber, and Andrew Jotischky.
2. *Responsiones ad dubitabilia circa communicationem christianorum cum sarracenis*, in Raymond of Penyafort, *Summae*, 3 vols., in *Universa Bibliotheca Iuris* I, ed. Xavier Ochoa and Aloisius Diez (Rome: Commentarium pro religiosis, 1976–78), vol. 3, pp. 1024–1036.
3. See Carlo Longo (ed.), *Magister Raimundus: atti del convegno per il IV centenario della canonizzazione di San Raimondo de Penyafort (1601–2001)* (Rome: Istituto Storico Domenicano, 2002); Stephan Kuttner, "Raymond of Penyafort as Editor: The 'Decretales' and 'Constitutiones' of Gregory IX," *Bulletin of Medieval Canon Law*, 12, 1982, pp. 65–80.
4. On the port of Tunis and its international commercial activities, see Tahar Mansouri, "Vie portuaire à Tunis au bas Moyen âge (XII–XVe siècle)," *Journal of Oriental and African Studies*, 9 1998, pp. 39–52. On the Catalan presence in Abū Zakarīyā's Tunis, see Charles-Emmanuel Dufourcq, *L'Espagne catalane et le Maghrib aux XIIIe et XIVe siècles: de la bataille de Las Navas de Tolosa (1212) à l'avènement du sultan mérinide Abou-l-Hasan (1331)* (Paris: Presses universitaires de France, 1966), pp. 93–110; on the Italians (in particular Venetians), see Bernard Doumerc, *Venise et l'émirat hafside de Tunis (1231–1535)* (Paris: L'Harmattan, 1999), pp. 13–26. For an introduction to medieval Tunis with an overview of scholarship, see Mounira Chapoutot-Remadi, "Tunis," in *Grandes villes méditerranéennes du monde musulman médiéval*, ed. Jean-Claude Garcin (Rome: Ecole Française de Rome, 2000), pp. 235–362. See also Ronald Messier, "The Christian Community of Tunis at the Time of St. Louis' Crusade, A.D. 1270," in *Meeting of Two Worlds: Cultural Exchange between East and West during the Period of the Crusades*, ed. Vladimir Goss (Kalamazoo, Mich.: Medieval Institute, 1986), pp. 241–255.
5. R. Brunschvig, *La Berbérie orientale sous les hafsides*, 2 vols. (Paris: Maisonneuve, 1940), vol. 1, pp. 20–38.

6. Olivia Remie Constable, *Housing the Stranger in the Mediterranean World: Lodging, Trade, and Travel in Late Antiquity and the Middle Ages* (Cambridge, England: Cambridge University Press, 2003).

7. Chapoutot-Remadi, "Tunis," p. 242.

8. Claude Cahen, *Orient et Occident au temps des Croisades* (Paris: Aubier, 1983), pp. 125–126, 133, 230.

9. Ibid., pp. 239–240.

10. Lateran III, canon 24, in *Les conciles œcuméniques: Les décrets. Tome II–1, Nicée I à Latran V*, ed. G. Alberigo et al. (Paris: Cerf, 1994), p. 480.

11. Lateran IV, canon 71, in *Les conciles œcuméniques: Les décrets. Tome II–1, Nicée I à Latran V*, pp. 572–575.

12. For the text of a trading agreement between the Almohads and Pisa (1186), see M. L. de Mas Latrie (ed.), *Traités de paix et de commerce et documents divers concernant les relations des chrétiens avec les Arabes de l'Afrique septentironale au Moyen Age*, 2 vols. (Paris: H. Plon, 1866; reprint New York: Burt Franklin, n.d.), vol. 2, pp. 28–29.

13. Muḥammad ibn Aḥmad Ibn Jubayr, *The Travels of Ibn Jubayr* (Leiden, The Netherlands: Brill, 1907).

14. See Benjamin Kedar, *Crusade and Mission: European Approaches toward the Muslims* (Princeton, N.J.: Princeton University Press, 1984), pp. 146–151.

15. "Naviganti vel eunti ad nundinas certam mutuans pecuniae quantitatem, pro eo, quod suscipit in se periculum, recepturus aliquid ultra sortem, usurarius est censendus. Ille quoque, qui dat X. solidos, ut alio tempore totidem sibi grani, vini vel olei mensurae reddantur, quae licet tunc plus valeant, utrum plus vel minus solutionis tempore fuerint valiturae, verisimiliter dubitatur, non debet ex hoc usurarius reputari. Ratione huius dubii etiam excusatur, qui pannos, granum, vinum, oleum vel alias merces vendit, ut amplius, quam tunc valeant, in certo termino recipiat pro eisdem; si tamen ea tempore contractus non fuerat venditurus" (X 5:19:19).

16. See Chapoutot-Ramadi, "Tunis," p. 241.

17. Mansouri, "Vie portuaire à Tunis," pp. 45–47.

18. The use of Catalan mercenaries is well documented for the period beginning in 1257; see Dufourcq, *L'Espagne catalane*, pp. 101–104.

19. C24 q1 c4–5. For analysis of Causa 24 and references to a new critical edition, see Anders Winroth, *The Making of Gratian's Decretum* (Cambridge, England: Cambridge University Press, 2000), pp. 50–92.

20. "Hereticorum consortia a catholicis sont fugienda," c24 q1 c2.

21. See John Tolan, *Saracens: Islam in the Medieval European Imagination* (New York: Columbia University Press, 2002).

22. Philippe Gourdin, "Les marchands étrangers ont-ils un statut de dhimmi? A propos de quelques statuts de marchands étrangers dans les pays chrétiens et musulmans de Méditerranée occidentale au XIIIᵉ siècle," in *Migrations et diasporas méditerranéennes (Xe–XVIe siècles)*, ed. Michel Balard and Alain Ducellier (Paris: Publications de la Sorbonne, 2002), pp. 435–46.

23. Latrie, *Traités de paix et de commerce*, vol. 2, p. 10.

24. Ibid., p. 11.

Bartolommeo Bulgarini, *Assumption of the Virgin with Saint Thomas*, c. 1360, now in the Pinacoteca Nazionale di Siena. Photo used with permission from the Ministero per i Beni e le attivit culturali, Siena.

3

BULGARINI'S *ASSUMPTION WITH DOUBTING THOMAS*

ART, TRADE, AND FAITH IN POST-PLAGUE SIENA

Anne McClanan

Bartolommeo Bulgarini's painting *Assumption of the Virgin with Saint Thomas* offers us a window into the interconnections shaping the visual and religious culture of the late medieval Mediterranean. This work, now in the Pinacoteca in Siena, was made about 1360 for the foremost charitable institution in Siena at the time, the Hospital of Santa Maria della Scala (the Spedale). The iconography of the painting was unprecedented, so how did such an unusual image come to be made in the conservative artistic milieu of Siena at the time? We will see that interactions among central Italy, Venice, and Constantinople drew Siena into a web of exchange and influence that ultimately yielded this extraordinary artwork.

In this painting, the Virgin Mary ascends to heaven surrounded by angels singing and playing music. Many compositional details of the painting follow Lippo Memmi's *Assumption of the Virgin* now in the Alte Pinakothek in Munich, especially the positioning of the Virgin encircled by musical angels. Below is Thomas, overwhelmed with awe. The apostle's central position is unusual in Assumption iconography. His back faces the viewer, but we only see him from the waist up as his torso bends upwards to the divine vision; his raised hands clutch the belt he has just received as the Virgin ascends to heaven. The viewer shares his moment of astonishment as we stand behind him facing the grand, serene vision of the Virgin.[1] In the spandrels, five prophets look down from each side; these lively clusters of men have exoticizing touches such as Phrygian caps and Pseudo-Kufic writing on their scrolls. The size of the panel measures a substantial 205 by 112 cm, and was likely cut down at some point from still larger dimensions. The apostle Thomas's presence in this tableau is dictated by two events, of a both general and specific nature. The devastating pan-Mediterranean epidemic of the Black Death had perhaps shaken the faith of some, and the image of Doubting Thomas became more prevalent in new artistic commissions at this time. More pertinent to this work though is the fact the Black Death, with its enormous casualties in Siena, had swelled the coffers of the Hospital of Santa Maria della Scala. Many families were completely wiped out and their assets donated to this institution that commissioned the painting by Bulgarini. With this new-found wealth, Siena acquired a set of prestigious relics from Constantinople, including the belt or girdle of the Virgin, which in the apocryphal tradition she casts down to Thomas as she makes her ascent. While trade in religious artifacts was an immediate inspiration for the iconography of this painting, other factors, as we shall see, shaped the work. The style, moreover, demonstrates the rather recherché cast that post-plague Sienese art took. The Byzantine style so eagerly embraced by the earlier generation of painters is now recast in an Italian framework to emphasize a harder, more abstract contour to the spiritual realities it depicted.

Bulgarini painted this altarpiece during Siena's much-maligned Rule of the Twelve (1355–68). Often characterized as ignorant and incapable, the Rule of the Twelve suffers in modern historiography from comparison with the preceding Council of Nine, since the upstart coalition of artisans and the aristocracy guided the city through an ordeal of recurring plagues and devastating mercenary raids. The level of change represented by the ascent of the Twelve may have been overstated in terms of the impact on everyday life in the commune. Major public projects continued, such as the Fonte Gaia planned in 1334 and finally realized in 1419 by Jacopo della Quercia. The vast scale of early fourteenth-century projects is evidenced by the fact that the city did not need to expand beyond its parameters of that time until the twentieth century, when its population finally equaled its early trecento high.[2] The ambitious Duomo plan to expand Siena's building to become the largest cathedral in Europe was finally abandoned in 1357, under both financial and technical problems. This diminution of plans for the cathedral suggests the environment in which Bulgarini painted: a Siena filled with reminders of its recent heyday and its current decline. Tragically for the Sienese, the Black Death of 1348 was only the first of numerous waves of the disease to visit the population, and these recurrences seem to have terrified artists and patrons even more than the first bout of the plague.

The Spedale emerged in this political environment as the leading institutional source of philanthropy and artistic commissions in Siena. In 1359 it paid the vast sum of three thousand gold florins to acquire a set of relics, and built a new chapel to honor this acquisition on the ground floor of the rector's palace with ready access to the piazza in front of the Duomo. The Chapel of the Relics was likely completed by the 1360s and was the original setting for the *Assumption* panel. In the seventeenth-century overhaul of the Spedale, the Rector Agostino Chigi noted a painting by Bulgarini that very likely was the work depicting the Virgin with Thomas.[3] Its patronage of other Marian imagery may also be evident in Niccolò di Buonnacorso's painting in which steps are inserted in the background, perhaps an inclusion of that venerable institution's favorite symbol.[4] Other alterations were also made to vaunt these newly purchased relics, including the construction of a special pulpit attached to the Spedale church. In addition to its serving as a hospital, the Spedale's place as a hostel for pilgrims en route to Rome was given another attraction by the possession of these prestigious relics.

We are lucky that fairly detailed records survive of the transaction that brought the relics to Siena. Documents attest that the deal was brokered by Pietro di Giunta Torrigiani, a merchant based in Constantinople who was born in the town of Signa near Florence.[5] Although Pietro purchased the collection of relics earlier, the transaction with the Sienese did not transpire until 1359. The empress of Emperor John VI Cantacuzenos (1347–54) testified to the authenticity of the collection to two of the bishops, and even claimed that the imperial family possessed nothing more valuable.[6] The treasures were given up for sale out of the Byzantine imperial family's state of chronic financial exigency, but perhaps an immediate financial crisis motivated this sale as well, for the imperial coffers had just been further depleted by two large ransoms paid to Genoese pirates and a Serbian governor.[7] The high status of the witnesses suggests the weight given this transaction in the Pera area of Constantinople in 1357: the Apostolic Nuncio to Constantinople, a Dominican inquisitor, and three bishops were all in attendance. The relic of the Virgin's belt had been an important one in Constantinople, for every 31 August, the end of the liturgical year, a feast was held in which the belt was placed on the altar of the Church of the Virgin in Chalkoprateia in the capital.

Andrea di Grazia represented the Spedale in the final transaction that took place in Venice on 28 May 1359. Cutler suggests that the high value of the pieces perhaps contributed to the delay, for no doubt the merchant wished to proceed judiciously in finding a buyer who could pay the daunting price tag the relics ultimately commanded.[8] To put the price of three thousand gold florins for the group of relics into perspective: the elaborately sculpted large fountain that Jacopo della Quercia produced for the Campo in Siena cost a full one thousand florins less in 1408. The transaction to sell the Byzantine relics seems to have provided the Italian merchant with something of a retirement plan, because the Spedale included in its compensation a house as well as payment of two hundred florins a year for the rest of his and his son's life.

In addition to the prized relic of the Virgin's belt, this group of religious artifacts was also desirable for several of the other items. One lectionary binding purchased then and now in the Biblioteca Communale in Siena, for instance, has fifty-two inset Byzantine enamels that appear to have been reset a few decades before the manuscript was sold to the Sienese. Its iconography is a bit jumbled, with multiple iterations of Christ and the Virgin, and it could have been made for a private patron.[9] Alternatively, in Venice some of the items such as this manuscript cover may have been prettified for the next phase of transactions. Paul Hetherington proposed, for instance, that the lectionary's silver gilt cover was crafted in Venice from a newly assembled set of Byzantine enamels.[10] The Spedale sale included other works such as the twelfth-century Byzantine enamel reliquary of the True Cross, a piece still housed in the Spedale, which today functions as a sprawling museum and temporary exhibition space. Additional items included in the deal were likewise associated with Christ: fragments of wood from the True Cross, rope used to remove the money-lenders from the Temple, his final garments, the lance and sponge from the Passion. In addition, there were other relics from thirty-three saints.

The moving of these sacred relics from Constantinople to Tuscany represents a broad shift of cultural and economic resources that impoverished the remnants of the Byzantine Empire. The sheer number of Byzantine manuscripts now in Italian collections compared with those remaining in Istanbul suggests a wholesale migration of a body of culture which occurred especially in the 100–150 years before the empire's final eclipse in 1453.[11] Cutler points out that at least twelve of the Byzantine works in the San Marco treasury that have long been assumed to be Venetian plunder from the Fourth Crusade (1204) may well have entered Italy as a result of financial transactions similar to the Spedale sale or as gifts.[12] Thus several of the most famous works of Middle Byzantine artistry in San Marco appear first in the 1325 inventory, but not in the 1283 inventory documents.

Although this major transfer of religious and cultural artifacts may not have happened immediately during the Fourth Crusade, the long-term consequences of the ensuing Latin occupation destroyed the Byzantine economy and created the conditions that led to this hemorrhage of Byzantine works. The medieval West had long cast an envious eye on Byzantium's wealth, and Constantinople's exalted status was clear. Robert of Clari, who saw the Fourth Crusade's depredations of the city in 1204, famously wrote:

> Never since the world was established was so great wealth, or so noble, or so magnificent, either seen or won ... Nor do I believe, of my own knowledge that in the fifty richest cities of the world could there be so much wealth as was found in the body of Constantinople. For the Greeks also bore witness that two-thirds of all the wealth of the world was in Constantinople, and that the other third was scattered throughout the world.[13]

The economic decline of Constantinople accelerated after the Latin conquest of the city and during its occupation from 1204 to 1261, primarily because of the crusaders' short-sighted disruption of the infrastructure and legal system.[14]

The roughly two centuries in Constantinople between the Byzantine reconquest of their capital and the beginning of Ottoman rule in 1453 were a grim time in which many of the city's remaining Christian artifacts were sold in desperation. The economy's collapse under Latin rule proved irrecoverable and the city probably contained only forty thousand inhabitants by the time these relics were sold to the Florentine merchant.[15] Even the wording used in prominent late Byzantine historians attests to the prominence of Italians in fourteenth-century Byzantium: these writers use the medieval Greek term for "Italians" when referring to the broader category of Western Europeans.[16] The overall pattern of Italian acquisition of the relics is not surprising, but it is unusual that a Florentine would broker a sale for the Sienese in Venice.[17] This flow of goods to Italy was almost inevitable given that country's dominance in eastern Mediterranean trade in the fourteenth century.[18]

Siena may have been particularly eager to acquire these religious items because of its longstanding, special devotion to the Virgin Mary. The battle of Montaperti in which Siena unexpectedly beat rival Florence in 1261 cemented the Virgin's role as protectress of the city.[19] The city's already fervent attachment to the Virgin received a new celebration after the purchase by the Spedale in 1359 – the most prized relics acquired from Constantinople were brought out to great fanfare at the feast of the Annunciation.

This intense reverence for the Virgin meant that she was a favored theme in art; remarkably, over half of the late medieval and Renaissance paintings made in Siena rendered the Virgin. Her image would be carefully calibrated for particular settings. For example, the original configuration of the Bulgarini altarpiece probably once included side panels of Saints Anthony Abbot and John the Evangelist.[20] Thus this altarpiece for the new chapel of the relics mirrors in its overall scheme the structure used in the main altarpieces at the nearby Duomo.

The altarpiece's lavish use of gold leaf combined with the finely worked surface treatment in some fundamental way brings the painting into harmony with the reliquaries honored elsewhere in the Spedale's chapel.[21] The great early trecento Sienese painter Simone Martini had developed this sgraffito technique to embellish the surface of his paintings, and the return to this process is typical of the revivalist mood in the later painter's milieu. Bulgarini even used colored glass and low-relief decorative modeling to embellish the area of the spandrels.

DOUBTING THOMAS

This adaptability to context is also expressed in Bulgarini's unprecedented composition for the depiction of Thomas in this *Assumption*. Thomas's position, which so closely echoes the posture of the Sienese officiants and worshipers honoring the Virgin in the new chapel, might have seemed surprising for its novelty to the original fourteenth-century viewers. Earlier paintings of the Assumption of the Virgin, when they included the apostle Thomas at all, depicted him tucked away modestly to one side, and often shown in profile, kneeling at prayer. A preoccupation with the Virgin and a newly acquired relic was the impetus for this shift from the customary iconography of the apostle Thomas. Whereas several studies explores his Christological iconography, relatively little scholarship considers the image of Thomas in Mariological imagery.[22]

Saint Thomas the Apostle is rendered in art in three different theological contexts. The most popular form depicts Thomas in his moment of doubt following the Resurrection, which has its most famous expression in Caravaggio's seminal painting *Doubting Thomas* (ca. 1601, now in Potsdam). There we see Thomas's dirty hand probe Christ's wound, the spectator vicariously absorbed into the apostle's maudlin curiosity, but the general outline of the scene follows the canonical text. The next two themes derive from apocryphal traditions. Thomas's missionary work was explored in art especially in India and churches connected to the Syriac tradition of Christianity followed there, but his role in the Assumption is actually the least common framework for Thomas's appearances in art.

In a Latin account of the Assumption attributed to Joseph of Arimathea, Thomas mirrors his role in the Gospel of John, but this time with several inversions in the story structure.[23] In John 20:25, Thomas demands rigorous proof of Christ's return: "Except I shall see in his hands the print of the nails, and put my finger into the place of the nails, and put my hand into his side, I will not believe." In the apocryphal account his status as the Doubter is reshaped. Mary on her deathbed gathers the apostles and Thomas does not appear, an absence explained by the other followers as punishment for his prior incredulity. Thomas, however, had been proselytizing in India, and arrived at the Mount of Olives as Mary was being born up and "the girdle with which the apostles had girt her body was thrown down to him."[24] Thomas manages to be the apostle honored with the most tangible proof of her miraculous ascent, but this time it is his colleagues who are the unbelievers: because they questioned his absence they have not witnessed the Assumption. The apostle Thomas's activities in India are recounted in the Syriac text of the apocryphal Acts of Thomas, now partially preserved in the British Library. Other later versions exist in Greek, Latin, Armenian, and Ethiopic but they generally follow the Syriac text in its main contours. Many other sources, including Eusebius and Gregory of Tours, refer to Thomas's missionary work in India, and there seems no reason to dispute the repeated assertion that he traveled as far as northern India. Moreover, the apocryphal tradition claims that Thomas was the twin brother of Jesus. The odd duality that Thomas shares with Jesus even carries over to the idea in the Acts of Thomas that the apostle, too, was a carpenter by trade, which leads to Thomas's eventual role as patron saint of architects.[25]

The apocryphal narrative of Thomas seems to have interested not just the Sienese but the Florentines as well. An amendment to the life of Thomas was made: before heading to India, Thomas by this account made a detour to Jerusalem, where he put the belt in the care of a holy man. Generations later, the belt was transmitted to Prato (soon to be annexed by Florence) as a dowry.[26] The couple kept the belt and on the husband's death in 1194 it was given to the local church of Santo Stefano, where the Virgin's belt soon wrought many miracles.[27] Documentary evidence supports that the relic of the belt was in the church by 1270, yet the popularity of the image of the Madonna with the belt culminates almost a hundred years later. Maso di Banco (d. before 1350) painted for the Duomo in Prato an altarpiece that includes an image of the Virgin handing her belt to Thomas (this panel is now in the Staatliche Museum, Berlin). Primarily after 1350, manuscripts of the legend of the belt proliferated, though, and Cassidy suggests that political forces pushed the relic into prominence. Moreover, we know that women turned to the Pratese relic to expedite their delivery, in a practice that taps into centuries of tradition connecting belts and maternity.[28] The belt's association with childbirth is manifest in one label given Artemis in ancient Greece – "She who loosens belts" (Lysizonos) – where the belt carried strong connotations of marriage and procreation.[29] Lavish examples of Byzantine marriage belts survive, and concurrently we see belts appear in several Byzantine and Western medieval *vitae* as turning points in accounts of miraculous rescues from dangerous and extended labors. In the late Middle Ages, Saint Margaret of Antioch, for example, was often sought as an intercessor in childbirth, and, for a woman in a dangerous labor, touching the relic of Margaret's belt was thought to be an especially efficacious expedient.

Florence had folded Prato into its territory in 1351, and that city contained the most prized relic of the Virgin in Tuscany – the belt (*cintolo* or *cingolo*) in the Pieve of San Stefano. This relic made the parish church an active pilgrimage site and we know that in the early fifteenth century the belt was processed around Prato to ward off the incursions by the Visconti Giangaleazzo. Perhaps the spate of Florentine artworks were made in response to an apotropaic use of the relic in the attacks in 1351 by the Archbishop Giovanni Visconti, though their existence could be more of a comment on the acquisition of Prato.[30]

Orcagna's marble tabernacle for Florence's Church of Orsanmichele, a sculpture made between 1352 and 1366, attests to an increased interest in the theme of the Assumption, in particular the version with the Virgin giving the belt to Thomas. Bernardo Daddi's painting of the Assumption of the Virgin was probably made for the altarpiece honoring the relic of the Virgin's belt in Prato, though it's not clear whether the painting was produced during the initial commission of 1337–39 or in the 1340s.[31] All that remains of the apostle in the panel today are his fingers grasping the belt, but his importance in the original image is clear from the fact that his hand appears the same scale as that of the Virgin. Moreover, at least twelve depictions of the Madonna del Parto survive from trecento or early quattrocentro Italy. Nine are from Florence and five of these images of the pregnant Virgin share a distinctive attribute – a cord-like belt. Perhaps Bulgarini's altarpiece, and indeed the desire for the acquisition of this relic by the Sienese, was inspired by the contemporary prominence of the belt for the Florentines.

SIENESE ARTISTIC CONTEXT

Bulgarini's painting for the Spedale addressed an immediately Sienese context as well. Duccio's *Maesta* includes a fairly traditional image of Saint Thomas with Christ after the Resurrection (1308–11, Museo dell'Opera del Duomo, Siena). Bulgarini reacted to this dominant tradition of depicting Thomas when he innovated in his conception of the altarpiece he created at a later moment in Siena's history, and the grand altarpiece would exert enormous influence over later Sienese art. The first half of Sienese fourteenth-century art is dominated by the workshops of great masters such as Duccio, the Lorenzetti, and Simone Martini. Millard Meiss's interpretation put forward in 1951 has dominated discussion of the Sienese art produced in the three decades following the Black Death. Meiss asserts that the more iconic, less naturalistic manner of representation, so at odds with the pre-plague years' experiments of the Lorenzetti, telegraphs in visual form the trauma that central Italy had experienced from the bubonic plague's ravages. Now more than anything the population sought atonement for their sins in hopes of averting a similar disaster. Meiss's ideas have been questioned in their broad contours but one of his thesis's most important consequences is that the relationship between the plague and potential consequences for artistic production has been tenaciously explored.

Rather than indicating that the years after 1348 were marked by a lull in the art market, analysis of Tuscan and Umbrian last wills shows actually an increase in individual patronage at the same time the power of the communes waned in this arena.[32] Most religious institutions probably had considerably reduced resources for artistic patronage in the 1350s.[33] Other factors were at play as well. Cohn has determined that artworks generally realized one-fifth the price they had before the Black Death, which relates to the fact that many more small-scale works seem to have been made.[34]

A careful analysis of usage patterns of punch marks suggests that the structure of artistic production shifted at the same time we see this transformation of patronage. Punch marks were the indentations left in the gold-leaf surface by specific tools deployed by painters. They serve as markers for the patterns in workshop production of these gold-leaf decorated paintings, because each punch tool was hand made and unique. Rather than being organized around a single master such as Duccio with his multiple apprentices, artists now worked together in fluidly organized teams called *compagnie*. From 1350 to 1362/63 the conservator Skaug noted the appearance of the same punch marks decorating the gold-leaf surfaces of different works in a way that indicated well-known artists shared tools and may have been working side by side.[35] Some of the punch tools used on Bulgarini's *Assumption* were also used in another iconographically innovative work, the Louvre's *Fall of the Rebel Angels* attributed to Naddo Ceccarelli.[36]

The Saint Victor Altarpiece, now in the Fogg Art Museum, may well represent the first example of this post-plague collaborative process, for we can detect the work of Bulgarini as well as the anonymous Master of the Palazzo Venezia Madonna.[37] We think that Bulgarini remained a central figure in this fluctuating constellation of artists for both artistic and technical reasons: his innovations were quickly disseminated among the other artists and he used an unusually large number of punch tools shared during the period of the *compagnia.*[38] It is this very complexity, this richness, that has made precise attribution of the works of Bulgarini and his Sienese contemporaries challenging. Many of the works such as *Assumption with Doubting Thomas* have been attributed in the past to anonymous entities such as the Ovile Master or an anonymous figure labeled "Ugolino-Lorenzetti."[39] Meiss himself made the leap of identifying from these works a coherent body of works and attributed them to the artist Bartolommeo Bulgarini known from textual records.[40] Bulgarini held an unusually high social status for an artist of his time, when his profession was firmly placed among other skilled crafts. He is the only fourteenth-century artist in Siena known to have emerged from a noble family, but his singular rank's impact on his artistic career is difficult to assess.[41]

The *Assumption* made for the Spedale is in fact the last datable extant work by Bulgarini, but it must have been well received because records indicate he went on to paint at least four additional altarpieces for the confraternity of the Spedale. In 1370 both he and his wife then joined their ranks.[42] The *compagnia* of Bulgarini and his associates fell apart with Bulgarini's admittance as a lay brother into the confraternity, Luca di Tommè's move to Pisa, and in 1363 Niccolo di ser Sozzò's death.[43]

As this collaboration ended in Siena, we can observe a city whose visual culture in the broadest sense had been transformed. The influx of ideas and specific religious artifacts from Byzantium stimulated one of its artists, Bulgarini, to seek a new iconographic form for the beloved and familiar image of the Assumption. This innovative painting of *Assumption with Doubting Thomas* depends on ever-extending waves of influence from factors within the city, elsewhere in Tuscany, the broader Italian context, and, ultimately, Byzantium.

NOTES

1. Henk van Os discusses the connection between the pose of Thomas and the celebration of the Eucharist. Van Os, *Vecchietta and the Sacristy of the Siena Hospital Church* (The Hague: Kunsthistorisches Studiën van het Nederlands Instituut te Rome 1974), p. 8, n. 20.
2. Michael P. Kucher, *The Water Supply System of Siena, Italy: The Medieval Roots of the Modern Networked City* (New York: Routledge, 2005), p. 12.
3. Judith Steinhoff-Morrison, "Bartolomeo Bulgarini and Sienese Painting of the Mid-Fourteenth Century" (Ph.D. diss., Princeton University, 1990), pp. 48–49.

4. Bruce Cole and Adelheid Medicus Gealt, "A New Triptych by Niccolò and a Problem," *Burlington Magazine*, 119, 1977, pp. 184–187.

5. Three articles by Giovanna Derenzini lay out the main contents and codicological issues about the text: "Esama paleografico del Codice X.IV.1 della Biblioteca Communale degli Intronati e Contributo Documentale alla Storia del 'Tesoro' dello Spedale de Santa Maria della Scala," *Annali della Facoltà di lettere e filosofia – Università di Siena*, 8, 1978, pp. 41–76; "Il codice X.IV.1 della Biblioteca Communale degli Intronati di Siena," *Milion*, 1, 1988, pp. 307–325; "Le reliquie da Constantinopoli a Siena," in *L'Oro di Siena: Il Tesoro di Santa Maria della Scala*, ed. Luciano Bellosi (Milan: Skira, 1996), pp. 67–78.

6. There is some debate about whether it was Empress Helena or Irene who participated in the sale, but Paul Hetherington leans towards identifying the empress as Helena. Paul Hetherington, "A Purchase of Byzantine Relics and Reliquaries in Fourteenth-Century Venice," *Arte Venete*, 37, 1983, p. 18.

7. Ibid., pp. 9–30, esp. p. 18.

8. Anthony Cutler, "From Loot to Scholarship: Changing Modes in the Italian Response to Byzantine Artifacts, ca. 1200–1750," *Dumbarton Oaks Papers*, 49, 1995, pp. 237–267, esp. p. 245.

9. Cod. X.IV.I, Complesso Museale di Santa Maria della Scala, Siena. Helen C. Evans (ed.), *Byzantium: Faith and Power (1261–1557)* (New York: Metropolitan Museum of Art, 2004), pp. 509–511.

10. Paul Hetherington, "Byzantine Enamels on a Venetian Book-Cover," *Cahiers archéologiques*, 27, 1978, pp. 117–145, esp. pp. 123–127.

11. Robert S. Nelson, "The Italian Appreciation and Appropriation of Illuminated Byzantine Manuscripts, ca. 1200–1450," *Dumbarton Oaks Papers*, 49, 1995, pp. 209–235, esp. p. 221.

12. Cutler, "From Loot to Scholarship," p. 246.

13. Robert de Clari, "The History of Them that Took Constantinople', ch. 81, in *Three Old French Chronicles of the Crusades*, ed. and trans. Edward N. Stone (Seattle: University of Washington Press, 1939).

14. Louise Buenger Robbert, "Rialto Businessmen and Constantinople," *Dumbarton Oaks Papers*, 49, 1995, pp. 43–58.

15. D. Jacoby, "La population de Constantinople à l'époque Byzantine: un probleme de demographie urbain," *Byzantion* 31, 1961, pp. 81–109, esp. pp. 103, 107.

16. Angeliki Laiou, "Italy and the Italians in the Political Geography of the Byzantines (14th Century)," *Dumbarton Oaks Papers*, 49, 1995, pp. 73–98, esp. p. 74.

17. Correspondence with David M. Perry about his forthcoming University of Minnesota dissertation "Venice, Stolen Relics, and the Aftermath of the Fourth Crusade."

18. Angeliki Laiou-Thomadakis, "The Byzantine Economy in the Mediterranean Trade System: Thirteenth–Fifteenth Centuries," *Dumbarton Oaks Papers*, 34–35, 1980–1981, pp. 177–222.

19. Diana Norman, *Siena and the Virgin: Art and Politics in a Late Medieval City State* (New Haven: Yale University Press, 1999), pp. 3–4. Even in 1215, however, the Ordo Officiorum Ecclesiae Senensis comments that the feast of the Assumption of the Virgin was the most well-attended church festival. Gerald Parsons, *Siena, Civil Religion and the Sienese* (Burlington, Vt.: Ashgate, 2004), p. 1.

20. In the eighteenth century, Girolamo Macchi noted that the Assunta altar included these two saints. Archivio di Stato, Siena, Ms D 108, fol. 295v, cited in Norman, *Siena and the Virgin,* p. 150, n. 82.

21. Diana Norman, *Painting in Late Medieval and Renaissance Siena* (New Haven: Yale University Press, 2003), p. 132.

22. Sabine Schunk-Heller, *Die Darstellung des ungläubigen Thomas in der italienischen Kunst bis um 1500 unter Berücksichtigung der lukanischen Ostnatio Vulnerum* (Munich: Scaneg, 1995); Glenn W. Most, *Doubting Thomas* (Cambridge, Mass.: Harvard University Press, 2005), pp. 155–213.

23. Most, *Doubting Thomas,* p. 112.

24. Narrative by Joseph of Arimathea, Sect. 17, in J. K. Elliott, *The Apocryphal New Testament* (Oxford: Clarendon Press, 1993), p. 715.

25. Most, *Doubting Thomas,* p. 97.

26. In addition to Siena and Prato, some other medieval churches that claimed to possess the relic of the Virgin's belt were Notre Dame de Montserrat, Notre Dame de Paris, Chartres, and Assisi. Patrice Boussel, *Des reliques et de leur bon usage* (Paris: Balland, 1971), p. 184.

27. The text of this addition to the Thomas narrative is edited in Anne Imelde Galletti, "Storie della Sacra Cintola (Schede per un lavoro da fare a Prato)," in *Toscana e Terrasanta nel Medioevo,* ed. Franco Cardini (Florence: Alinea, 1982), pp. 317–338, esp. pp. 323–338.

28. Brendan Cassidy, "A Relic, Some Pictures, and the Mothers of Florence in the Late Fourteenth Century," *Gesta,* 30, 1991, pp. 91–99, esp. p. 97. Boussel notes that the relic of the Virgin's belt in France was also evoked by women in labor. Boussel, *Des reliques,* p. 184.

29. Sue Blundell and Margaret Williamson, *The Sacred and the Feminine in Ancient Greece* (New York: Routledge, 1998), p. 34.

30. Brendan Cassidy argues for the military inspiration in "The Assumption of the Virgin on the Tabernacle of Orsanmichele," *Journal of the Warburg and Courtauld Institutes,* 51, 1988, pp. 174–180, esp. p. 179.

31. John Pope-Hennessy, *The Robert Lehman Collection,* vol. 1, *Italian Paintings* (New York: Metropolitan Museum of Art, 1987), pp. 48–50; Giuseppe Marchini, "Vicende di una pala," *Studies in Late Medieval and Renaissance Painting in Honor of Millard Meiss,* ed. Irving Lavin and John Plummer (New York: New York University Press, 1977), pp. 320–324, esp. pp. 321–322.

32. Samuel Cohn, *The Cult of Remembrance and the Black Death: Six Renaissance Cities in Central Italy* (Baltimore: Johns Hopkins University, 1997), p. 249.

33. Judith Steinhoff, "Artistic Working Relationships after the Black Death," *Journal for the Society for Renaissance Studies,* 14, 200, pp. 1–45, esp. p. 43.

34. Cohn, *The Cult of Remembrance,* pp. 265–269.

35. Erling Skaug, *Punch Marks from Giotto to Fra Angelico. Attributions, Chronology, and Workshop Relationships in Tuscan Panel Painting with Particular Consideration to Florence, c. 1330–1430* (Oslo: Nordic Group, the Norwegian Section, 1994), pp. 254–257. For views that balance some of the suggestions made by Skaug regarding the punches used on the *Assumption,* see the reviews by Carl Brandon Strehlke in *Burlington Magazine,* 137, 1995, pp. 753–754, esp. p. 754 and Norman E. Muller in *Journal of the American Institute for Conservation,* 35, 1996, pp. 66–69, esp. pp. 67–68.

36. Joseph Polzer, "The 'Master of the Rebel Angels' Reconsidered," *Art Bulletin*, 63, 1981, pp. 563–584, esp. p. 572.
37. Steinhoff, "Artistic Working Relationships after the Black Death," p. 4. Note that this author has a book due to appear in 2007 that will expand the arguments put forward in this article.
38. Steinhoff, "Artistic Working Relationships after the Black Death," p. 9.
39. Bernard Berenson, "Ugolino-Lorenzetti," *Art in America*, 5, 1916–17, pp. 259–275; 6, 1917–18, pp. 25–52
40. Millard Meiss, "Bartolomeo Bulgarini altrimenti detto 'Ugolino Lorenzetti'?" *Rivista dell'arte*, 18, 1936, pp. 113–136.
41. Steinhoff, "Bartolomeo Bulgarini and Sienese Painting," p. 18.
42. Henk van Os discusses Bulgarini's (though he uses the designation corresponding to "Ovile Master") status as the Spedale's prime artist at the time. Van Os, *Vecchietta*, p. 6.
43. Steinhoff, "Artistic Working Relationships after the Black Death," p. 44.

4

THE SAINT IN THE HAREM

THE COMMERCE OF INTER-RELIGIOUS RELATIONS IN THE FLORENTINE *RAPPRESENTAZIONE DI ROSANA*

Margaret Aziza Pappano

Rosana, the subject of legends and popular vernacular plays in late medieval and early Renaissance Italy, enjoyed a healthy cult until her feast was suppressed by Rome in 1661. According to papal authorities, Rosana was never actually a saint but a fictional heroine descended from the most promiscuous of European romances, *Floire and Blancheflor*.[1] This romance, widely considered to be of Eastern origins, is found in most vernaculars, sometimes in multiple versions, across western Europe.[2] In Italy, Boccaccio reworked the romance into *Il Filocolo*, named after the male hero, who adopts this pseudonym meaning "labor of love" as he seeks out Biancafiore, sold by his meddling parents into the Sultan's harem in Egypt. In Boccaccio's version, the heroine's experience is secondary to that of the hero, as his "pilgrimage of love" to be reunited with his beloved becomes the organizing motif of the text. Alas, as she is a woman, imprisoned in a harem, Biancafiore can do nothing but wait to be rescued by her childhood sweetheart. Her chief role in the romance tradition becomes preserving her virginity so that when she is finally reunited with her lover she will still be a white flower and hence worthy of his labors.

Yet, this romance, rewritten so frequently, sometimes served causes beyond the exaltation of steadfast love. Most of the romance versions locate Floire's realm in Spain and, since Blancheflor's parents are captured by a Saracen king while on pilgrimage to Santiago de Compestela, the romance also concerns itself with Christian–Islamic conflict and the eventual conversion of Spain into a Christian king-dom. *Floire and Blancheflor* then joins a larger group of medieval romances, such as the Constance romances, *King of Tars*, and *Fierabras*, in which the woman, even a passive one like Blancheflor, becomes the agent of conversion in the ongoing medieval struggle to Christianize Europe and the Mediterranean. Perhaps it was this element of the romance that leant itself to hagiographic interpretation.

Concentrating on the twelfth-century French version, often thought to represent one of the original three strands of this complex literary tradition, Sharon Kinoshita posits that *Floire et Blancheflor* depicts a Mediterranean world not so much in conflict as in contact.[3] Reading the romance through its participation in a network of commercial circulation encompassing East and West, Islam and Christianity, in the greater Mediterranean, Kinoshita sees the text's work in terms of a "destabilization of fundamental categories of faith, class, and gender" which are recuperated only at the end with the forcible conversion of the Muslims of Spain. In the romance tradition, Floire and Blancheflor are represented as perfect look-alikes with identically beautiful faces, so much so that when the Egyptian Emir discovers Fleur sleeping at Blancheflor's side in his harem he first thinks that Fleur is a girl. Their destined conjoining is thus represented at the level of physiogamy, reaffirming their fate to be one. Floire's Saracen identity becomes a mere afterthought, since he is clearly intended to be a Christian just like Blancheflor and but awaits a moment in his action-packed journey to be sprinkled with the holy water. His incipient and latent Christianity, already inscribed on his body in blond tones, is thus signaled by his uncanny resemblance to the pale Whiteflower. Floire's journey to be reunited with his Blancheflor can thus be read as his recovery of his true self, the pale European Christian he is meant to be. In these versions, Blancheflor does not so much bring Christianity to Spain as, rather, provide the means by which Floire travels to Egypt to realize that he is not in fact a Saracen like the Sultan and needs to recover his Christian self by bringing her back to Spain. In the French and English romances, though the Sultan promises him wealth and dominion, Floire just wants to grab Blancheflor and head home. One role of the Egyptian episode seems to be to affirm Floire's difference from the Muslim Sultan. How indeed can a hero so singularly devoted to his one beloved be related to a faithless Saracen who keeps a harem of women to satisfy his perverse pleasures?

Il Filocolo provides a critical hinge between the romance and hagiographical traditions in Italy. Boccaccio fills out the prehistory of the heroine, especially through elaborating the character of her mother, and shifts their native land from France to Rome, changes and expansions that will become part of Rosana's *vita* as a popular saint. As in the play and *legenda*, the King and Queen of Rome (the parents of the heroine) are traveling to a shrine to give thanks for the Queen's pregnancy when their party is ambushed, the King killed, and the Queen taken captive. Boccaccio's text, thickly encrusted with classical allusion, is slippery on the issue of their confessional identity. Their pilgrimage is to "the holy temples of the blessed diety, placed on the furthest western shores" of Spain;[4] while this sounds like Santiago de Compestela, Boccaccio resists couching the meeting as a conflict between Christian and Saracen. However, when the party is vanquished by the Spanish army, the Queen laments over her dead husband, "Alas, Lelio, where have you abandoned me? Where have you left me? Amid an Arab race alien to our customs, where I know no one."[5] Yet, ethnic rather than religious difference is accentuated, since the Queen is referred to as a Roman rather than a Christian. Having omitted definitively Christianizing Biancafiore's mother, Boccaccio also fails to pass on Christianity to the daughter. Hence, *Il Filocolo* does not establish confessional difference between the otherwise identical Florio and Biancafiore as the underlying motif of their tumultuous love affair.

In Boccaccio's version of the romance, religious identity surfaces only at the end, functioning as a move toward a more perfect love after Florio and Biancafiore are reunited. When Florio/Filocolo unfolds his story to the angry Sultan after being discovered in the harem, in bed with Biancafiore, the Sultan recognizes him as his own nephew, son of his sister. In this way, Boccaccio affirms a Saracen genealogy for Florio, though the Sultan's practices are depicted more as pagan than as Muslim. Consequently, Boccaccio adds an extended conversion scene in Rome, where the couple go to reclaim Biancafiore's heritage and become Christian before they return to Spain. It is really only at this point that Biancafiore discovers that she is herself Christian; religious conversion is thus figured through place as an apotheosis of their love, since Florio and Biancafiore need somewhere to go now that they have been reunited. Having already gone eastward, the only direction left is upward from Rome, so their earthly love is conjoined with a spiritual love and devotion to God.

Rewritten in trecento Italy as a *legenda*, Blancheflor was eventually transformed into Saint Rosana and her feast celebrated with plays sponsored and organized by Italian religious confraternities beginning in the late fifteenth century.[6] Liberated from the romance, Rosana and her identically named mother become more active agents of conversion in the *legenda*, reading scripture, preaching to crowds, leading their men to the baptismal font. The hagiographical tradition also relocates the action from Spain to the Anatolian peninsula, where Rosana's father is killed and her mother captured on pilgrimage not to Santiago de Compestela but to the Holy Sepulcher in Jerusalem. Floire, now transformed into a youth named Ulimentus, is the heir to Caesarea, and Rosana is the heiress of Rome, her confessional identity located squarely at the center of Catholic Christendom. Confessional conflict is thus shifted eastwards in the Mediterranean, staging encounter not just between Muslims and Christians in the Iberian peninsula but also between Europe and the Levant and indeed between Islam and Christianity across the Mediterranean. Although the play *La Rappresentazione di Rosana* represents a notably more passive saint than the *legenda*, it follows a similar story-line and clearly uses the *legenda* as a source, adapting its basic changes from the romance. Although the dating of both *legenda* and *Rappresentazione* is imprecise, they can tentatively be placed in late trecento and late quattrocento Florence, respectively. There is documentary evidence that the confraternity of Saint Anthony of Padua put on a play of "Sancta Rosana" in the Church of the Carmine for Carnival in 1485.[7] We cannot be certain that this production refers to the play that has been preserved in the early printed editions, but it is quite possible that it was. In fifteenth-century Florence, *sacra rappresentazione* were put on by boys' confraternities like that of Saint Anthony as part of the moral and religious education of the youths; but they also served, as Lorenzo Polizzotto argues, "to communicate, to both performers and audiences, messages ... that were specifically political."[8]

While the anonymous authors of the *legenda* and play, the latter of which is sometimes attributed to Antonia Tanini Pulci, clearly knew *Il Filocolo*, they drew from the romance tradition as well, perhaps because this tradition was more firmly grounded in religious encounter than Boccaccio's classicizing text. By making Rosana's parents new converts to Christianity who are traveling to the Holy Sepulcher in Jerusalem when they are ambushed in Caesarea, the *legenda* and play set up a clear opposition between Christian and pagan. Rosana is baptized at birth and in turn baptizes Ulimentus, transforming their love into a matter of Christian righteousness rather than romantic fatalism.

At this point, a short summary of the Rosana plot may be helpful: The King and Queen of Rome are childless, but upon conversion to Christianity the Queen immediately conceives. They make a pilgrimage to the Holy Sepulcher to give thanks; en route to Jerusalem, the King and his retinue are killed and the Queen is captured by the King of Caesarea. The Queen, in captivity, gives birth to Rosana, has her baptized, and then dies; meanwhile the Queen of Caesarea gives birth to Ulimentus. The children grow up together and fall in love. Rosana secretly converts and baptizes Ulimentus. The King and Queen of Caesarea become alarmed by Ulimentus's love for Rosana; they send him to Paris and then sell Rosana to merchants bound for Babylon. The merchants sell her to the Sultan. Ulimentus discovers that his beloved has been sold and seeks her out in Babylon with a troop of armed men. Bribing the gatekeeper of the harem, Ulimentus rescues Rosana and returns, with the gatekeeper, to Caesarea; they convert his parents and the entire realm of Caesarea by sword.

Although the *Rappresentazione* and *legenda*, like *Il Filocolo*, represent Ulimentus's realm as vaguely pagan rather than Saracen,[9] its identification with Caesarea and Cappadocia may have guided the audience to more specific interpretations. It is significant that the Italian hagiographical tradition shifts the locale from Spain to the Anatolian peninsula, for in the late fifteenth century this is precisely where the hotbed of interconfessional relations lay for the Italian republics.

In the *legenda* and play of Rosana, two distinct eastern realms are depicted, Caesarea and Babylon, seemingly corresponding to the historical configuration of the two contemporary Islamic powers of the eastern Mediterranean: the Ottoman Empire centered in Anatolia and the Mamluk state in Egypt and the Levant. Babylon, or Egypt, is represented as a place far more alien than Caesarea, where the King, although depicted with stereotypical Eastern bombasity and cruelty, is refined enough to send his son to Paris to learn "balli e giostre e torniamenti" (jousting, dancing, tournaments). In addition, we are informed at the beginning of the play that Caesarea has just been conquered by Roman armies; although this clearly does not guarantee safe passage for the Roman King and Queen and reference to this incident subsequently vanishes from the text, it does indicate something of the complex history of territorial relations between Rome and the former Byzantine Empire. In contrast, Babylon is more clearly marked out as an alien space than Caesarea in the *legenda* and play. The religious difference of Babylon is represented most succinctly through the Sultan's harem, a garden in which he keeps virgins locked up to use at his will. (Meanwhile, the King and Queen of Caesarea appear to have a conventional monogamous marriage.) Although the play omits the detail from the romance tradition that the Sultan marries each harem girl for a year after which time he puts her to death – an echo perhaps of the frame story of the Arabic *The Thousand and One Nights* – the Sultan's sexual deviance is signified through his willingness to pay ten thousand gold ducats for a "daughter of the royal blood of Rome." The enormous price that the Sultan is willing to pay for Rosana signifies his eagerness to defile the purity of Christianity.

For the romance of Floire and Blancheflor to be recast in hagiographical terms and refocused eastwards in the Mediterranean in quattrocento Florence resonates with the reconfiguring of Christian–Muslim relations in the context of the rise of the Ottomans. While papal policies urged military response and favored depictions of the Ottomans as threat and scourge to Christianity, particularly after the Ottoman conquest of Constantinople in 1453, Florentine response was more complex. In point of fact, the conquering Mehmed II specifically favored the Florentine merchants in his expanding empire, using them to displace the Venetians. In 1469 he granted new trade privileges to Florence, having opened up a direct trade route through Ragusa so that Florentines no longer had to depend upon their rival Venice as intermediary in their eastern Mediterranean trade. The Ottoman market was a major source of Medici wealth, and Lorenzo di Medici, an important patron of Florence's religious plays, attached great importance to his friendship with Mehmed II.[10] Although many Florentines favored the hard-line papal policy, and crusade was preached in Florence, there were also rumors and accusations of Florentine collaboration with the Turks. The Ottoman capture of Otranto in Apulia in 1480, a momentous event that the alarmed Pope Sixtus IV proclaimed had positioned the Turks to strike at the very heart of Christianity, was even attributed by Florence's rival city-states to Lorenzo di Medici's intervention[11]

In late fifteenth-century Florence, representations of Ottoman power were highly charged but deeply ambivalent. On the one hand, a letter from the Signoria dubbed the Florentines "the most faithful and obedient sons of his Majesty" in response to Mehmet's capture of one of the Pazzi conspirators in 1470;[12] on the other, the Ottomans could be characterized as "hard and inhuman ... barbarians."[13] However, given the nature of the Italian republics' rivalries with each other, their reliance on the Levantine trade, and their wariness of papal political ambitions in the peninsula, other Italian city-states expressed similar reluctance to formulate military policies against Mehmed II. As James Hankins has recently pointed out, there was an enormous outpouring of exhortatory crusade literature in quattrocento Italy, even beyond that produced during the height of crusading in the twelfth and thirteenth centuries. The threat of the Turks and necessity for crusade in fact constituted one of the most popular themes of humanist writing.[14] Yet, at the same time, Italian city-states were deeply imbricated in economic – and to some extent political – relations with the Ottomans. At Mehmed II's request, the Doge of Venice sent Gentile Bellini to fresco the palaces in Istanbul, and the Florentine Francesco Berlinghieri sent the Ottoman Sultan a copy of his *Geographia*, so there was a growing tradition of cultural exchange as well.[15] As much as existed a rhetoric of the "Turkish dogs" intent upon devouring Christendom, the Italian republics had intricate connections with the Ottomans to the extent that the Turkish "threat" played into the delicate balance of power among metropolitan and mercantile rivals in the Italian peninsula. As I will argue below, the late fifteenth-century *Rappresentazione di Rosana* responds to this ambivalence. It walks a fine line, trumpeting the crusading position but ultimately relying upon networks of exchange to redraw confessional boundaries in the eastern Mediterranean, incorporating some and expelling other Saracens from the Christian body.

THE CALL TO CRUSADE

The dominant mood at the end of part 1 of *La Rappresentazione*, at the close of the first day of a two-day performance, is vengeance against the "pagans" for the killing of Rosana's parents, the King and Queen of Rome, as they make pilgrimage to Jerusalem. The play departs from the *legenda* here and exploits theatrical resources to issue a rousing call to arms. No such scene is included in the *legenda* (or even in romance analogues), while the play moves away from the scene of Rosana's birth and mother's death in childbirth back to the battlefield for the final scene of the first day's performance. The stage directions inform us, "Un Romano ferito si riza e dice da se [a wounded Roman rises and says to himself]." Although the action of the play has long since taken us away from the bloody battlefield and into the refined court, the play's abrupt return to the battlefield frames the actions in contemporary terms: it must be remembered that Christians have been slaughtered and action must be taken. The spectacle of the wounded soldier rising on the battlefield, calling for vengeance for the "superbi cristian" seems intended as a galvanizing call to the contemporary audience:

> O vanagloria, o invidia maladetta!
> O superbia che mai può far buon frutto!
> Qual ingiuria fa far tanta vendetta
> Che'l Re con tutto 'l popol sia distrutto?
> [O haughtiness, O envy curst, O pride,
> That cannot ever any good fruit bear,
> What injury produced revenge so great
> That the King and all his folk should be destroyed][16]

The soldier concludes his speech by announcing that he will go to Rome to see that vengeance is carried out for this great injury, his own wounded body standing on stage as a powerful visual reminder of the wound inflicted on Christendom. Rome is here constructed not just as the realm of the fallen King and vanquished people, but as the center of Christianity, responsible for protecting its followers across the Mediterranean. From its inception in the speeches of Urban II, who drew a vivid picture of hapless pilgrims slaughtered on their way to Jerusalem, crusade was frequently justified as a necessary recourse to protect the pilgrimage route to the Holy Land.

In Rome, the soldier's news finds an audience that immediately takes up his call to arms. The lieutenant (*il luocotenente*) announces (seeming to address the present members of the audience), "Ciascun di voi in punto ben si metta / Oggi a un anno a far questa vendetta [Let each of you with care prepare yourselves / To be revenged by one year from this day!]."[17] He continues,

> Va' porta questa lettera in Borgogna,
> Tu in Francia, in Ungheria e'n Inghilterra,
> Tu ne la Magna, e tu ne va'n Guascogna,
> E tu in Brittagna a nunziar la guerra;

Tu in Ispagna, Ascalona, e tu'n Sansogna,
Chè ciascun guidi gente di suo terra,
E venga a Roma ognun con la sua setta,
Chè s'à ire in Cesarea a far vendetta.
[Go, take this letter to Burgundy; you
To France, to England, and to Hungary;
To Germany you go; you, to Gascoigne;
You go to Brittany – announce the war.
You, Spain and Ascalon; you, Saxony –
That each may guide the people of his land,
And let each with his legion come to Rome
To march on Cesarea to seek revenge.][18]

Reflecting the crusading literature produced and popularly circulated during the era generally, this stanza more specifically echoes, as the play's recent editor has pointed out, Petrarch's famous call to arms in his *Canzioniere* 28.[19] This poem, composed in response to Philip VI's announcement that he would lead a crusade to recover the Holy Land in 1334, is characteristic of Petrarch's fervor for crusade, a topic he was passionately devoted to, writing in support of crusade in different contexts over much of his life.[20] Although Philip's crusade was never launched, in this poem Petrarch calls upon Christians throughout Europe to take up arms for "la vendetta" against "turchi, arabi et caldei, / con tutti quei che speran nelli dèi [Turks, Arabs, and Chaldeans / and all who place their hope in pagan gods]."[21] Petrarch's quest for vengeance here is, as Nancy Bisaha observes, for the theft of Christian land.[22] *La Rappresentazione di Rosana* adopts this language of vengeance; while, on one hand, it refers to vengeance for the killing of the King and Roman people, on the other, by linking itself with Petrarch's crusading poem, it participates in a larger discourse of Christian claims to lost eastern territories and injuries inflicted by the infidel. When the lieutenant calls upon the European realms to unite together in Rome to march on the enemy to seek "revenge," he clearly transgresses the narrative fictions of an ancient Roman *legenda*. The play then reproduces contemporary crusading rhetoric that urges Europe to set aside differences to unite against the common enemy; in so doing, like Petrarch's poem, the play inscribes a contest between East and West, slicing the world into halves: Christians and their threatening others.

In the play, the call to arms is not answered, or not answered directly, for the Caesareans are not killed in revenge for the slaughter of the Roman King and his retinue. However, after the King's daughter Rosana is sold to the Sultan of Egypt, her rescue is brought about by military assault on Babylon. In a move that is not unfamiliar to us today, retaliation for the assault by one "infidel" group is displaced onto another. The hagiographical tradition radically departs from its romance sources in remaking the hero, Ulimentus, into a brave and daring soldier. In the romance, Floire lives up to his name, remarkable for his passivity and, as I have already noted, even mistaken for a girl. He returns with Blancheflor to his native land not because he steals her from the Sultan and defeats his troops, but because the Sultan rewards the devotion of the lovers and bids them farewell. Although such passivity in which star-crossed lovers are victims of twists and turns of fate is typical for the genre of the Greek romance,[23] which may well have influenced *Floire and Blancheflor*, the hagiography demands a hero capable of rescuing Christianity from its enemies. If indeed *La Rappresentazione di Rosana* was performed by the boys' confraternity of Saint Anthony of Padua, as the records suggest, then it appears designed to inculcate the masculine crusading ideal in the youthful performers. However, even as it promotes crusading, particularly against Mamluk Egypt in order to recover Jerusalem and avenge injuries to Christian pilgrims, *La Rappresentazione* offers a complex view of Christian–Muslim relations, since conversion via the virginal body of Rosana ultimately serves to extend the influence of Christianity across the Mediterranean.

VIRGIN FOR SALE

The play's attempt to allay the threat of economic power coupled with religious difference represented by the new Mediterranean power of the Ottomans is worked through the romance of Rosana and Ulimentus, which depends upon her maintenance of sexual purity. Even when finally reunited with the hero, Rosana maintains a steadfast chastity that ultimately becomes the key to converting Caesarea to Christianity, at least in the *legenda* version. Although Rosana might be circulated around the Mediterranean by Egyptians, Turks, and undefined pagans, her virginal body stands as a boundary marker for the uncontaminability of Christian identity. Whatever monetary price she fetches, and whatever devotion Ulimentus demonstrates, Rosana's value supersedes both, as she remains representative of a fantasy of Christian indelibility – a representation suggesting that, despite the networks of trade and economic dependencies Florentines had with Muslim realms, they remained free from Muslim cultural and spiritual influences. The *legenda* and play have to rewrite the romance tradition to make this point: Rosana's devotion is not to Ulimentus, as Blancheflor's was to Floire, but to the Virgin Mary and Christ who miraculously protect her body from penetration. The hagiographical tradition thus excises the often-titillating romance scene in which the lovers are discovered sleeping together in the Sultan's harem, for the focus must be not on restoration to the proper beloved but rescue from the improper one, the accursed Sultan of Egypt.

In the play and *legenda*, Rosana's body becomes the ground upon which religious encounter is imagined and enacted. When Ulimentus finally manages to get a message to her in the harem, Rosana's response is to announce that she remains a virgin – "i'son vergine e casta mantenuta [I'm a virgin and remain chaste]" – which also conveys that Christianity has withstood assault from the menacing Saracens. Rosana has been miraculously protected, for through the intervention of Christ and the Virgin Mary the Sultan fell ill on the day she entered the harem. The threat of penetration stands for the fear of the instability of religious identity, imagined through the improper mingling of Saracen and Christian, the collapse of boundaries between confessional bodies and identities.

Conversely, Christianity represents a threat to the "infidels'" imagined genealogical purity. When the Queen of Caesarea sees Rosana's influence over her son, a love that she imagines will impede a proper dynastic marriage, she seeks to have her killed. Instead, the King of Caesarea sells Rosana as *mercatanzia* (merchandize) for a thousand doubloons to some merchants bound for Babylon. In turn, the merchants sell her to the Egyptian Sultan for ten thousand gold ducats. At each transaction, her virginal status is sworn or tested and affirmed. For the pagans/Saracens, Rosana's body can be subjected to a value system in the market economy; they misread her virginity as a form of currency rather than as a sign of Christian purity and power – and, most importantly, fixity. Mercantilism is of course the ultimate model of mixing, since goods are subject to a value system that wrenches them free from their originary contexts, relativizing all values through the shifting worth of coinage and the demands of different markets. Even through the different prices she fetches, one sees that Rosana's value for the Saracens is contextual – one price in Caesarea, another in Egypt. Her Christianity, high lineage, beauty, and virginity make her a hot commodity, but a commodity nevertheless and thus subject to the valuations of the Saracen terms of exchange.

Significantly, however, it is Rosana's virginity that becomes the critical factor in her exchange value, determining her purchase price. The merchant says to the King, "Se vergine è, come ci fai capace, / Prendei ciò che tu vuoi, ch'ella ci piace [If she's a virgin, as you'd have us believe / Take what you want, for she well pleases us]."[24] Likewise, the Sultan is ready to pay enormous sums "s'ell' ha il corpo mondo e netto [if clean and pure her body is]."[25] However, this is precisely where the irony enters the story, for this virgin cannot be penetrated and thus is beyond value – worth both nothing and everything. As Caroline Bynum describes, "set apart from the world by her intact boundaries, her flesh untouched by ordinary flesh, the virgin (like Christ's mother, the perpetual virgin) was also a bride, destined for a higher consummation."[26] As an impenetrable female body, Rosana is valueless to the Sultan, who buys her only for consummation, for his own sexual pleasure; but as a body chosen by Christ she has a transcendant value, unquantifiable in human terms. By selling Rosana, the King of Caesarea equates her with commodities whose worth fluctuates as they pass from hand to hand, market to market; but Rosana proves that, despite being sold as a slave, Christianity cannot be devalued, even in Saracen markets.

Although the romance traditions of Floire and Blancheflor and the *legenda* all contain the scene of the buying and selling of the virginal girl, *La Rappresentazione di Rosana* contains several other scenes of merchandizing that invite more extended consideration of the role of trade in inter-religious relations. For Kinoshita, the trafficking of Blancheflor "makes visible modalities of encounter and exchange far beyond the field of Roncevaux" and "revalues" the Christian girl (who is illegitimate in the French romance tradition) through the medium of Saracen currency.[27] Likewise, the hagiographical tradition hints at ways in which networks of trade provide the nexus of inter-religious exchange in the Mediterranean. However, unlike the romance tradition, in the hagiographical tradition there is no revaluation, for the Christian identity is marked by its stability and sameness across geographical contexts.

In a text obsessed with boundaries and enclosures, merchandizing becomes the vehicle to cross over into guarded spaces. In a scene specific to the hagiographical tradition, the wife of the innkeeper (*l'ostessa*) enters the harem to bring a message to Rosana from Ulimentus. She is able to do this because she customarily brings goods to sell to the women of the harem. Here it is important to recall that merchants enter into the palace garden to carry off Rosana from Caesarea. Indeed, it is no accident that the two spaces from which Rosana is taken are both described as gardens: the garden of the palace at Caesarea and the Sultan's harem, referred to as a "giardin serrato" (locked garden) in the play. Such imagery is significant, since in quattrocento Florence, the *hortus conclusus* figures prominently in iconography of the Virgin Mary.[28] By relating the Virgin to an enclosed garden, the artists evoke the notion of salvation, everlasting life, enclosed in her impenetrable body. The use of garden imagery is intended ironically by the playwright: both gardens are penetrated by merchants who steal the virgin Rosana from them. Since the gardens are located in the hostile Saracen spaces of Caesarea and Egypt, it is clear that they are not the firm boundaries against threats to Christian salvation that the Virgin's body stands for. In the play, Rosana's body is the only space that resists penetration.

The play includes a rather curious scene in which the girls (*le fanciulle*) of the harem bargain with the hostess over the silk dress she brings as a pretext to enter the harem. The girls demonstrate that, as isolated as they are behind harem walls, they know how to examine and bargain for merchandize. The dress that the hostess brings has already been worn, which the girls immediately recognize, noting that it has been splashed by puddles, is faded, and has "pezza a men di venti [no less than twenty patches]."[29] One girl considers buying it to please the Sultan, "per suo amore / Per poter poi da lui più grazie avere" [for his love/ so that I can have more favor from him then]."[30] This scene displays the imbrication of Saracen female sexuality in commercial relations. The harem girl is represented as seeing herself as a sexual object of the Sultan's lust – she is merchandize, just like the dress. Her desire for the gown is to increase her value in the Sultan's eyes. Unlike the priceless virgin, her value fluctuates. For this reason, the girl rejects a visibly worn dress, as if a new dress could give her a virginal value, like Rosana. The worn dress in fact appears to reflect the status of the harem maidens, whose bodies have been penetrated and commodified as slaves in the harem system in contrast to the Christian Rosana. In this way, the play suggests that, just as Saracen spaces are penetrable, so too are the bodies of Saracen women, whose sexuality stands in sharp contrast to the inviolable Christian – and, by extension, Christian lands. The mercantilism of the eastern Mediterranean is thus represented as symptomatic of its unstable value system, as confessional territories potentially vulnerable to the power of Christian truth.

THE TURK AS GATEKEEPER

In both *legenda* and *Rappresentazione*, the Sultan of Egypt employs a "Turco" as the gatekeeper of his harem, named Alisbec (a bowdlerization of "Ali Beg") in the play version. Although both texts are spare on this point, it seems that the Turkish gatekeeper is to be differentiated ethnically from the Sultan and his men, for he is first described as "il Turco" to identify him. (Turks were among the largest group of slaves in Egypt during this period.)[31] In both versions, the Turkish gatekeeper functions as the key figure who enables the rescue of the Christian virgin from the Saracen harem. In the play, Ulimentus approaches Alisbec with a bribe: high rank, wealth, and honor in exchange for Rosana. Although Alisbec at first resists because he does not want to be thought a traitor, Ulimentus prevails upon him to exchange his lowly state of slavery for lordship, and Alisbec agrees to help him. However, after Ulimentus departs, the play contains the following soliloquy by Alisbec:

> O maladetta e perfida avarizia!
> O cupidigia del mondano onore!
> Ve' che'l danaio corrompe ogni giustizia!
> Ogniuno esser vorre' superiore!
> I' cometto oggi troppa gran nequizia,
> Ma pur errar con molti è manco errore;
> Per aver liberta, regno e tesoro
> Si de' far paragon d'ogni martoro.
> [O cursèd avarice perfidious!
> O desire for honors in the world,
> Every justice, money will corrupt,
> And everyone would be of higher rank;
> Today I do a great iniquity,
> But when one errs with many, error's less,
> To have a realm and treasure, liberty,
> Will bear comparison with any pain.][32]

This speech endows Alisbec with a consciousness of his mercenary activities: unlike the merchants and Sultan, he understands the power that money has to destabilize values. While he curses the system, he also rationalizes it to gain his freedom and wealth. It is clear, however, that he understands money as utilitarian – the means to an end – rather than value in and of itself. In the context of the play, his consciousness is coded as incipiently Christian, for it has been the infidels who construct values solely in economic terms. Alisbec intimates that there should be certain values – like justice – that cannot be bought and sold like commodities.

The figure of Alisbec is key to the play, more so than to the *legenda*, and for this reason *La Rappresentazione di Rosana* seeks to establish a moral framework for his character. Indeed, in the play, he displaces the figure of Rosana as the focus of the story. Rosana's function ends when she is rescued from the harem; she faints upon greeting Ulimentus and must be carried away by Alisbec. She is mentioned for the final time but several lines later, when Ulimentus asks her to pray for them during the battle scene as the Sultan's troops give chase to Ulimentus and his men. The play departs significantly from the *legenda* here, both in staging a battle with the Sultan's troops and in banishing Rosana from the narrative. The narrative returns to the call to arms of part 1: male military power supplements the power of the virgin as the ballast against Saracen corrosion. Significantly, Alisbec is depicted as the military leader as he cries,

> Ciaschedun s'armi e lass'ir prima mene
> Ch' i'ho la fè rotta e la figlia ho rapita,
> Et or ci vo' per voi metter la vita.
> [Each one, to arms, and let me lead the fray.
> For I have broken faith and stolen the girl
> And now I lay down my life for you.][33]

Having rescued Rosana from the harem, Alisbec has literally saved, by carrying off in his arms, the image of Christianity; hence, as he breaks faith (*fè*) with the Sultan, by extension he also breaks with the faith of Islam. It thus comes as no surprise that Alisbec converts, asking to be baptized as soon as they return to Caesarea. What is surprising is that Rosana is displaced as the medium of conversion as Ulimentus takes on the proselytizing role, converting first Alisbec, then his parents, and the entire realm of Caesarea to Christianity. (At Ulimentus's command, the King announces, "fra tre di ognium si battezassi,/A pena delle forche a chiunque errassi [within three days all must be baptized/the gallow's pain for all who stray from this].")[34]

In the *legenda*, however, Rosana retains an important role in the story, responsible for converting Ulimentus's parents and their kingdom. Near the end of the narrative, after they have been returned to Caesarea for some time, Ulimentus seeks Rosana in her room to ask his beloved to become his wife. Rosana agrees, but only on the condition that his parents, barons, household, and all the people ("lo tuo padre e la tua madre e ... la sua baronia e famiglia, e tutto il populo")[35] convert to Christianity. Such an act is consistent with the bodily dynamics of the hagiographical narrative. Rosana's virginal body that could not be valued now is given a value: the price of a kingdom's conversion. Like Christ, she makes a sacrifice of her flesh: she will literally shed blood to redeem the infidel nation and bring them to salvation. As she exchanges her virginity for marriage, she becomes instead the priceless gift of salvation to the pagans. Hence, her body, like the body of Christ, is penetrable only to be incorporative: it can both withstand assault by infidels and open to taken them in.

La Rappresentazione leaves out any mention of the couple's matrimony; Rosana is simply dropped from the story. To understand why the play departs so dramatically from its primary source we might set it in the context of late quattrocento Florence. Rather than continue to exalt the miraculous powers of Rosana's body to withstand, protect, and convert, the play turns toward the crusading rhetoric of the first part, as the men win Rosana back by their swords and convert the kingdom of Caesarea by force. This fantasy is only made possible, however, by Alisbec, the Turk who becomes assimilated to Christianity and leads the charge. The play thus seems to construct the Turk as a liminal figure, quite different from the irredeemable Egyptian Sultan and his men. It is therefore notable that the language of devotion between Ulimentus and Rosana is replaced by a similar language between Ulimentus and Alisbec, who vow love and commitment to each other. Although a symbol of Christian indelibility, Rosana's function is also, as a woman, to mediate between men; her virginal body not only keeps apart Christianity and Islam but also brings together Christian and Turkish men, who realize their common bond as they unite to save her. It is likely that the performance of the play made this point especially powerfully. After they defeat the Sultan's men, Alisbec, Ulimento, and the latter's retinue return to Caesarea "cantanda questa lauda" (singing this *lauda*),[36] according to the stage directions. The play contains a popular *lauda,* "Ave, vergin benedetta," which the performers sang as they walked across the stage, perhaps still carrying the virgin Rosana, who now functions as a processional image more than an active character. Since many confraternities functioned as *laudesi* companies, or included the singing of *laude* to the Virgin among their activities, the play gestures toward the larger social function of the performance: to unite together the male members in shared spiritual pursuit. While singing praises to the Virgin Mary provided the ostensible reason for the *laudesi* companies, they also functioned to forge social, political, and economic ties among the men of Florence. The Virgin becomes the convenient facilitator for Florentine male bonding. By including Alisbec in the group singing the *lauda,* the play makes the point that participation in these communal exercises will bring about spiritual renewal and enlightenment, even for unbelievers.

The play has prepared us for Alisbec's important role through his critique of the commercial system, mentioned above. In the final scene of the play, after Ulimentus has offered him a realm of his own, Alisbec refuses:

> O signor mio, i' ti sono obligato
> E non creder ch'i tema di ristoro;
> Chè val più il sacramento che m' hai dato
> Che tutto quando il mondo e'l suo tesoro;
> Come tu vuoi, i'ti son sempre allato
> Disposto a far per te ogni lavoro,
> E sono a quel che vuoi contento e sazio,
> E d'ogni cosa sempre ti ringrazio.
> [I'm very much obliged to you, my lord,
> Though I don't think I'd compensation seek
> That's worth more than the sacrament you gave
> To me – beyond all else the treasure of
> The world. As you desire, I'll ever stay
> Beside you, set to do your every task.
> I'm satisfied and glad to do your will,
> And ever give you thanks for all you've done.][37]

Alisbec recognizes the transcendental value of the sacrament, worth more than all the treasure in the world. Alisbec's faithfulness to Christianity is signaled through this faithfulness to Ulimentus: both are beyond any sort of commercial quantification, since they are seen as stable and enduring values. While originally relations with Alisbec the Turk were facilitated through a monetary exchange, such relations have to be superseded by another language, here notably one in which religion and friendship are merged as the male bonds, having proven spiritually efficacious in their rescue of the Christian virgin, are now sacralized.

Although relations between Florence and the Ottoman Empire were chiefly economic, the play holds out a fantasy that the economic might facilitate more sincere bonds through which trust and knowledge would lead naturally to spiritual affiliations. Both the *legenda* and play involve the motifs of recently converted Eastern sovereigns violently imposing Christianity on their subjects as powerful Christianizing Oriental despots. James Hankins points to some fifteenth-century Italian sources that advocated conversion rather than crusade for the Ottoman Turks, arguing that the Ottomans were only recently Islamized and still had many Christian elements in their midst.[38] According to Robert Schwoebel, Mehmed II's "generally humane treatment of Christian subjects, for him a matter of politics and economy, was interpreted as a sign that he was enlightened and ripe for conversion to Christianity."[39] Still others constructed a Trojan genealogy for the Turks, and thereby assimiliated them to the major European – and, indeed, Italian – narrative of origins.[40] Although geographic identity in the *legenda* and *Rappresentazione di Rosana* is somewhat vague, as is characteristic of hagiographical genres, they nevertheless depict an eastern Mediterrenean that is not wholly and homogeneously other but demonstrates distinct differences in the permeability and adaptability to Christian culture, while attempting to deploy the virginal body of Rosana to mark a religious and cultural boundary under threat from commercial and political entanglements with the Muslim world. It remains to be observed, however, that since it is likely that the romance of Floire and Blancheflor was adapted from an Eastern tale – perhaps Persian, perhaps Arabic – it is in fact the literary culture of Islam that through the circulations and transactions of Mediterranean contact and exchange had permeated the Christian liturgical calendar in the figure of the spurious Saint Rosana.

NOTES

1. Hippolyte Delahaye, *The Legend of the Saints*, trans. Donald Attwater, 2nd edn. (London: Chapman, 1962), p. 87. I would like to thank Ariel Salzmann for her help in researching this article.
2. See Patricia E. Grieve, *Floire and Blancheflor and the European Romance* (Cambridge, England: Cambridge University Press, 1997) for a discussion of the

wide range of the romance across Europe; see René Basset, "Les sources arabes de Floire et Blanchefleur," *Revue des Traditions Populaires*, 22, 1907, pp. 241–245, and Sharon S. Geddes, "The Middle English Poem of Floriz and Blauncheflur and the Arabian Nights Tale of 'Ni'amah and Naomi': A Study in Parallels," *Emporia State Research Studies*, 19(1), 1970, pp. 14–24, for a discussion of the romance's possible Eastern origins.

3. Sharon Kinoshita, "In the Beginning Was the Road: *Floire et Blancheflor* and the Politics of Translation," in *The Medieval Translator*, ed. Rosalynn Voaden, René Tixier, Teresa Sanchez Roura, and Jenny Rebecca Rytting, vol. 8 (Turnhout, Belgium: Brepols, 2003), pp. 223–234, esp. p. 233. See Grieve, *Floire and Blancheflor*, pp. 15–50 for a discussion of theories of the romance's complex redaction history.
4. Giovanni Boccaccio, *Il Filocolo*, trans. Donald Cheney (New York: Garland, 1985), p. 23.
5. Giovanni Boccaccio, *Il Filocolo*, trans. Donald Cheney (New York: Garland, 1985), p. 33.
6. The earliest mention of a Saint Rosana is from the twelfth century, but the Tuscan *legenda* is the earliest known written account of her life. There is a nineteenth-century edition of the *legenda: La Legenda della Reina Rosana e di Rosana Sua Figliola*, ed. Allessandro D'Ancona (Livorno: Francesco Vigo, 1871). This has been translated into English as *The Tale of Queen Rosana and of Rosana Her Daughter and the King's Son Aulimento*, trans. Mildred Mary Blance Mansfield (London: David Nutt, 1909). All references to the *legenda* will be to D'Ancona's text. The play has been edited as "La Rappresentazione di Rosana," in *Sacre rappresentazioni dei secoli XIV, XV, e XVI*, ed. Alessandro d'Ancona (Florence: Successori Le Monnier, 1872), vol. 3, pp. 361–414. All references will be to this edition by page number, since the edition does not include line numbers. The English translation is titled "The Play and Festival of Rosana," in Antonia Pulci, *Florentine Drama for Convent and Festival: Seven Sacred Plays*, trans. James Wyatt Cook (Chicago: University of Chicago Press, 1996), pp. 215–276. All translations will be from this edition by page number. Alfred Cioni, *Bibliografia delle sacre rappresentazione* (Florence: Sansoni Antiquariato, 1961), pp. 264–220, lists twenty early editions from Florence, one from Siena, one from Venice, one from Pistoia, and two from Orvieto, all printed between the sixteenth and early seventeenth century. The fifteenth-century edition has been lost.
7. Nerida Newbigin, *Feste d'Oltrarno: Plays in Churches in Fifteenth-Century Florence* (Florence: Olschki, 1996), pp. 147–149. Because the extant *Rappresentazione di Rosana* is a two-part play, intended for performance over two days, it has also been suggested that it may have been performed on the feast of Saint Giovanni, which was celebrated as a two-day feast in Florence.
8. Lorenzo Polizzotto, *Children of the Promise: The Confraternity of the Purification and the Socialization of Youths in Florence 1427–1785* (Oxford: Oxford University Press, 2004), pp. 77–93, esp. p. 84. Unfortunately the records for the Florentine confraternity of Saint Anthony of Padua have not been preserved, so it is not possible to provide a nuanced sense of the performative conditions of their 1485 "Sancta Rosana" play or even to know much about them as a specific social group.
9. Of course the often purposeful confusion of the Muslim religion with paganism was widespread in medieval literature. Frequently the "Saracens" were represented

as worshipping idols, such as the infamous trinity from *La Chanson de Roland*, "Mohammed, Tervagant, and Apollo."

10. Halil Inalcik, *The Ottoman Empire: The Classical Age 1300–1600*, trans. Norman Itzkowitz and Colin Imber (London: Weidenfeld & Nicolson, 1973), p. 135.

11. James Hankins, "Renaissance Crusaders: Humanist Crusade Literature in the Age of Mehmed II," *Dumbarton Oaks Papers*, 49, 1995, pp. 111–207, esp. 126.

12. Kenneth M. Setton, *The Papacy and the Levant (1204–1571)* (Philadephia: American Philosophical Society, 1978), vol. 2, p. 337.

13. Poggio Bracciolini, *Opera Omnia*, quoted in Hankins, "Renaissance Crusaders," p. 131.

14. Hankins, "Renaissance Crusaders."

15. Setton, *The Papacy and the Levant*, p. 329; Franz Babinger, *Mehmed the Conqueror and His Time*, trans. Ralph Manheim (Princeton, N.J.: Princeton University Press, 1978), p. 506.

16. *La Rappresentazione*, p. 381; *The Play and Festival of Rosana*, p. 239.

17. *La Rappresentazione*, p. 382; *The Play and Festival of Rosana*, p. 240.

18. *La Rappresentazione*, p. 382; *The Play and Festival of Rosana*, p. 240.

19. *The Play and Festival of Rosana*, p. 240.

20. See the excellent analysis of Petrarch's crusading ideology in Nancy Bisaha, "Petrarch's Vision of the Muslims and Byzantine East," *Speculum*, 76(2), 2001, pp. 284–314.

21. *Petrarch's Songbook: A Verse Translation*, trans. James Wyatt Cook (Binghamton, N.Y.: Medieval and Renaissance Texts and Studies, 1996), pp. 57–63, lines 55–56.

22. Bisaha, "Petrach's Vision," p. 289.

23. See Mikhail Bakhtin's discussion of the Greek romance in *The Dialogic Imagination: Four Essays*, trans. Caryl Emerson and Michael Holquist (Austin: University of Texas Press, 1981), pp. 86–110.

24. *La Rappresentazione*, p. 389; *The Play and Festival of Rosana*, p. 248–249.

25. *La Rappresentazione*, p. 393; *The Play and Festival of Rosana*, p. 253.

26. Caroline Bynum, *Holy Feast and Holy Fast: The Religious Significance of Food to Medieval Women* (Berkeley: University of California Press, 1987), p. 20.

27. Kinoshita, "In the Beginning," p. 233.

28. John R. Spencer, "Spatial Imagery of the Annunciation in Fifteenth Century Florence," *Art Bulletin*, 37(4), 1955, pp. 273–280.

29. *La Rappresentazione*, p. 405; *The Play and Festival of Rosana*, p. 266.

30. *La Rappresentazione*, pp. 404–405; *The Play and Festival of Rosana*, p. 266.

31. Kate Fleet, *European and Islamic Trade in the Early Ottoman State: The Merchants of Genoa and Turkey* (Cambridge, England: Cambridge University Press, 1999).

32. *La Rappresentazione*, pp. 408–409; *The Play and Festival of Rosana*, p. 270.

33. *La Rappresentazione*, p. 410; *The Play and Festival of Rosana*, p. 272.

34. *La Rappresentazione*, p. 413; *The Play and Festival of Rosana*, p. 275.

35. *La Legenda*, p. 67.

36. *La Rappresentazione*, p. 410. Cook omits this section from his edition.

37. *La Rappresentazione*, pp. 413–414; *The Play and Festival of Rosana*, p. 276.

38. Hankins, "Renaissance Crusaders," pp. 127–131.

39. Robert H. Schwoebel, 'Coexistence, Conversion, and the Crusade against the Turks," *Studies in the Renaissance*, 12, 1965, pp. 164–187, esp. 170.

40. Hankins, "Renaissance Crusaders," pp. 136–141.

5

TWO RABBINIC VIEWS OF OTTOMAN MEDITERRANEAN ASCENDANCY

THE *CRONICA DE LOS REYES OTOMANOS* AND THE *SEDER ELIYAHU ZUTA*

K. E. Fleming

The history of the Iberian expulsions has long remained within the purview of Jewish history. Yet their domino effect – the numerous communal transformations and geographical movements that came in their wake – is not solely or specifically a part of Jewish history. The final fall of Byzantium and the rise of the Ottomans as a European and a Mediterranean power; increasing ties between Europe and the Americas; intensification of commerce in the Indian Ocean; decline of Catholic power in the Mediterranean; the unification of Spain and the mass exile of European Jewry to all corners of the world – all were interconnected and had an impact on one another. The expulsions from Sepharad were an event in "global" as well as Jewish history. Only within this broader context can developments within the various *kehilot* of the south Balkans be properly understood. Equally, the broader historical context is complete only if the history of the Jews is included as one of its central components. The Jewish communities of the south Balkans were at the heart of many of its transitions, and eye-witnesses to a number of its major transformations.

No wonder, then, that it is during this period, and particularly in the western Ottoman provinces and the Mediterranean, that we witness a sudden renewal of historical writing by Jews after fifteen centuries of near complete historiographic silence. As Yosef Yerushalmi has so famously written, "The resurgence of Jewish historical writing in the sixteenth century was without parallel earlier in the Middle Ages ... Only in the sixteenth century do we encounter within Jewry a cultural phenomenon that can be recognized with little hesitation as genuinely historiographical."[1] Given the dramatic concatenation of cultural currents within which they found themselves, it is no surprise that rabbinic and communal leaders of the period began to engage, along with their more strictly religious and communal functions, in writing and recording the historical events of their period, analyzing their causes and crafting historical narratives that sought to explain the dramatic changes all around them.[2] History-writing was part and parcel of a broader literary efflorescence that characterized the Jewish communities of the period. While consisting largely of strictly "religious" writing,[3] it also pointed to a new interest in the broader world in which south Balkan Jewish communities found themselves.

The new trend toward Jewish historiographic writing is typified by two great rabbis of the period, one Romaniote and the other Sephardic, the first from Crete and the other from Salonica. Both wrote accounts of Ottoman ascendancy, but with different purposes and varying interpretations of the meaning of the sudden growth of Ottoman power in the Mediterranean.

> Account of the last war undertaken by our grand senor Sultan Suleiman,[4] he who is in glory ... [and] his battle against Hungary, and the method of rule of his son Sultan Selim, may God make him prosper ... Written in Constantinople, on Wednesday, 28 Kislev, in the year 5327 of the world's creation, the 11th of December.[5]

So opens the *Cronica de los Reyes Otomanos* of Moshe ben Baruch Almosnino, a great Salonican Sephardic rabbi, political counselor, and sometime historian of the sixteenth century.[6]

The *Cronica de los Reyes Otomanos* is a unique document, a contemporary historical account of the Ottoman Empire at its territorial and administrative apogee. The reigns of Selim I (1512–20) and his son Suleiman I (1520–66) marked the most intensive period ever of Ottoman expansion. They also overlapped precisely with the remarkably swift consolidation of Sephardic culture in Salonica, and with a staggering efflorescence of Salonican Sephardic Jewish writing of all sorts. Among Almosnino's direct intellectual contacts were Rabbi Joseph Caro (1488–1575), the compiler of the *shulhan 'aruch*, a codification of Jewish law authoritative to this day; and the rabbi and halachist (legal scholar) Shmuel di Medina (1506–89). Both spent portions of their careers in Almosnino's Salonica. His broader intellectual points of reference ranged from Aristotle to Aquinas, while his cultural and communal sense of identity drew potently on the experience of the expulsions and the memory of Sepharad.

Almosnino's most immediate context, however, was that of Ottoman ascendancy and the might of the Turks. These topics frame his history. Both in genre and content, Almosnino's *Cronica* marked a departure from the forms of Jewish literature that had been dominant during previous centuries. Its relative breadth of interest – in a history that was not specifically Jewish – is signaled not just by its content, but also by the fact that the first published edition was in Spanish.[7] *Extremos y Grandezas de Constantinopla* was published in Madrid in 1638.[8] Almosnino's text was of relevance and interest not only, and perhaps not primarily, to a Jewish audience.

In the year 5327 of the creation of the world – 1566, the year of Suleiman's death – Moises Almosnino sat down to write his account of the Ottoman ruling house. Even without the perspective so often offered only by hindsight, Almosnino grasped that the death of Suleiman was to bring a tidal, if gradual, shift to Ottoman fortunes.[9] Three weeks before beginning the *Cronica*, Almosnino had witnessed the arrival of Suleiman's remains, brought in state to Istanbul for burial. The sight was clearly one to make an impression. The beauty of the Spanish with which Almosnino describes the events adds to the drama of the account:

> El rey muerto entraron en Constandina día de viernes a diez de quislev, que fueron 22 de november, al cual salieron a recibir el *muftí* ... Y como llegaron con el rey muerto a la puerta de la civdad, lo sacaron de el caro puesto dentro de su ataúd y lo tomaron los más principales y entraron con él por la civdad alzado muy en alto sobre las palmas de las manos; y ansí lo trujeron mudándolo de unos en otros de los más principales leídos, con gran multitud de gente y grandes señores que lo acompañaban todos a pies, y siempre sobre las palmas de las manos en alto, con mucha cantidad de leídos que iban leyendo delante dél a altas voćes, hasta que allegaron a la marata.[10]

> [The dead king entered Constantinople on Thursday, the 10th of Kislev, which was the 22nd of November ... And as they reached the gates of the city with the dead king, they took him from the carriage ... and carried him into the city with their hands held high, passing him from one to the other ... until they reached the tomb (lit., the area outside the tomb where mourners would give alms to the poor[11]).]

The story of Suleiman's rise some four-and-a-half decades earlier had been chronicled by another Jewish historian and rabbi, the Cretan Romaniote Eliyahu ben Elqana Kapsali (ca.1490–1555[12]). Kapsali, from Candia (present-day Herakleion) in Crete, is the author of the *seder eliyahu zuta*, the "The Order of Little Eliyahu" (that is, "the younger" – in distinction to his grandfather, also Rabbi Eliyahu Kapsali).[13] The term *seder* (order) refers to the order of the world. The book is a global history – a history of the globe as it looked from Kapsali's vantage point.[14] As the subtitle described it: "The History of the Ottomans and of Venice and that of the Jews in Turkey, Spain, and Venice."[15]

As with Almosnino's *Cronica*, the subject of Kapsali's study was relatively new in the context of earlier Jewish literary tradition. In form, though, it echoed the well-established approach of situating the entirety of human history on a distinctly Jewish timeline. The fourth book of Kapsali's chronicle is devoted to the topic of Suleiman's ascendancy to power, but the work as a whole begins in mythic time, with the creation of the world. The *seder eliyahu zuta* doesn't make a distinction between mythic time – what Kapsali calls "matters of the world" (*dvarim 'olamim*; that is, the creation of the world, the sins of Adam and Eve in paradise, the flood, and so on) – and lived historical time as he experienced it. The creation, the flood, the rise of Muhammad, the conquest of Constantinople – all were events that existed on the same continuum.[16] All had equal significance as divinely guided occurrences.

MYTHIC TIME AND SECULAR HISTORY

These two texts, Kapsali's *seder eliyahu zuta* and Almosnino's *Cronica*, both in some sense "Jewish," give us two different views of the meaning – historical and religious – of Ottoman ascendancy. For Kapsali the rise of the Ottomans was nothing short of a miracle, one harbinger of a coming messianic age. Almosnino, by contrast, saw the Ottomans in pragmatic and political terms, as a temporal refuge for the ejected Jews of Iberia.

The differences stem from a number of factors. These include Kapsali's status as a Romaniote in distinction to Almosnino's as Sephardic; Kapsali's fixity of place over several generations in contrast to Almosnino's sharp memory of the expulsions; Almosnino's perception of the Jewish community of Salonica as in the ascendant as compared with Kapsali's view of the Cretan Romaniote community as threatened by new elements; and Salonica's status as an Ottoman city versus Candia's subjugation to Venetian rule. Finally, the different immediate circumstances that gave rise to the creation of the two texts shaped their content: while Almosnino wrote to pass the time, almost as a form of entertainment, Kapsali used his writing as a means of meditating upon the admonitory signs of trouble – earthquakes, famine, the plague – that he saw all around him.[17] The two together provide a useful introduction to the central distinctions between Romaniote and Sephardic communities at the time, just as comparison of sixteenth-century Salonica and Candia shows the wide-ranging effects of Ottoman ascendancy across an array of communities. While Romaniotes and Sephardim would soon clash on cultural grounds, at the beginning of the sixteenth century their sharpest differences stemmed from their radically different histories.

For Almosnino, the rise of the Ottomans was an event in human history – *historia profana*. For Kapsali, the staggering growth in Ottoman power was an event in the gradual unfolding of the divine plan on earth – what we would call *historia sacra*. This distinction is reinforced in the intentionality underlying each text. Almosnino did not have the initial aim of writing a history at all; he wanted simply to give a journalistic account of a visit to the Ottoman capital. Kapsali, in contrast, wanted expressly to write a history of the Ottoman Empire, and to situate it on a spectrum of events that he saw as having particular significance for the Jews. Almosnino's text is a straightforwardly descriptive work, Kapsali's more deeply interpretive. Kapsali has a specifically transcendent view of the Ottomans – they had been brought to power by the hand of God – while Almosnino regards them from a largely bureaucratic and administrative standpoint.

Both authors, though, are united by the basic fact that neither one wanted to write a history of the Jews per se, even though both wrote largely for a Jewish audience. Their texts aren't exclusively – or even predominantly – about Jews or Jewish matters. When compared with other Jewish histories of the period, such as Ibn Verga's *shebet yehudah*[18] or Gedalia Ibn Yahia's *shalshelet hakabala*,[19] the *Cronica de los Reyes Otomanos* and the *seder eliyahu zuta* stand out for the breadth of their interest in the non-Jewish world. This is the case even within the context of Kapsali's explicitly Jewish historical framework. Kapsali's interest in *dvarim 'olamim* (matters of the world) is in distinction to what he calls *dinim tori'im* (legal matters) and *divrei hachmei hamekubalim* (kabbalistic knowledge) – that is, religious matters.[20] These "matters of the world" are what we today would term "history," in a secular, or at least proto-secular, sense, and the *'olam* – the world – about which he writes, though God's creation, is not an exclusively Jewish sphere.

The different conditions under which Kapsali's *seder* and Almosnino's *Cronica* were composed gave rise to divergences between them. Kapsali, as a member of a family of longstanding residence in Crete, relied heavily on anecdotal information, personal experiences, and communal memory. His fascination with the Ottomans was based on the immediate evidence he had of their rise to power – the stories of refugees from Rhodes (who came to Crete after the Ottomans took Rhodes in 1523), and the frantic building of fortifications throughout Crete undertaken by the Venetians in the 1500s in the ultimately futile effort to ward off the arrival of the Ottomans on Cretan shores.

Kapsali interviewed eyewitnesses, among them the refugees from Rhodes, and drew on the testimonials of "reliable" individuals. For his information on the rise of the Ottomans, he spoke with "old and knowledgeable Turks" ("togarmim zekenim veyod'im"); for his accounts of the battles of Constantinople and Malta he relied on the memories of his grandfather, "who knew the awesome and awful story" ("ve yada' et kol ma'ase kostandina hagadol vehanorah"). Finally, for tales of Sepharad he personally interviewed the scores of expelled Jews who passed through the port of Candia:

> And for the stories of Sepharad – there were always poor people [as guests] in our house, and the expelled who came to find shelter under our roof. And now, the exiled and beloved Sephardim would always pass by us, and we would put out for them a bed and a table and a chair and a lamp ... And when they come to us, they tell me all about the great and awful[21] story of the expulsion from Spain.[22]

Almosnino, on the other hand, claimed that official Ottoman court histories were the basis for his text; all his interlocutors had knowledge of these authoritative documents.[23]

Kapsali's approach is a form of proto-ethnography, while Almosnino, with his reliance on documents and texts, uses the techniques of modern historiography. More important, though, is that this difference of approach points to the vast difference Kapsali and

Almosnino had experienced of Ottoman ascendancy. For Almosnino the rise of the Ottomans was something that had happened, something to be researched; for Kapsali it was an event to be awaited, the harbingers of which could be seen everywhere.

Kapsali furnishes his writing with heavy use of biblical formulations – a greater portion of his text consists of direct biblical citation than of other material. Almosnino, by contrast, while using occasional Hebrew phrases, doesn't make any allusions whatsoever to biblical material, and doesn't connect the Ottomans to Jewish prophetic tradition. Kapsali's *seder* is written within an explicitly eschatological and messianic framework, while Almosnino's *Cronica* is purely secular. Kapsali asks for the help of God in writing his history, and the appellation *seder* – that is, "order" – reflects his attempt to place the historical events of his time within the greater divinely mandated order of the world. Almosnino writes his *historia* without a title, in his own free time, as a way to pass the time.[24]

The protagonists of Almosnino's *Cronica* are the Ottoman rulers, while in Kapsali's *seder* the ultimate protagonist is God and the *seder* is the history of the intervention of the divine in the world of his creation. Compare, for example, the respective accounts of Suleiman's persistent interest in conquering Hungary. Almosnino writes, "It was the third war that the grand senor had waged against Budun ... Going into Hungary, which of old they called Panonia, he decided to go into Bech, which they call Vienna, and not come out without taking it."[25] The account is concerned with military logistics, Suleiman's tactical considerations, and the sequence of events. In contrast, Kapsali is concerned with Suleiman's actions as guided by the hand of the divine:

A stormy wind is doing His word, because this was the word of God regarding the king of Hungary, and God said: "Who will seduce the king of Hungary so he will rise and then fall from the heights of Gilead?" ... And the wind came out and stood in front of God, and said, "I will seduce him. You will get him from the palm of my hand." ... And [God] said, "You will seduce and you will succeed, go forth and do so." ... The wind of God started to animate Sultan Suleiman, and ordered him to summon his troops and go.[26]

The two works had different motivations, different contexts, and different agendas. The differences between them can – in the most general of terms – be seen as resulting from the fact that the one was written by a Romaniote and the other by a Sephardic refugee in Ottoman lands. In the context of the sixteenth century, these categories should be taken as geographical as much as cultural. The Sephardim (Almosnino among them) had come in contact with the Ottomans because of the Jews' forced movement from the west to the east. Romaniotes like Kapsali, on the other hand, had come in contact with the Ottomans because of Ottoman expansion from east to west. Almosnino writes as one who had been forced to flee to Ottoman territories, Kapsali as one who awaits liberation through the arrival of the Ottomans in the territory in which he lived.

The differences between the Romaniote and Sephardic communities were to become a stage for conflict, debate, and, ultimately, a large degree of assimilation. But in the mid sixteenth century, when the immediate effects of the expulsions were still ongoing, the dissimilarities between the two communities were perhaps seen most clearly in the different views that they had of the rise of Ottoman power.

THE SALONICAN DELEGATION TO CONSTANTINOPLE, 1566

Almosnino's intention was not to write a history of the Ottomans. His initial interest in the dynasty was pragmatic, the product of the complicated economic circumstances in which Salonica's Jews found themselves at the end of Suleiman's reign. In 1537 Sultan Suleiman had granted the Jews of Salonica privileged status (*mu'af ve müsellim ra'aya*), largely because they provided the fabric used for the Ottoman janissary corps' military uniforms.[27] (Textile manufacture dominated the economic life of Salonica in the centuries following the expulsions; *responsa* of the period reflect this industry's centrality to Salonican Jewish life.[28] Shmuel de Medina, for example, described in one *responsum* the entire process by which raw wool was processed into fabric.[29])

Initially, those directly involved in the textile industry were granted tax exemptions; ultimately all Salonican Jews, interconnected as their community was, were able to claim input into the fabric production. As a result, all Jews in sixteenth-century Salonica enjoyed the benefits of privileged status. After 1537, however, Salonica's textile trade began to decline, the victim of competition from new fabric imports from the Italian city-states and England. In the context of external competition, the privileged status the Jews enjoyed became a bind: by the terms of the arrangement with the Porte (the Ottoman government), the Salonicans couldn't trade with anyone other than the Ottomans, while the Ottomans were free to obtain their textiles from whomever they pleased. So long as the Jews of Salonica had been the sole providers of textiles, the arrangement had been to their benefit. In the context of increased competition, however, the arrangement was problematic.[30] Moreover, it appears that the official document guaranteeing certain privileges for Salonica's Jews was lost in a great fire that destroyed portions of the city in 1545.[31]

Adding to this already burdensome economic state, in 1566 the Ottoman authorities placed an unprecedented fiscal demand on the Jewish community of Salonica: 7,800 head of sheep were to be delivered annually to Constantinople. In previous years the Jews had had to provide livestock as tribute (although the requirement had been suspended from 1537 to 1545[32]), but never before in such quantity. Almosnino explains:

> [The Ottomans] did not give us rest and imposed on us innumerable taxes and levies, and what was particularly heavy on us was the issue of the head of sheep, which was without precedent among the Jews and was intolerable. Because the Jews of Saloniki were day and night working for the service of the king, making the cloth for his slave [troops], the janissaries. And despite that, we were ordered to lead seventy-eight hundred head of sheep every year to Constantinople.[33]

In the summer of 1566 Almosnino was sent to Istanbul as head of a delegation that set out to intercede with the Sultan.[34] The delegation spent a year and a half in Constantinople, returning to Salonica only in 1568. Suleiman's continuing siege on Hungary, followed by his death and the transfer of power to Selim II, made the timely conclusion of the delegation's business impossible.

Almosnino put the extra time in Constantinople to good use. While there he wrote three historical texts, all related to the history of the Ottoman ruling house. They were published together in Spain in the early seventeenth century under the collective title *Cronica de los Reyes Otomanos*. At the time of writing, however, Almosnino's impulse was simply to write an eyewitness account of what he saw in Constantinople. All of his texts were written in Spanish, in Hebrew letters (in distinction to Ladino). The first, composed in December of 1566, includes the account of Suleiman's death and burial. It also provides a genealogy of Ottoman rulers and information about new appointments made by Selim II upon his ascension to power. Four months later, in April 1567, Almosnino wrote a second text, which he defined as "a sort of history" (*como historia*).[35] It concerns the rule of Sultan Suleiman, and was written, it seems, only because *ʿid al-fitr*, the three-day holiday marking the end of Ramadan, imposed a delay on the delegation's work.[36] Almosnino's third text provides a detailed report of the activities of the Salonican delegation in Constantinople, and an account of conditions in the city – climate, sanitation, economy, etc. Yet despite his prolixity, Almosnino regarded his writings as secondary to his role as political emissary: "I am very busy negotiating the request of our republic with the court."[37] Almosnino's three compositions were apparently printed or hand-transcribed in Salonica, and somehow landed in the hands of a Jewish translator working in the service of Spain, in Oran in North Africa. This Ya ʿacov Kansino, the descendant of a family of translators who worked for the Spanish crown, published the book in Spanish in 1638, under the title *Extremos y Grandezas de Constantinopla*.[38]

The setting and inspiration for the composition of Almosnino's work were thus markedly different from the context that inspired Kapsali's; it is perhaps not surprising that the secular nature of Almosnino's work is in sharp contrast to Kapsali's *seder eliyahu zuta*. Almosnino wrote in the context of what was in effect a business trip, while Kapsali wrote with the explicit aim of finding religious meaning in the historical events to which he was witness. Yet this difference, too, is better seen as a product of the broader difference of context that divided the Romaniote and Sephardic communities of the time. To the Romaniotes – particularly those who, like Kapsali in mid-sixteenth-century Crete, were not yet under Ottoman rule – the rise of the Ottomans was experienced much more immediately than it was for the Sephardim. In the Iberian context, the rise of Ottoman power was a distant occurrence. The Sephardim encountered the Ottomans only as a result of their own movement hundreds of miles eastward. For the Romaniotes, on the other hand, as for other communities of the south Balkans and the Mediterranean, the rise of Ottoman power was a wave that crashed over them. The urgency to understand the deeper, divine meaning behind the Ottomans is reflected in Romaniote and Greek Orthodox writings alike, and sets the Mediterranean commentary of the period apart from that of western Europe.

THE SULTAN AS MESSIAH: KAPSALI'S APOCALYPTIC
READING OF OTTOMAN HISTORY

The *seder eliyahu zuta* stands apart not simply for its inclusion of mythic events alongside contemporary historical ones, but for Kapsali's overall treatment of Suleiman, which presents him as a messianic deliverer – not just of the Jews, but of all peoples. Kapsali's style of writing draws heavily on the formulations of Davidic kingship found in the biblical books of Kings and Chronicles. (In this respect, then, Kapsali's *historia* – his *seder* – is based on the *chronica* of the Davidic line, while Almosnino's *Cronica* is more a true "history.") The theme of divine intervention and involvement, direct and indirect, in the rise and reign of Suleiman is a pronounced feature of the *seder*. Kapsali compares Suleiman to Kings Solomon,[39] David, and Herod;[40] he states that he is the "wind" of God (*ruah elohim*)[41] and the "sword" of God (*herev elohim*);[42] he describes Suleiman as "animated by the spirit" of God ("ruah adonai lefaem et sultan Suleiman").[43] His descriptions of the Sultan give some sense of the poetic style in which the entirety of the *seder* is written: "The spirit of wisdom and sagacity, a spirit of heroism and resourcefulness, descended on the King of the Turks, and he made his wars wisely and cunningly ... that is why he was able to crush his enemies."[44]

Kapsali's *seder* sees Suleiman as fulfilling a number of specific prophetic traditions. Kapsali notes, for instance, that Suleiman was Sultan Selim's only male descendant. This was in accordance with traditions that the anointed one was to be a sole male child (Catholic doctrine maintains to this day that Jesus was the only son of Joseph and Mary, and that New Testament references to "brothers" are in fact to the male children of Joseph's first wife). Suleiman's unique status as male heir is linked to the celibacy – or at least near celibacy – of his parents, another theme common to messianic thought. By way of explanation for Selim's apparently limited powers of procreation, Kapsali conjectures that Sultan Selim "thought only of wars" and of the greatness of his people, and as a result "was not interested in the love of women" or, more accurately, "did not succumb to the coveting of women" ("ki merov heshko ve haftso bamilhamot ha'atsumot, lo natan libo ki im 'aleihem, uvahem yehege yomam valila, ve'al hemdat nashim lo yavin").[45] Of further significance is the fact that Suleiman, the only son of near-celibate parents, was the tenth ruler in the line of Ottoman succession: "The tenth King of the Turks will be holy to God, and in his days Judea and Israel will be saved, and the deliverer comes to Zion" ("vehu hamelech ha'asiri latogarmim, veha'asiri yihie kodesh ladonai uveyamav yivasha' yehuda veisrael uva letsion goel").[46]

In this passage Kapsali invokes three different biblical passages at once, the first from Leviticus, the next from Jeremiah, and the third from Isaiah. In *seder eliyahu zuta* Kapsali's vast knowledge of biblical narrative is woven into Ottoman history, or, rather, Ottoman history in Kapsali's history is written as part of biblical narrative – itself a historical narrative, albeit of a different sort. The fact that Suleiman is the tenth ruler is understood as a fulfillment of Leviticus, in which God commands that "all tithes of herd and flock, every tenth one that passes under the shepherd's staff, shall be holy to the Lord" (Leviticus 27:32). In its Levitican context, the verse in and of itself carries no prophetic value – it is part of the book's long closing discursus on agricultural and animal tithes – but Kapsali uses it in order to render new meaning to Suleiman's place within the Ottoman dynastic line. Suleiman, as the auspicious tenth, will guarantee the safety of the people: "In his days Judea and Israel will be saved." Here, the biblical allusion is to Jeremiah 23:5–6, "The days are surely coming, says the Lord, when I will raise up from David's line a righteous branch, who shall reign as king and deal wisely, and shall execute justice and righteousness in the land. In his days Judah will be saved and Israel will lie in safety. And this is the name by which he will be called: 'The Lord is our righteousness.' " This Jeremian passage is explicitly prophetic. The entirety of Jeremiah 23:1–8 was in Kapsali's day (as today) understood as a messianic oracle in which God, having reproached the leaders of Judah for scattering their people, then promises to establish a righteous king, born of David's line, to rule over a restored Israel.

Finally, Kapsali ends his introductory discourse on Suleiman with yet another messianic prophecy, this time from the book of Isaiah (59:20): "He will come as a redeemer to Zion." Situated within the explicitly prophetic and messianic context of Jeremiah and Isaiah, the Levitican material casts Suleiman's status as tenth Ottoman ruler in a similarly prophetic light. In short, by Kapsali's interpretation, Suleiman – the only son of his father, the righteous tenth king in the Ottoman dynastic line, the protector of the Jews – is *mashiach*, the Messiah.

The rise of Ottoman power was remarkably swift, and to Kapsali's mind could only have been brought about through the direct intervention of God. That intervention, however, hadn't been undertaken on behalf of the Ottoman ruling house so much as for the Jews, as a critical paving stone on the path to the long-awaited age of grace.

JEWISH MESSIANIC HISTORY IN ITS EARLY MODERN MEDITERRANEAN CONTEXT

Such tropes, of course, are not unique to Kapsali. The blending of mythic and historical time is arguably the central characteristic of Jewish historical writing – the thing that most makes it "Jewish." Yet even more, perhaps, it is the Jewish view of history that makes Judaism what *it* is: a profoundly historical worldview, in which "even God is known only insofar as he reveals himself 'historically,' " in history.[47] Kapsali's approach – his fusion of eternal time with lived history; the patterning of his narrative on the kingly formulations of Chronicles; his rereading of messianic prophecy – is familiar from a number of other important Jewish histories, almost all Sephardic, of the period. Abraham Zacuto's *sefer yuhasin* (Book of Genealogies), Solomon Ibn Verga's *shebet yehudah* (The Scepter of Judah), Samul Usque's *Consolaçam as tribulaçoens de Israel* (A Consolation for the Tribulations of Israel), Yosef Hakohen's *dibrei hayamim lemalkei zarefat umalkei bet ottoman hatogar* (History of the Kings of France and of the Kings of the Ottomans) – in approach, themes, and motivation all echo Kapsali's *seder eliyahu zuta*.

Yet, in reading the history of Suleiman as a prophetic messianic history, Kapsali was not simply being a "Jewish" historian. He was also being a quintessentially early modern Mediterranean one. Reading the rise of Ottoman power as an apocalyptic event, an irruption of transcendent time into the realm of historical time, was not uniquely Jewish. It was a major preoccupation of Christian and Muslim writers of the period as well. Eastern Orthodox writers, particularly, shared this interpretive prism. After all, the Orthodox Christian populations of the southern and eastern Mediterranean had only fifty years earlier suffered what they, too, regarded as a sort of exile and destruction: the final demise of the Byzantine Empire, brought with the fall of Constantinople to the Ottoman Sultan "Fatih" Mehmet I – Mehmet the Conqueror – in 1453.[48] The collapse of Christian temporal power in the region was viewed by Orthodox Christian thinkers through the lens of biblical prophetic tradition, just as the expulsions were by their Jewish counterparts.

The religio-apocalyptic dimensions of such lines of interpretation took multiple forms. Millenarian thought attached itself to the events of 1453, according to which the fall of Constantinople – a "thousand-year city"[49] – was one of the sufferings and lamentations foretold by biblical prophetic tradition as forerunners to a messianic age. Numerous apocalyptic Greek Orthodox folk traditions derived from the Ottoman conquest of the city. For example, the absence of any record of the death of Emperor Constantine XI Palaiologos (last spotted in battle against the Ottomans on the city ramparts on 29 May 1453), combined with the fact that the Emperor's body was never found, fed a millenarian belief that he had been occulted, lifted up by God, and would be returned to earth only upon the restoration of the city to the Greeks.

Similarly, one strong strand of early modern Greek Orthodox apocalyptic thought argued that "ítan thélima theóu i póli na tourképsi" (it was the will of God for the city to fall to the Turks).[50] By this reading – as by Kapsali's – the Ottoman dynasty had been raised to power by the direct act of the hand of God, and the domination of the region by the Muslim Turks was taken as one of the signs of the end times, a harbinger of the coming apocalypse. While by Kapsali's account the Ottomans had been sent by God to establish a reign of peace and safety, by most Christian readings the Turks had been sent to punish the Christians and warn them to mend their heretic ways. As with Kapsali, the Christian interpretation drew heavily on the prophetic texts of the Hebrew Bible – particularly Jeremiah and Isaiah, with their detailed accounts of the wickedness, punishment, and ultimate redemption of God's people.[51]

In both cases – Mediterranean Jewish and Greek Orthodox alike – the Catholic West stood as the ultimate symbol of aggression, heresy, and hate. Here too was another factor that drew Jewish and Greek Orthodox thought together. Almosnino's preoccupation with Suleiman's battles with "Siguetvar" and particularly with Vienna ("que llaman *Bech*")[52] reflects his joyous fascination with the prospect that the Catholic West – the cause of so much Jewish suffering – might be brought to its knees.

For the Greek Orthodox, the doctrines of Catholicism were a heresy, and the Greeks were being punished by God for dabbling in it. The Council of Florence (1438–45), which met successively at Ferrara (1438–39), Florence (1439–43), and Rome (1443–45), had as its prime aim to reunite the churches of the East and West. In the context of Byzantine decline, reunion would clearly have been desirable to the leaders of Constantinople, who desperately needed military assistance against the looming threat of the Ottomans. But the council's Decree of Union, signed by Greek and Roman representatives on 5 July 1439, was purely cosmetic, and the majority of Constantinopolitans regarded it as an act of betrayal on the part of their church.[53] The fall of the city was read as a punitive act, aimed at the heresy of those Greeks who had allowed union, however superficial, to be pursued.[54]

So it is that the two great ruptures of early modern Mediterranean history – the successive expulsions of the Jews from the Iberian peninsula and the conquest of Constantinople – were understood by their respective communities as being intimately linked to the same constellation of factors. In both cases, the horrors of Catholic doctrine were read as an underlying cause – in the Sephardic instance, of course, most explicitly. Sephardic historians claimed that the expulsions were a punishment for Jewish conversions to Catholicism;[55] Orthodox thinkers interpreted the fall of Constantinople as a punishment for Orthodox conversions to Catholicism. Both events were intimately linked to the rise of Ottoman power in the region. For the Jews, the Ottomans were an instrument of redemption; for most Greeks, a tool of punishment. For both, however, the Ottomans represented hope that the Catholic West might at last be overcome. Finally, both the expulsions and the fall of Constantinople, in their respective contexts, were read through the prism of biblical prophetic tradition, as alternatively apocalyptic, millenarian, and messianic events.

From the outset, the Jewish and Greek Orthodox communities of the western Ottoman provinces were at once bound together and set apart from one another by the experience of Ottoman subjugation. On the one hand, Jews and Christians alike were subject peoples: both were organized according to confession; both were subject to specific economic and social strictures. On the other hand, the official Greek Orthodox narrative (propagated largely by the Church and its representatives) was that subjugation to Ottoman rule was an enslavement, punishment, and burden, an oppressive condition from which deliverance was ultimately to come. But for the Jews subjection to Ottoman rule was (comparatively, at least) a form of liberation, the first step in the gradual progress toward a messianic age in which all Jews would be safe and free and vindicated to the world.

THE MEDITERRANEAN EAST AS ISRAEL

Again, the broader global context framed and conditioned these interpretations. Most salient is that the sixteenth-century rise of Ottoman power in the Mediterranean came largely at the expense of Catholic European powers. The most significant island conquests of the sixteenth and seventeenth centuries saw the Knights of Saint John lose Rhodes (1522–23) and the Venetians lose Cyprus (1571) and Crete (1645–69). The (largely Romaniote) Jewish populations of these islands, like the ejected Sephardim, had a powerful memory of the experience of subjugation to Catholicism. (Other Jewish communities of the region, most notably Corfu's, were to remain continuously under Catholic rule until the modern period.)

Jewish identity, like Greek Orthodox identity, was negotiated in a complex and relatively heterogeneous context. Catholicism, Orthodox Christianity, and Islam all exercised – at different times and in different ways – varying degrees of social control over the Jewish communities of the south Balkans. But they also were in competition with one another. The social and political competition among different communal groups shaped Jewish identity just as strongly as did the presence of any one form of political domination.

It is within this context that Kapsali is best understood, a context that allowed his *seder* to accomplish two narrative tasks at once: the *seder eliyahu zuta* simultaneously contributes to the ongoing narrative of Jewish history – the biblical narrative of destruction, punishment, prophecy, and redemption – *and* provides a wholly new historical narrative, a contemporary and distinctively Mediterranean account of the sixteenth-century apogee of Ottoman power.

The means through which Kapsali accomplished this did not rely merely on clever exegetical interpretation. The key "source text" for the *seder* wasn't the Bible, but more potently the living history of which he was a part: the history of the fall of Constantinople, the rise of the Ottomans, the expulsion of the Jewish populations of the Iberian peninsula (and, later, Italy), and their "redemption" and "salvation" in Ottoman lands. The books of Jeremiah and Isaiah, both of which are dominated by the theme of a scattered people searching for physical safety and spiritual redemption, seemed to Kapsali's mind not merely prophetic, but accurate in their description of his contemporary time.

The promise of Jeremiah was the promise that just as the Israelites were led by God out of the land of Egypt, so too would they in future generations "live in their own land" (Jeremiah 23:8). In the context of early modern Mediterranean apocalypticism – Jewish and Christian alike – such traditions were connected to the notion of an "Israel" more conceptual than literal; a place that was characterized by safety and peace. Again, they were based on a prophetic outlook that was more presentist than futuristic. For Eliyahu Kapsali, who daily saw the expelled Jews from Sepharad arriving at the waterfront in Candia, it was no leap to read Venetian Crete – and, even more, the Ottoman domain of Suleiman, of which he hoped Crete would soon be part – as a sort of Israel, the promised land of peace and deliverance, ruled over by a just and righteous king.

The Jewish literature of the period is replete with examples of this vision. Eliyahu of Pesaro, an Italian Jew who traveled the Mediterranean in 1563, is typical in this regard. That year Eliyahu wrote a letter describing his trip from Venice to Famagusta, Cyprus.[56] His destination had been the Holy Land, but a rumor of pestilence prevented him from getting there. He stayed on instead in Famagusta, where he made the acquaintance of Rabbi Eliezer Ashkenazi (later chief rabbi of Krakow), with whom he studied for two years.[57] In the process he fell in love with the island, which he came to regard as a promised land. He wished only to bring his friends and family: "I would not ask for more from God than he might implant the idea in the heart of some decent personalities from the provinces of Italy to decide to come to us and live here. For there is nothing better for them and for their descendants than this." The pleasures of Cyprus were both material and divine, the realization of prophetic promise. Quoting from the Song of Songs, he continued, "The man who will decide to stay in the courts of Famagusta ... will eat precious fruits, Henna with spikenard plants" (Song of Songs 4:13).[58] Cyprus was the land of deliverance, a place of freedom for the "enslaved" Jews of Sepharad. As Eliyahu concluded, "In truth – whoever lives here belongs to those who eat manna."[59]

Given the status of Jews in sixteenth-century Europe and the recent memory of the expulsions, it is easy to understand how Kapsali and Eliyahu of Pesaro could come to such conclusions. More potent, however, is the fact that the expulsions – horrible though they were – had provided the catalyst for the eastward movement of hundreds of thousands of Jews. While this movement did not take most of them as far as the literal Jerusalem, many felt that they had found the promised land simply by moving from the west toward the east. For some south

Balkan Jews, such as the Sephardim of Salonica, this feeling was to continue for well over three hundred years. For others, however, like the Romaniotes of Crete, the next several centuries would be marked by instability and loss of identity. While the sixteenth and seventeenth centuries marked the consolidation of Sephardic communal power and identity, for the Romaniotes they were the beginning of a long period of uncertainty and decline.

NOTES

1. Yosef Hayyim Yerushalmi, *Zakhor. Jewish History and Jewish Memory* (Seattle: University of Washington Press, 1989), pp. 57–58.
2. An overview of Jewish historical writing of the period is provided by Maria Bel Bravo, "The Expulsion of the Spanish Jews as Seen by Christian and Jewish Chroniclers," in *The Jewish Communities of Southeastern Europe. From the Fifteenth Century to the End of World War II*, ed. I. K. Hassiotis (Thessaloniki: Institute for Balkan Studies, 1997), pp. 55–73. Note, though, that the article is more useful as a bibliographic overview than as a source for factual information, a certain amount of which is incomplete or incorrect.
3. An overview of Sephardic presses and literary production in Ottoman territories can be found in Jane S. Gerber, *The Jews of Spain: A History of the Sephardic Experience* (New York, Free Press, 1992), pp. 158–161.
4. Suleiman "Kanuniye" (the Lawgiver), 1520–66.
5. Moises Almosnino, *Cronica de los Reyes Otomanos*, ed. Pilar Romeu Ferre (Barcelona: Tirocinio, 1998), Libro I, 1, p. 59. (Romeu Ferre notes that there is an error in the date conversion: 11 December 1566 was 29 rather than 28 Kislev.) A history of the various versions of the text and their composition and translation is provided in Romeu Ferre's "Introducción," pp. 15–27. The sole existing original copy of the entire text is in the Biblioteca Ambrosiana de Milan (signatura x – 126 – sup, ant. Ms. III 32). All references to Almosnino's *Cronica* are to Romeu Ferre's edition. ("Proceso de lo sucedido en la guera última que hizó nuestro gran señor sultán Suleimán, que esté en gloria, y de su falecimiento estando su exército dando la batalla sobre Siguetvar, y del modo de reinar su hijo sultán Selim, que el Dio lo prospere, hata tornar del campo y entrar en Costandina en su palacio, con todo lo que en su entrad sucedió. Escrito en Constandina, dia de miércoles 28 de quislev, año de cinco mil y trećientos y vente y siete a la criación del mundo, onće de dećembro.")
6. Almosnino's dates are estimated as 1515–80. Meir Zvi Benaya, *moshe almosnino, ish saloniki* [Moshe Almosnino of Saloniki] (Tel-Aviv: University of Tel-Aviv, 1996), p. 11. Benaya's is the most comprehensive biographical overview to date of Almosnino, but its primary focus is on his writings (particularly his rabbinics) rather than on his life. It devotes minimal attention to the *Cronica*.
7. Or, more accurately, a version in Roman letters – the original had been written in Spanish (that is, not in Ladino or in Hebrew), but with Hebrew letters.
8. Moysen Almosnino, *Extremos y Grandezas de Constantinopla*, trans. Iacob Cansino (Madrid: Francisco Martinez, 1638). Jacob Cansino was a translator and

interpreter in the employ of the Catholic court of King Felipe IV, and also translated Hebrew, Arabic, "Chaldean" (*caldea*), and a number of other languages as well. Needless to say, there were in 1638 few Jews in Spain likely to read the text; clearly it was published because of its broad appeal as a work of Ottoman history, a major interest in Europe at the time. Its transposition into Roman letters shows that the audience for the Madrid edition was entirely non-Jewish. The title page identifies Almosnino as "Rabi Moysen Almosnino, Hebreo." An account of the Cansino edition is provided in Romeu Ferre, "Introducción," pp. 19–21.

9. Contemporary "declinist" theories of Ottoman history point to 1566 as the year that marked the beginning of the long, slow end of the Ottoman Empire.

10. *Cronica*, Libro I, 9, p. 75

11. The term used by Almosnino, *marata*, may come from the Arabic *'imāra*, meaning "building." It is unclear whether the term refers to the tomb itself, a mausoleum, or the area outside the tomb where mourners traditionally gave alms to the poor. Based on context, the last seems most likely.

12. Benayahu, based on the rate of Kapsali's literary output, estimates the year of his birth as 1490. He conjectures 1555 as the year of his death, since 1550 is the last year in which Kapsali is recorded as literarily active. Meir Benayahu, *rabi eliyahu kapsali, ish kandia: rav, minhag, ve historian* [Rabbi Eliyahu Kapsali of Kandia: Rabbi, Scholar, and Historian] (Tel-Aviv: Tel-Aviv University Press, 1983), pp. 73, 86. Benbassa and Rodrigue give his dates as 1450–1523, surely an error, given that we have *takanot* (communal ordinances) authored by Kapsali dating from the mid sixteenth century (the last *takana* that bears his signature is from 1549). Benbassa and Rodrigue may have based their estimate on the fact that it is known that the plague struck Crete in 1523, and that the Jewish community was particularly hard-hit. Kapsali, however, wrote a lengthy account of the plague (in which he describes his fears that he, too, might succumb), and also wrote an account of the siege of Rhodes, which concluded in favor of the Ottomans in December of 1523. Benbassa and Rodrigue, *Sephardi Jewry*, p. 55.

13. Of his grandfather Kapsali wrote, "My venerable master, my eminent ancestor, Rabbi Eliyahu Kapsali, of blessed memory ... my name is the same as his; may my path resemble his!" ("Mon vénérable maître, mon ancêtre éminent, Rabbi Eliahou Capsali, de memoire bénie ... mon nom est le même que le sien, puisse mon parcours ressembler au sien!"); *no'am ve hobalim*, cited in Simone Sultan-Bohbot, "Introduction," in Eliahou Capsali, *Chronique de l'expulsion*, trans. Simone Sultan-Bohbot (Paris: Cerf, 1994), p. 16, n. 21.

14. Somewhat surprisingly, the title has been more often translated incorrectly than correctly; it is usually rendered as either "The Little Order of Eliyahu" or "The Book of Little Eliyahu" – the latter exhibiting a clear misreading of *seder* for *sefer*, the former a misplacing of the adjective *zuta* (little). Kapsali makes clear in his introduction why he refers to himself as *zuta* (n. 43, above). Examples of this confusion are found in Yerushalmi, who translates Kapsali's title as "The Minor Order of Elijah" (*Zachor*, p. 57), and Bel Bravo, who does not translate the title but cites it as *sefer* [rather than *seder*] *eliyahu zuta* ("The Expulsion of Spanish Jews," p. 62, n. 19).

15. The manuscript as transcribed by Aryeh Shmuelevitz has been published collaboratively by the Yad Ben-Zvi Institute, Hebrew University Jerusalem, and the Diaspora Research Institute of Tel-Aviv University.

16. Eliyahu Kapsali, *seder eliyahu zuta A'* [*Seder Eliyahu Zuta* by Rabbi Eliyahu ben Elqana Capsali. History of the Ottomans and of Venice and that of the Jews in

Turkey, Spain and Venice], ed. Aryeh Shmuelevitz, Shlomo Simonsohn, and Meir Benayahu (Jerusalem: Hebrew University/Ben-Zvi Institute, 1977), vol. 1, pp. 12–13. Here Kapsali outlines the contents of his book.

17. A view of other factors informing Kapsali's viewpoint is provided by H. Ben-Sasson in *Sefer zikaron li-Gedalyahu Alon* [Gedalia Alon Memorial Volume], ed. Mehahem Dorman, Shemuel Safrai, and Menahem Stern (Tel-Aviv: Tel-Aviv University Press, 1970), pp. 276–291.

18. First published in Adrianople in 1554.

19. First published in Venice in 1587.

20. "velif'amim nitkavanti lirshom biktsat min hamekomot ktsat dinim tori'im, veshemets davar me'at mis'er lo kabir midivrei hachmei hamekubalim [And at some times {in this text} I intended to write in a few places a few legal precepts, and a little bit smaller than small – nothing big – from the words of the kabbalists]." Kapsali explains that religious knowledge is divided into two categories – legal precepts and kabbala – and that his *seder* is only concerned with these to a very small extent. The real topic of inquiry is something other than religious knowledge. It is *dvarim 'olamim* (matters of the world). *seder eliyahu zuta A'*, vol. 1, p. 12.

21. Note here the repeated use of the construction *hagadol vehanora* (the great and awful), to describe both the expulsion of the Jews from Iberia and the fall of Constantinople. The parallelism locates both events on the same spectrum – both are simultaneously awesome and awful, and both are brought about through the direct intervention of the divine. The use of the phrase furthers the messianic/apocalyptic tone of Kapsali's text (for more on this theme see the further discussion of Kapsali below), for it is a quotation from the book of Malachi (4:1): "Lo, I will send you the prophet Elijah before the great and awful day of the Lord comes." Malachi 4:1 is itself a commentary on Malachi 3:1: "See, I am sending my messenger to prepare the way before me, and the Lord whom you seek will suddenly come to his temple ... But who can endure the day of his coming, and who can stand when he appears?" In Christian tradition, the three synoptic gospels (Matthew, Mark, Luke) use this material as the framing prophetic for John the Baptist, the forerunner to the Christian Messiah. In Kapsali's text, it is used as framing prophetic for the general history of the rise of the Ottomans, and the specific history of the reign of Suleiman the Magnificent.

22. *seder eliyahu zuta A'*, vol. 1, p. 11. ("ve sippurei sepharad – tamid hayu 'ani'im bnei beitenu, vehagerushim mistofefim betsel koratenu. Vehine hasfaradim hahamudim vehanifradim 'ovrim 'alenu tamid vesamnu lahem mita, veshulhan, vekise, umenora, vehaya bevoam elenu yasuru shama, vayesapru li et kol gerush sefarad hagadol vehanora.")

23. Almosnino, *Cronica*, p. 107. ("[T]engo oído haber en su tiempo sucedido dignas de ser notadas, están por estenso especificadas por su cronista, aunque no son hata aquí divulgadas por su autoridad, que según dicen es escritura de gran cantidad y traerlo aquí sería una inportuna prolijidad.")

24. Ibid. ("Por haber visto algunos de mis señores de esta noble civdad y lugar tan famado el proceso que yo acaśo hiće por lo pasado, notado a recreimiento y istancia de algunos mis íntimos amigos, que el Dio sustente, que ne hićieron ser contento de escribir lo que sucedió.")

25. Ibid., *Cronica*, p. 111. ("Fue la tercera guera que este gran señor hizo sobre Budún, que es haćia la miśma parte que hizó la primera, camino para

la Hungaria, que antigamente llamaban Panonia, donde pensó tomar a Bech, que se llama Viena, y no salió con ello.")

26. *seder eliyahu zuta B*, p. 21.

27. Shaar Asher Covo, *Responsa, yore de'a*, no. 13. Also Halil Inalcik, "Jews in the Ottoman Economy and Finances, 1450–1500," in *The Islamic World From Classical to Modern Times: Essays in Honor of Bernard Lewis*, ed. C. E. Bosworth, Charles Issawi, Roger Savory, and A. L. Udovitch (Princeton, N.J.: Darwin Press, 1989), pp. 513–550; I.-S. Emmanuel, *Histoire des Israélites de Salonique*, vol. 1, *140 BC–1640* (Paris: Librairie Lipschutz, 1936), pp. 210–216; and see also the same author's supplementary text included therein, *L'Histoire de l'Industrie des Tissus des Israélites de Salonique*, pp. 15, 23.

28. See, for example, De Medina, *Responsa* IV, nos. 45, 262, 422; Avraham de Boton, *Responsa, lechem rav*, no. 139; Yosef ben Lev, *Responsa* III, no. 33.

29. De Medina, *Responsa* IV, no. 45.

30. To have a sense of how religiously enshrined the fabric industry was in early modern Salonica, see the *haskama* transcribed by Almosnino ca. 1560, published in France in 1900, that describes the history of the profession, and the duties of the community involved in it. The text is reproduced in entirety in Emmanuel, *L'Industrie des Tissus*, pp. 31–32.

31. Emmanuel, *Histoire des Israélites*, vol. 1, p. 212.

32. Ibid.

33. Cited in Meir Zvi Benaya, *moshe almosnino ish saloniki: po'alo veyetsirato* [Moshe Almosnino of Saloniki: His Deeds and His Works] (Tel-Aviv: Tel-Aviv University Press, 1996), p. 62. ("lo natnu lanu manoah vehitlu 'alenu ensfor missim vearnonot ubifrat hichbid 'alenu 'inyan rashei hatson shelo haya lo takdim etsel hayehudim vehaya bilti nisbal: mishum she yahudei saloniki hayu yomam valel lesherut hamelech ba'asiat habadin layanicherim 'avadav, velamrot zot nitsdavenu lehovil shiv'at alafim ushmoneh me'ot rashei tson kol shana lekonstantina.")

34. Other members included Yacob ben Nachmias and Moshe ben Baruch.

35. "Solo diré muy breve la universalidad de lo que tengo a memoria, que será como historia de la vitoria que hubo en los reinos y rejonas muy nombrados, tieras, villas y fortaleźas famadas que en su tiempo fueron tomadas por su intercesión" (*Cronica*, pp. 107–108).

36. The first of Iyar 5327, was 10 April 1567; in 1567 Ramadan began on 12 March, and Eid fell on 9–10 April ("por deporte en estos días de ocio forzado por haber comenzado hoy, primero día de iyar, año de 5327 de ser el mundo criado, la pascua de los turcos, que llaman Bairam"). *Cronica*, p. 107.

37. *Cronica*, p. 107. ("[S]oy muy ocupado en el negocio de las súplica de nesa república en esta corte.")

38. Romeu Ferre, "Introducción," pp. 19–20. See also, above, note 5.

39. *seder eliyahu zuta B'*, p. 11.

40. Ibid., p. 15.

41. Ibid., p. 20.

42. Ibid., p. 21.

43. Ibid., p. 22.

44. Ibid., p. 24. ("Ruah hochma uvina / ruah 'etza ugvurah / naha 'al melech togarma / vaya'as be'orma uvehochma / milhemet ha'ir halaz harama ... lachen ramas oyvav ve 'ochrav.")

45. *seder eliyahu zuta B'*, p. 7.

46. Ibid., p. 7.
47. Yerushalmi, *Zakhor*, p. 9.
48. Indeed, the development of modern Greek nationalism and of Zionism some four hundred years later were to follow remarkably similar trajectories, in large part because both groups would come to understand themselves as exiled. For the Greeks, this sense of exile began with the 1453 fall of Constantinople. For the Jews of the western Ottoman provinces the longstanding biblical exilic tradition would be historically instantiated first by the expulsions from Spain, then by the Greek conquest of Salonica.
49. The year 330 marks the formal establishment of the city, under Constantine I ("the Great"), but it was widely understood as being one thousand years old at the time of the Ottoman conquest.
50. In *tis Agias Sophias* [of Saint Sophia], in *Eklogai apo ta Tragoudia tou Ellinikou Laou* [Selections of Songs of the Greek People], ed. N. G. Politis (Athens: E. G. Vagionaki, 1978), p. 13, l. 11.
51. There were, however, Greeks who saw the rise of the Ottomans as a continuation and revivification of Roman imperial tradition – much as Mehmet the Conquerer seems to have viewed himself. Kritoboulos, for instance, appointed governor of the Aegean island of Imbros by Mehmet I, embraced the events of 1453 as a sign of ongoing continuity of Cesarean rule.
52. That is, Beç, the Turkish name for Vienna. *Cronica*, p. 61.
53. See K. E. Fleming, "The Question of Union and the Fall of Constantinople," in *Modern Greek Studies Yearbook*, 12–13 (1996/97), pp. 35–48.
54. Conversely, those Greeks who supported union read the fall as a punishment directed against the opponents of union. Doukas, an obscure figure in Genoese employ, was a Greek supporter of union with the West who wrote a contemporary account of the fall of Constantinople. In his work, the biblical books of Isaiah and Amos function as the prophetic sources that forecast the fall of the city, and the sense that the Turkish conquest is a just fulfillment of prophecy runs throughout his account. Mehmet, the agent of punishment, is a "flesh-eating devil," "a fierce and bloodthirsty tyrant," and the very embodiment of Nebuchadnezzar.
55. For a very quick overview, see Bel Bravo, "The Expulsion of the Spanish Jews," pp. 55–73, esp. p. 71. (Note, though, that Bel Bravo incorrectly identifies Kapsali as "a descendant from the Jews expelled from Sefarad" [p. 62].)
56. Joseph Shatzmiller, "Travelling in the Mediterranean in 1563: The Testimony of Eliahu of Pesaro," in *The Mediterranean and the Jews: Banking, Finance and International Trade (XVI–XVII Centuries)*, ed. Ariel Toaff and Simon Schwartzfuchs (Ramat Gan, Israel: Bar Ilan University Press, 1989), pp. 237–248.
57. Ibid., p. 239.
58. Ibid., p. 240.
59. Ibid., p. 240.

6

TRADING IDENTITIES

THE SIXTEENTH-CENTURY GREEK MOMENT

Molly Greene

Scholars of the early modern Mediterranean have successfully argued for the existence of what can be called a "Jewish moment" in the sixteenth century.[1] This refers to the extraordinary wealth and influence that various Jewish communities enjoyed during this time. Several factors contributed to this efflorescence. Following the disaster of the explusion of 1492, Sephardi Jews fanned out across the Mediterranean, settling first in the various states of the Italian peninsula and then gradually making their way to the Ottoman Empire. This scattering of the population allowed for the emergence of a powerful commercial diaspora stretching from Istanbul in the east to Livorno in the west and Tunis in the south. At the same time, the consolidation of Ottoman rule in the eastern Mediterranean, after centuries of fragmentation between Byzantine, Italian, and Turkish statelets, led to a decline in Italian power – principally Venetian and Genoese – in the east. By the sixteenth century the Italian states were searching for intermediaries who could maintain the links with commerical entrepots such as Alexandria, Aleppo, and Istanbul that they had traditionally enjoyed. The Jews, who moved back and forth with relative ease between the Ottoman Empire and the Italian peninsula were the perfect candidates. As Benjamin Ravid pointed out, Ancona, Venice, and Livorno all fought fiercely to attract Jewish merchants to their city.[2]

The Ottomans, like their Italian counterparts, were well aware of the value of their new Jewish subjects. Their social and political system, however, was far more open. As a result, some of the more accomplished newcomers moved quickly to the very pinnacles of Ottoman society. The most famous individual was Joseph Nasi, the Portuguese Marrano who settled in Istanbul in 1554 and became a banker to the court as well as political adviser to the Sultan. These highly placed Jews were able to assist their brethren in various ways and their exalted status contributed to the general perception of Jewish wealth and power in the sixteenth-century Mediterranean.

It is equally true, although less remarked upon, that the Greeks enjoyed a sixteenth-century moment of their own. In that century the Greeks developed a truly pan-Mediterranean presence. The two phenomena are not unrelated. Although the Greeks and the Jews each possessed their own particular history, both were an integral part of an international commercial order that emerged in the sixteenth-century Mediterranean. One aspect of this new order has been described by Peter Earle in an article he wrote on Ancona. He said:

> This development marks a stage in the resurgence of the commercial vitality of Islam and indeed of the eastern Mediterranean as a whole, which lies between the late medieval pattern of Italian and Catalan domination of eastern Mediterranean commerce and the pattern from 1600 onwards of domination by the new maritime powers of the Atlantic and the North Sea.[3]

Earle is correct to point to Ottoman strength as an essential part, perhaps the essential part, of this equation. Its complement, however, was the determined attempt of the Italians to either hold on to power (in the case of Venice) or to acquire power by staking out a position in the Mediterranean (in the case of Livorno). Ottoman power and an incongruous mixture of Italian weakness and ambition combined to create opportunities for the Jews; the same combination also opened up horizons for the Greeks.

THE DEMAND FOR MARITIME LABOR

Writing in 1589, the Venetian Provveditore Generale of Crete, Zuanne Mocenigo, informed the Senate that few boats were being built in Candia's arsenal and he went on to explain why:

> The necessary workers are not to be found in this Kingdom, due to the tremendous expense involved as well as the dearth of these past years. [There is also a] lack of commercial traffic and therefore profits are

low. As a result of this, few boats are being built. These workers, seeing that they won't be able to exercise their profession here because of the difficult situation, turn to other professions in order to earn their living, or they go to other countries, principally Constantinople, where workers are paid well and money circulates easily.[4]

In 1608 another provveditore, Agostino Sagredo, reported with satisfaction that he had been able to increase the number of caulkers, carpenters, and oar-makers in the Cretan shipyards by raising salaries. This had the effect of bringing back the workers who had been scattered "and not only in the Kingdom; many had also been overseas in foreign countries."[5]

Venetian difficulties were Greek opportunities. It was difficult to retain skilled workers in Crete (hence the salary increase) precisely because they had so many opportunities elsewhere in the Mediterranean. The Venetian officials mentioned Constantinople; he could also have included Livorno and Venice itself. Greek naval expertise was in demand in all the major Mediterranean ports, and probably in minor ones as well for which little or no documentation has survived. Like the Jews, the Greeks were sought after. Unlike the Jews, however, Greeks were courted mainly (although not exclusively, as we shall see) for their seafaring rather than their commercial skills.

Livorno

In 1564 the Medici ruler Cosimo I invited Greeks to settle in his new city of Livorno. The invitation went out through the mediation of a Basilian monk by the name of Dionisio Paleologo. Cosimo wanted the Greeks in order to man and service the Tuscan galleys and the ships of the Knights of Santo Stefano in particular.[6] The first settlers were sailors, pilots, bombadiers, and caulkers and they remained at the heart of the community. They were granted first one church, then another, to use as their own and in 1601 they received permission to build a new church, SS. Annunziata, which would be the cultural and religious anchor of the Greek community.[7]

In the meantime, recognition "come corpo nazionale" came in 1589, with the nomination of a "protettore della nazione greca" who was none other than the Governor of Livorno himself, one Manoli Volterra of Zante (Zakynthos).[8] In the same year (and before those granted to the Jews) privileges were granted to Greeks currently residing in Livorno, as well as to those who might settle there in the future.[9]

The exceptional skills of the Greeks, and hence their exceptional treatment in Livorno, are apparent in the biography of a Cypriot named Aloisyo di Nores who came to Livorno after the battle of Lepanto in 1570. He enjoyed a long and illustrious career serving a series of grand dukes for over fifty years as the head bombardier of the flagship galley.[10]

The need for Greek labor, and Greek maritime labor in particular, came from Medici ambitions to build up Tuscany's naval power. This ambition had several sources. First, Spanish troops – Spain conquered the Republic of Florence in 1530 – had been stationed in the citadel of Livorno as recently as 1543 and Cosimo was determined to build up Tuscany's independence vis-à-vis Spain. All of his Medici descendants would share the same ambition.[11]

The second concern was more defensive. Right until 1565, when the seige of Malta was successfully resisted, the Ottoman naval advance in the central Mediterranean seemed unstoppable. The city of Tripoli fell to the Ottoman armada in 1551 and in 1558 the Ottomans slaughtered an entire contingent of Spanish troops stationed on the Algerian coast and raided the island of Minorca. Truly alarmed, Philip II sent his galleys into the central Mediterranean, where they met a spectacular defeat at the island of Gerba (Jerba) in 1560. Alongside these major engagements, Muslim forces routinely raided the Italian coastline.

Defense, then, was very much on Cosimo's mind in 1561, the year that he established the military-knightly Order of Santo Stefano. In a solemn ceremony held at Pisa the following year, Cosimo I became the first grand master. The express purpose of this new naval order – which was funded and supplied with galleys by Cosimo himself – was to fight "per le fede di Cristo."[12] Three years later Cosimo issued the official invitation for Greek settlement in Livorno; as stated earlier, Greek labor was intended primarily for the galleys of this new order.

Finally, Medici ambition to make Livorno into an international Mediterranean port is well known. Enticing foreign merchants and foreign shipping to the port was an essential part of that plan and in this aspect the grand dukes were wildly successful. Only eight hundred people resided in the city around 1570; by 1622 that number had grown to over ten thousand.[13] This once sleepy fishing village became one of the busiest harbors in the seventeenth-century Mediterranean, as well as the main port of call for ships on their way to and from the Levant.

Less well known, because it failed, is the Medicis' hope that Tuscan commercial power would grow along with the growth of Livorno. This would include the development of an indigenous merchant class. Part of this attempt included a turn to the eastern Mediterranean where, in the medieval period, the Florentines had been so prominent. In 1574, one year after work had begun on Livorno's new harbor, Francis I moved to renew the capitulations that Florence had signed with Mehmet the Conqueror more than a century ago.[14] This attempt, like all the others of its kind, failed. Nevertheless, given chronic shortages of manpower in the early modern Mediterranean, the grand dukes would also have been keen to retain Greek maritime labor in order to man Tuscan commercial vessels if they ever got into the water.[15]

Venice

The Venetian Provveditore writing from Crete in 1589 was tactful enough not to include Venice among those places that he said were taking away Greek labor from Crete. Yet it is certain that the metropole was a magnet for Greeks with maritime skills.

The most important Greek overseas colony in the early modern Mediterranean was in Venice. By the second half of the sixteenth century that community was four thousand strong and seamen were well represented among them.[16] Most of the members of the Greek Fraternity in Venice, which will be discussed more below, were involved in commerce and maritime affairs, and sailors were well represented among them.[17] Greek seamen were in high demand in Venice, both for their skill and for their knowledge of the Ottoman world which made them the perfect go-betweens.[18]

There was plenty for Greek sailors and caulkers and carpenters to do in Venice. The Venetians had been shocked by the size of the fleet that Mehmet the Conqueror put to sea in 1470.[19] They responded by expanding the capacity of their arsenal. The reserve was raised from twenty-five to fifty light galleys, and ships were churned out of the arsenal at a steady clip throughout the sixteenth century. Peak production was reached in the 1560s.[20] Frederick Lane has called the Venetian arsenal "the biggest industrial establishment in all of Christendom" if not the world.[21] Although we lack studies on the specific question of Greek labor in the arsenal, it is inconceivable that the Greeks – with their reputation as skilled shipbuilders – would not have been in demand as production at the arsenal soared.

Greek sailors served on both Venetian war galleys and merchant ships. The Venetian Admiral Cristoforo da Canal, writing at mid-century, evaluated the free labor available for the navy and said that the Greeks were the very best. They could outrow the Dalmatians and were rarely ill.[22] At some point in the sixteenth century, the crews of the war galleys had become so heavily Greek that a Venetian commander argued for placing a Greek priest on board, since the Latin clergy could not properly hear their confessions.[23] In its clashes with the Ottoman navy, Venice followed a two-pronged policy toward the Greeks found on board enemy vessels. Those who were slaves were freed, while mercenaries were killed. This brutal policy was not simply an expression of outrage but must be seen in the larger context of the fierce competition between Venice and the Ottoman Empire for Greek labor. Frederick Lane observed that killing the Greek mercenaries was one of the ways that "Venice tried unsuccessfully to deprive the Turks of the services of the Greeks."[24]

Of course, the demand for Greek maritime skill had its darker side. Raising salaries – as advocated by Sagredo in Crete in 1608 – was one method of obtaining labor but there were many others. Both the Venetians and the Ottomans were perfectly willing to raid the islands and coasts of Greece and force the Greek population into service on their ships. The historical record is replete with such behavior, which has received a good deal of attention from historians.[25] Venetian administrators in Crete, for example, did not hide the desperate situation from their superiors in their reports back home. Recruitment for the galleys should begin in February, not May as had become the custom, wrote one official, because the peasants were hungry in February.[26] The peasant response was laid out in other reports. Entire families were destroyed as people frantically sold vineyards, fields, and cattle in an attempt to find the money to pay for substitutes. In the course of one recruitment drive, a villager hung himself rather than be taken away to the galleys.[27]

The salutory effects of the competition have been much less remarked upon. What remains unclear is how the balance between free and coerced labor was determined. It seems likely that skilled labor – such as the Cypriot bombardier who served the grand dukes of Livorno for half a century – would have fared better than those Greeks whose skills were less specialized. This is borne out by Venetian reports from Istanbul in the middle of the century. Antonio Barbarigo, writing in 1558, said that, in case of need, the Sultan found it easy to recruit skilled workers for the dockyards. Just two years later another Venetian official in the Ottoman capital observed that – despite casting a very wide net – the Ottomans could never find enough rowers and thus had to resort to slaves.[28]

The Venetian merchant marine reached its peak in the 1560s.[29] The sailors of the Greek community in Venice clearly found ample employment opportunity on these ships. Increasingly, the crews on Venetian ships were of mixed nationality and Greeks predominated. In 1602 Venice passed the Navigation Laws which were intended to boost faltering Venetian navigation by requiring that ships of Venetian registry have crews that were two-thirds Venetian. Venice's dependence upon Greek sailors is made clear by the fact that an exception was made for the Greeks who, for the purposes of this law, could be counted as Venetian.[30]

Istanbul

In 1521 a Venetian official in Istanbul wrote home that he had never seen such a large fleet in the works. One hundred large galleys and ninety-two smaller ones had already been built and were in the arsenals at Gallipoli and Istanbul, and still the work continued.[31] Suleiman was preparing, of course, for the attack on Rhodes which would come the following year and would successfully oust the Knights of Saint John from the island. But this was just one of many large-scale sea battles over the course of the sixteenth century. At Algiers, at Gerba, at Malta, the Ottomans and the Hapsburgs fought each other for control of the Mediterranean, all the way through to the epic battle of Lepanto in 1570. Clearly, the Ottoman need for manpower was just as great, if not greater, than that of the Venetians and they drew on the same pool of Greek labor. As with the Venetians, much of the service was forced and the relatively unskilled rowers must have fared the worst.[32]

But not all Greeks were rowers. As early as 1474 we know that Greek rowers and shipbuilders each had their own guild at the arsenal at Gallipoli.[33] The recruitment orders sent out in 1521 included a general levy for rowers (one man out of every ten in the targeted Greek communities) but also a request for skilled craftsmen from Mytilene and Chios.[34] Later on in the century, two hundred technicians were employed full-time in the arsenal.[35] And conditions in the Ottoman Empire were clearly attractive enough to draw Greeks from beyond the Sultan's domains. A Venetian report from 1558 noted that both Cretans and Ionian islanders were settled in Istanbul, working for the navy, and another report written just a few years later explained that the Greeks preferred to work for the Turks because they could earn in four months what it took a year to earn in Venice.[36] The Venetians were, of course, very alarmed by Greek participation in the Ottoman navy. Thus, when one official wrote that the Ottoman navy would not be able to operate without the participation from Greek subjects of Venice, we can wonder whether he was trying to shock his superiors into action. Nevertheless, Greek-Venetians did work for the Ottomans and in sufficiently large numbers that the Venetians developed a particular word – *mariol* – to distinguish those Greeks from their Ottoman brethren. The Venetians claimed there were enough such Greeks to fill up thirty Ottoman galleys.[37]

THE WORLD OF COMMERCE

Scholars of the Ottoman Empire, and of the early modern Mediterranean more generally, are well aware that the Ottoman conquest of Istanbul in 1453 bolstered Greek commercial fortunes and upset longstanding Italian commercial domination in the eastern Mediterranean. Just as the Ottoman sultans favored the Greek Orthodox Church over the Catholics in the religious sphere, they also bestowed commercial privileges on the Greeks – who, after all, were Ottoman subjects – and denied them to the Italians. The closing of the Black Sea to non-Ottoman shipping is only the best-known example of a very wide-ranging policy.

This framing of the issue, while not incorrect, is incomplete and, despite its emphasis on the Greeks, fails to capture the full extent of Greek commercial fortunes in the sixteenth century. It presents the upturn in Greek commerce and shipping as a purely internal Ottoman affair, one that is the result mainly of Ottoman policy. In fact the Greeks were operating on a much wider stage than this. In the sixteenth century Greek shippers and sailors and shipowners benefited not just from Ottoman strength, but also from the slow ebbing away of Venetian power. Venice was increasingly unable to restrict the lucrative Levantine trade between the metropole and Venetian colonial possessions – Cyprus, Crete, to name just the most important ones – to Venetian citizens alone. This allowed Venice's colonial subjects, who were overwhelmingly Greek Orthodox, to break into these previously exclusive circles. Ottoman Greeks as well streamed into the city.

In addition, to complete the picture, and to recognize its truly international dimension, we must include the cooperation between Ottoman Greeks and Venetian Greeks in managing the trade of the eastern Mediterranean. The Jews benefited from their ability to move back and forth between, principally, Venice and the Ottoman Empire. The extent to which the Greeks could, and did, do the same has been insufficiently appreciated. This raises the question of whether there were not one but two diasporas in the sixteenth century, the Jewish and the Greek. Here I think the differences outweigh the similarities. The Jewish communities scattered across the Mediterranean were truly a diaspora in the sense that they all owed their existence to the common tragedy of expulsion from the Iberian peninsula after centuries of existence there. The commercial benefit that accrued to them from the tight networks that stretched across the inland sea were the inadvertent result of a sometimes desperate search for a safe place to settle.[38] The Greek networks were not the result of any such upheaval. Rather they owed their existence to the fact that, between the two of them, two great powers, the Venetian Republic and the Ottoman Empire, controlled the areas that constituted the Greek heartland. The complicated relationship between Venice and the Ottomans – sometimes at war, other times at peace, but always trading no matter what the conditions – created nearly unlimited opportunities for mediation. The Jews were ideally placed to offer such mediation but so were the Greeks since they were spread out across both Venetian and Ottoman territory.

Venice

The Greek commercial community in Venice was the creation of two factors: Venice's increasing openness to foreign merchants, which was forced upon the republic by historical circumstance, and Venice's declining control over its colonial possessions. The first factor benefited both Greeks and Jews; the second was more specific to the Greeks.

In the sixteenth century Ancona, Livorno, and Venice all competed for the same Jewish merchants who, they hoped, would be able to create or maintain Italian trading links with the Levant.[39] Of these three, only Venice had long boasted a strong native merchant class. Indeed, Venice was synonymous with merchants. But by the sixteenth century this once powerful group was in retreat and, increasingly, foreign merchants residing in the city handled much of the commercial traffic.

Both Greeks and Jews benefited from Venice's increasing openness to foreign merchants. But the particular circumstances that brought the two groups to the city were somewhat different. However reluctantly (Venice certainly was not as liberal as Livorno), Venice did make increasing accommodations for Jewish merchants out of a desire to attract this valuable group to the city.

The Venetians did not recruit Greek merchants with the same determination.[40] Ottoman Greek merchants gained access to the city within the larger context of Venetian–Ottoman confrontation. Venice's steady loss of territory to the Ottomans meant that Venice had little choice but to grant, and enforce, commercial reciprocity between the Most Serene Republic and the Ottoman Empire. In 1419 – long before the expulsion of the Jews from Iberia – the capitulations granted by Sultan Mehmet included rights for Ottoman merchants trading in Venetian-ruled areas.[41] Early in the sixteenth century, the Venetians relaxed their monopoly on trade between Venice and Venetian territories in the Levant. For many centuries this trade had been reserved for citizens of Venice; now Venetian subjects living in the overseas *stato da mar* and Ottoman subjects as well were permitted to trade between Venice and the ports of the eastern Mediterranean.[42]

Encouraged by these developments, Ottoman merchants, both Christian and Muslim, became regular visitors to the *Serenissima* in the sixteenth century. In the 1540s the Ottoman Grand Vezir Rüstem Pasha was so inundated with complaints by Ottoman merchants about damages suffered in Venice that he felt compelled to write to the Doge on this matter. In his letter he referred to the Ottoman traders who went "constantly from the well-protected lands of the Sultan to those parts for trade."[43] Frequent references in the sources to Ottoman merchants in Venice continue throughout the century.[44]

The most prominent, and hence the best-documented, Greek merchants in the city, however, were not Ottoman Greeks, at least not in the sixteenth century. Here we must return to the subject of the Greek Fraternity of Venice which was mentioned briefly earlier. The Greek Fraternity of Venice was founded in 1498.[45] It came into being when the Greeks approached the Council of Ten and – citing their recent military contribution in the conquest of Dalmatia – asked that they be allowed to organize, legally, as a *confraternita* or *scuola*. The motivation behind this request was the desire to secure the community's religious freedom and to clarify their legal situation. Up until this time the Greeks had chafed under the control of the Latin clergy. Now, with their own *confraternita*, they gained the right to draw up their own charter, to elect their own priests, and to take any decisions that they saw fit to make provided they did not contravene the laws of the republic. They were granted the right to worship in the church of Agios Vlasios and they chose Saint Nicholas as their protector.

The similarities with Livorno are immediately apparent. Official protection was followed by the construction of a church that would lie at the center of the emerging (official) community. But there were also differences. The relationship between the Medici grand dukes and the Greeks was created almost ex nihilo out of the contingencies of the sixteenth century. This was certainly not the case in Venice, which had ruled over extensive areas of the Greek East for centuries. Part of the willingness to grant the Greeks relative autonomy in Venice owed to the general commercial trends that I have been discussing, but specifically colonial concerns also figured into the mix. As the Ottomans continued to advance in the Mediterranean, conquering Greek territory that had formerly been Venetian, the Venetians steadily liberalized their treatment of their Greek subjects.

The Greek Fraternity of Venice was very much the creation of, first, merchants and, second, merchants from Venetian-controlled territory. Of the thirty-six individuals who held the post of president (*gastaldos*) between 1498 and 1558, at least sixteen were merchants. Between 1558 and 1570 eleven individuals held that position (some more than once) and all of them were merchants.[46] Merchants and shipowners were the most prominent contributors to the fund for the construction of the church of Saint George and, when that was not enough, a tax was imposed in 1546 on every Greek ship that weighed anchor in Venice.[47]

Most of the Greek merchants in Venice in the sixteenth century – and certainly the prominent and wealthy merchants who founded the Greek Fraternity – were from either the Ionian islands or Crete.[48] Representation from other locations changed in response to particular events. The third Ottoman–Venetian war (1537–40) produced a stream of refugees from the Aegean town of Nauplion as sovereignty passed from Venice to the Ottomans. In the early years of the Fraternity many members hailed from the Ionian island of Leukada, but that number dropped steadily in the sixteenth century following the Ottoman conquest of the island.[49] Although the Fraternity was in theory open to all Greeks, its membership drew almost exclusively on those Greeks who were Venetian subjects. In other words, the Greek merchant community in Venice – as embodied in the Greek Fraternity – had a particular quality that set it apart from the other foreign merchant communities of the city. The community was the result not only of Venetian decline in general, which opened the city up to foreigners, but also of Venice's declining control over its colonial possessions, which created opportunities for her colonial subjects, who were, in the overwhelming majority, Greek.

Information on confraternity members show that they moved easily between the metropole and the provincial capitals from which they had originally come.[50] This was the case whether they chose to settle in Venice, or to maintain their base in their city of origin. They pursued commerce at multiple levels, from the local – carrying goods between the Ionian islands and Venice – to the regional – between the eastern Mediterranean and Venice – and the international – carrying the wine of Crete or the currants of Corfu to England. The most important commodity they dealt in was grain, which they fetched from the ports of the Ottoman Empire and brought to grain-starved Italy.[51]

Markos Defaranas (1503–75) was born in Zakynthos. He came to Venice in his early thirties and became a member of the Greek Fraternity in 1534. By the late 1530s he was working as a secretary (*scrivan*) on a ship named the *Luna* that sailed regularly between Venice, Crete, and Cyprus. He then advanced to being a shipowner and continued his trips across the eastern Mediterranean, as well as the smaller orbit between the ports of the Ottoman Balkans, the Ionian islands, and Venice. All this time he continued to reside in Zakynthos, despite his membership in the Greek Fraternity. In 1550, however, he became a permanent resident of Venice and sailed that summer with the Venetian *muda* to Alexandria. On another trip to Alexandria in the mid 1550s the ship was blown off course all the way to the North African coastline and he, along with the rest of the crew, was enslaved. Defaranas spent fifty-six days in Alexandria before being ransomed by unidentified Christian merchants. In 1558 his name appears among a list of sea captains in the city. This list was compiled by the Venetian government, which wanted to know how many ships were available for the transport of wheat and salt to the city.[52]

The Samarianis family was originally from Methone, in the western Morea, but when that city fell to the Ottomans they moved to Zakynthos. Markos Samarianis is listed as a member of the Fraternity from the early 1520s. He was a shipowner and prominent member of the Fraternity. He contributed generously to the construction of the church of Saint George and served in many high positions.[53] He was a grain merchant who used his family connections in the Ottoman Morea (his sister was married and living in Patras) to secure grain for Venice.

The Vergis family from Corfu appears in Venetian records as early as 1511 when Matthew Vergis sailed from Venice to Constantinople. Other journeys – to Crete, to Cyprus, to Alexandria – were made in the following decade. Throughout the sixteenth century different members of the Vergis family regularly supplied Venice with wheat from various Ottoman ports and salt from Cyprus and far-away Ibiza. In 1559 another Matthew Vergis had a ship built in Venice which measured nine hundred *botti*. In 1569, on a trip back from Southampton with this ship, loaded down with cloth, salt, and tin, Vergis was captured by Huguenot pirates and taken to the port of La Rochelle. He and his crew were freed thanks to the efforts of Queen Elizabeth.[54]

These individual and family stories were replicated over and over again throughout the sixteenth century. They all point to the fact that Venice's Greek subjects moved easily throughout the Venetian and Ottoman East. In some cases they took advantage of Venice's pre-existing connections with cities in western Europe and traded as far west as England.

Historians have written a great deal about the foreign competition that Venice began to suffer in the sixteenth century. The English, the Jews, the Ragusans, and the Genoese all moved in on traditional Venetian territory. Genoese competition for the sweet wine of Crete, for example, led to a fifty percent drop in freight rates on the Crete to England route. Closer to home, Ragusans were bidding cargo away, even in Venice's backyard, the Adriatic.[55]

It is strange that the Greeks are largely absent from the list of competitors.[56] Strange because so many Greeks still lived under Venetian rule and one might reasonably ask whether Venice's difficulties opened up possibilities for its subjects. In fact they did, as I have shown above. Long resentful of the Venetian monopoly on trade, Greek merchants moved quickly to capitalize on Venice's weakness. They were helped by a dramatic, although little-mentioned, shift in the relationship between ruler and ruled in the Venetian domains. It is striking that even scholars who work on the history of the Greeks under Venetian rule have very little to say about the declining import-ance, for commercial history, of the distinction between *sudditi* (sub-jects) and *cittadini* (citizens). This stands in stark contrast to the attention lavished on the changing status of the Orthodox Church under the Venetians.[57]

For many centuries the lucrative routes of international trade had been reserved for Venetian citizens. The Greeks, as subjects but not citizens, were excluded. Thus a Cretan merchant named Costa Michel managed to ship a cargo of pepper to Venice early in the fourteenth century, but when he reached the city the pepper was seized because his name did not appear on a list of Venetian citizens.[58] This wall between subject and citizen, while still standing, was in a state of near collapse at the beginning of the sixteenth century. And over the course of the next one hundred years it would disappear all together. Venetian writing at the time makes it clear that now the critical dis-tinction was between "foreigners," on the one hand, and "Venetians" and "subjects of Venice," on the other. Although the distinction between Venetians and subjects was usually (but not always) retained, they were one group, in terms of rights and privileges, while the foreigners were another.[59]

One of the few scholars to even allude to this critically important development is Chyrssa Maltezou, the historian of Venetian Crete. She says, somewhat cryptically, that "the local population was eman-cipated economically."[60] This "emancipation" was yet another factor that contributed to the wide stage on which the Greeks operated in the sixteenth century.

A CRETAN DISAPORA?

The Cretans represent a special case within this larger sixteenth-century moment that I have been describing. Here we may be able to speak of a diaspora. The reason for this is that the Cretans were so prominently represented in the most important Greek overseas communities. It does seem that, more than other Greeks, the Cretans fanned out across the Mediterranean and constructed commercial connections that were very wide-ranging as well as highly profitable.

We know the least about Livorno. But a notarial document from 1621 does provide an important piece of information. The notary registered the "consensum" of about sixty Greeks that property belonging to Greeks who had died intestate would go, not to the Prince, but for the benefit of the Church. Each signatory gave his place of origin and the largest group came from Crete.[61]

The Greek community in Venice, as mentioned earlier, was heavily weighted toward those Greeks who were Venetian subjects. Among those, the Cretans were always prominently represented. Throughout the sixteenth century the records of the Greek Fraternity – which provide information on the geographical origins of its members – put the Cretans somewhere in the top three regions in terms of numbers represented. Only the Cypriots consistently outnumbered them.[62]

The Cretans surely benefited from the fact that they came from the island that produced one of the most sought-after products of the early modern Mediterranean, that is, the sweet wine known as *malvasia*. They sold it throughout the Mediterranean and in places as far away as London.[63] Braudel described sixteenth-century Crete as an island where "we must imagine a countryside converted by man for the cultivation of the vine, producing raisins and the wine known as malmsey."[64]

Already at the beginning of the sixteenth century a Venetian merchant noted that Cretans brought the island's wine, honey, cheese, silk, and cotton to the ports of the eastern Mediterranean, as well as to North Africa, Puglia, and Naples.[65] Foscarini, writing toward the end of the same century, said, "Many go from here to Constantinople and to the *mar maggiore*, and quite a few go to Alexandria where they drink no other wine than Cretan wine."[66]

Thanks to the work of A. Pippidi, we do have one study, albeit brief, of a Cretan merchant in the wine trade which suggests how far afield the islanders ventured, and how high they could rise, thanks to *malvasia*.[67]

Constantinus Corniactus was born in Candia, Crete, in 1517. His family must have been quite prominent because his sister married Leonin Servo, a Cretan as well, who appears in the historical record as a wealthy merchant settled in Constantinople. Servo was influential enough that he submitted a memorandum to the Council of Ten in Venice in 1575, through the good offices of the Bailo, which suggested steps that Venice might take to improve the religious situation of the Cretans.[68] Corniactus made his money selling Cretan wine in Lwow and he was settled in nearby Moldavia. Pippidi notes that many other Cretans were in Moldavia as well, also selling the sweet wine of their native island. Writing in 1578, the Venetian Bailo estimated that between 1200 and 1500 bottles of Cretan wine arrived in Istanbul every year, headed for Poland. After 1563, when his brother was murdered by the Moldavian princes, Constantine settled in Lwow.[69] He prospered in Poland as well; he became a money-lender to the Prince of Poland and he restored an Orthodox church in Lwow that had been part of the foundation of the Moldavian Prince Alexander Lapusneanu. Born a subject of Venice, he died a member of the Polish nobility.

Corniactus was certainly one of the most illustrious, if not the most, of the Cretan merchants of Lwow, but there were others. About forty Cretans were active in the city between 1560 and 1603.[70] The Cretan colony in Istanbul has received much less attention from historians. Scholars of Venetian Crete have preferred to focus on the island's ties with the West, even though it is clear that ties with the empire of the East were developing rapidly, long before the arrival of Ottoman armies in 1645.[71] Leonin Servo, mentioned above, is just one example of a wealthy Cretan merchant who left his native land to settle in Istanbul. A story of love gone awry in sixteenth-century Istanbul begins with the unlucky fiancé returning to Crete to fetch good wine for the wedding.[72] We lack numbers, but the anecdotal evidence suggests that it was a very important community indeed.

The Latin community in Ottoman Istanbul was based in Galata, just as it had been under the Byzantines. The Genoese initially dominated the area, but over time Venice recovered her position and then surged ahead. The republic signed capitulations with the Ottoman Empire in 1482 and over the course of the sixteenth century the *nazion Veneta* became one of the most important foreign communities. The Venetian resurgence swept many Greeks into the city. Many of the "Venetians" in Galata were, in fact, Greek subjects of the republic.[73] As early as the fifteenth century Cretans especially enjoyed prominent positions in the community, the better to facilitate trade between Constantinople and Crete. Sanudo mentions that it was "Cretans of the Venetian nation" who were in charge of defense in Galata.[74] Writing in 1612, a Venetian official estimated that there were over three thousand Venetian subjects in Galata and most were from Candia.[75] Although there does not appear to be any formal break-down of the Greek-Venetian population of Istanbul by area of origin, the strong Cretan presence is also indicated by the fact that many of the documents generated by the Bailo's office refer specifically to Cretans.[76]

ISTANBUL AND MEDIATION

The Greeks of Ottoman Istanbul were closely associated with com-merce, with shipping, and indeed with all the trades having to do with the sea.[77] The neighborhood of Galata, just across the Golden Horn to the north, quickly re-emerged after 1453 as the new commercial cen-ter of the city, just as it had been under the Byzantines, and it was very much a Greek neighborhood. Its population was more Greek than Muslim and the institutions associated with Christian life, from churches to taverns, lined the streets in ways that would have been considered scandalous within the walled city of Istanbul.[78] Michael Kantekouzenos had his residence in Galata, as did many other members of the Greek elite.[79] As studies too numerous to relate have shown, the Ottoman victory in 1453 signaled the end of Italian domination of the eastern Mediterranean and the Black Sea, and cleared the way for the emergence of a strong Greek commercial class.[80] Istanbul, and Galata in particular, was at the very heart of this community.

Mehmet the Conqueror and his successors aspired to make Istanbul the new center of East–West trade and the activities of the city's Greek merchants reflect those aspirations. From the Black Sea the Greeks brought timber, furs, dried fish, and caviar to Istanbul. On the return trip they carried the luxury goods of the Mediterranean – such as wine from Crete – to the Black Sea ports where they were picked up and sent on to the cities of central Europe.

From Istanbul Greek merchants carried the goods of the Black Sea to western Europe, mostly Italy. The Italian cities, chronically short of grain throughout the sixteenth century, also depended on Greek merchants to bring them precious foodstuffs from the eastern Mediterranean. For the trip home the Greeks loaded their ships with a wide variety of finished products from the West, such as wool fabrics, glassware, and paper.

Trade with Venice was of course particularly active. We lack a comprehensive study of the Greek merchants of sixteenth-century Istanbul in their international context. But the scattered biographical details of certain prominent mercantile families suggest a web of commercial, family, and religious ties to Venice. They also suggest that, like the Jews, Greek merchants mediated the relationship between the Ottoman Empire and the Venetian Republic.

The Marmaretos family were wealthy Greeks, leaders of the Istanbul community, who resided in Galata.[81] By the 1530s, one member of the family, Dimitrios Marmaretos, was established in Venice as part of the family business. He was a member of the Greek Fraternity and was trusted enough by the Venetian state that he was asked to give them a report on Ottoman war plans in 1537, on the eve of another Ottoman–Venetian war, which he did.[82]

The Koresse were also residents of Galata; the family's size and scope were so great that one historian has called them a dynasty.[83] Family members and family property were spread out across the Aegean, the Black Sea, and the Balkans. The Koresse probably had their origin in Chios, but by the sixteenth century they were landowners in Crete; they traded with Italy, France, Moldavia, the ports of the Black Sea, and many points in the East. Their ties to Venice ran very deep. The family enjoyed the status of *cittadinanza Veneta originaria* for services they had rendered to the republic. These included spying and the management of Venetian debt vis-à-vis the Sultan. One Antonios Koresse was established in Venice at mid-century, where he was one of the most active members of the Greek Fraternity. The Venetian Bailo referred to him as "cittadino nostro venetiano."[84] At the same time, he had a close relationship with the famed Ottoman naval commander Hayreddin Pasha.[85]

These are just a few examples. Many of the most illustrious merchant families of Galata established themselves in Venice as well. The pattern is striking enough to suggest that service to both the Venetians and the Ottomans was considered an effective way to augment and preserve the wealth of the family.[86] A court case in front of the Venetian Bailo reveals that Manoles Kantekouzenos established himself in Venice, where he was a member of the Greek Fraternity, while his brother, Antonios, stayed behind in Istanbul to handle that branch of the family's business. When the Bailo ruled against Antonios in a commercial dispute the latter took advantage of his status as a *haraci* or Ottoman subject to dodge the judgment.[87]

The Greeks of Venice also maintained their ties with the Orthodox Patriarchate in Istanbul and their connections allowed them to function as go-betweens in matters concerning Venice, the city's Greek community, and the patriarch. Recourse to the patriarch was common in the event of disputes within the community. During a particularly bitter dispute in the early 1540s the patriarch went so far as to excommunicate a priest named Nicholas Trizentou. For its own reasons, Venice wanted to support this priest and asked Mathaios Vareles, a prominent grain merchant and member of the Greek Fraternity, to go to Istanbul to gain Trizentou's reinstatement.[88] Although Vareles declined to undertake this mission, the government's request suggests that the city's Greek subjects were viewed as mediators not just in matters with the Ottoman government, or for private business, but could also negotiate the complicated world of the Greek Orthodox Church.

BEYOND THE SIXTEENTH CENTURY

The Ottoman imperial moment and the Italian Indian summer created a constellation of forces that was exceptionally favorable for both the Jews and the Greeks.

By gaining control of most of the eastern Mediterranean basin, the Ottomans came to rule over the sea and land routes that had long been the focus of Italian commercial activity. The Italians had no choice but to treat with the empire if they wished to maintain their presence in the East. At the same time the Italian city-states, both old and new, no longer boasted their own merchant classes as they had in the late medieval period. The Greeks and the Jews moved in to fill the gap. At times they were actively courted, in other cases only grudgingly tolerated, but the opportunities were there.

At the same time, the sixteenth century was marked by repeated military clashes between the two superpowers, the Hapsburgs in the West and the Ottomans in the East. Add on to that the many wars between the Ottomans and Venice as the latter slowly lost her empire in the East, plus the fact that the Mediterranean basin became an extension of the intense rivalries of European politics in the sixteenth century, and one can grasp that the demand for galleys and men to row and command these galleys was intense throughout the century. This demand was of fundamental importance in the internationalization of the Greek community in the Mediterranean of the time. Warfare and international rivalry also created the need for spies and for mediators and both Greeks and Jews were called upon to perform these services.

The Jewish presence on both the Italian peninsula and in the Ottoman Empire was mostly a new one. It was the result of the diaspora from the Iberian peninsula. In the Ottoman Empire, unlike in Italy, certain elite Jews moved to the very highest levels of government and this only increased the conviction in places like Venice that the Jews were valuable, indeed essential, go-betweens. But both the Ottomans and Italians valued the Jews for their ability to move between East and West.

The spread of Greek communities was the result of a somewhat different dynamic. From their home base on the Balkan peninsula, in the islands, and along the shores of the Aegean – as well as their important presence in the Ottoman capital – Greeks moved out to the West as Italian power receded. These Greeks included both Venetian and Ottoman subjects. It has long been appreciated that the consolidation of Ottoman rule meant a boost in the fortunes of Greek commerce within the Ottoman Empire. But the international dimension of the Greek revival has been missed.

A changing international situation in the seventeenth century affected Jews and Greeks alike. This century saw the final collapse of Italian commercial power as well as the rise of northern shipping and commerce: Dutch, English, and (to a lesser extent) French. This process was gradual and should not be unduly compressed. After all, Venice held on to Crete until 1645 (and only lost it definitively in 1669) and commerce between the island and the metropolitan capital continued to be important.[89] Nevertheless, it was increasingly the case that northern ships, rather than Italian ones, connected the Ottoman Empire to other ports in the Mediterranean (as well as to points further afield). These rising powers had both their own ships and their own merchants, and did not need (or want) the services of either the Greeks or the Jews. The window of opportunity which the Italian Indian summer had created for Greeks and Jews was now closed.

In the seventeenth century, too, great-power conflict moved out of the Mediterranean. The Hapsburgs and the Ottomans disengaged and a by-product of this disengagement was that intra-European rivalries (such as the one between the French and the Spanish) were less likely to involve the Mediterranean basin.[90] Turning to the Italians: over the course of the century the Medici in Livorno gradually gave up their attempts to become a seapower to be reckoned with. The Ottomans did fight two more major maritime wars (in 1645–69 and 1683–99) but the age of galley warfare, and of Mediterranean seapower more generally, was coming to an end. This meant less demand for the maritime labor that had contributed so enormously to the internationalization of the Greek community.

The Jewish historical moment proved to be a singular one. Particular Jewish communities – most notably the Livornese Jews – continued to enjoy great prominence. But as the sixteenth turned into the seventeenth century, the tight links that had united the sprawling Jewish diaspora began to atrophy and Jewish life in the various communities took on a decidedly more local character. The decline in their international cohesiveness went hand in hand with a decline in the wealth, importance, and visibility of the Mediterranean Jews overall. Their revitalization would have to wait until the opening decades of the nineteenth century and then under very different conditions.

There were many reasons for the singularity of this moment. One in particular stands in contrast to the Greek experience. The Jewish advantage in the sixteenth century was an ephemeral one. One of their great strengths, in Ottoman eyes, was their connection to Europe. They knew European languages and European ways and were extremely valuable in this regard. Ironically enough, through their settling in the East, it was inevitable that these connections would begin to weaken over time and thus take away the singular qualities that had made the Jewish refugees, or at least their upper classes, so attractive to the Ottomans in the first place. As we shall see below, the fortunes of the Greeks would prove to be cyclical, rather than singular, in nature.

The Greeks also entered into a period of retraction in the seventeenth century. We know very little about the process whereby the community, so very international in the sixteenth century, became more provincial. One of the reasons for this is that the seventeenth century overall is a very murky century.[91] The other is that the "Greek moment" of the sixteenth century – which I have spent this article describing – is not yet recognized in the literature. Therefore there would appear to be no contraction to explain.

There is slight, but very intriguing, evidence that at least some of the sixteenth-century patterns continued, albeit on a much reduced scale. Daniel Panzac's study of eighteenth-century commerce in the

Ottoman Empire has revealed that over seventy percent of Muslim shippers in Istanbul were not native to the city. Of those seventy percent, an astonishing forty percent were from Crete.[92] Let us recall that in the sixteenth century, when Crete was still under Venetian rule, most of the Greeks in the Ottoman capital were Cretans. Is it possible that these eighteenth-century Cretan merchants, now Muslim, represent a commercial tradition stretching back at least two centuries? Panzac also found that Cretan Muslim merchants were a prominent community in Alexandria, controlling the traffic between Egypt, Thessaloniki, and Istanbul. It seems likely that the diasporic habits of the Cretans endured in the seventeenth and eighteenth centuries.

In the second half of the eighteenth century, Greek commerce exploded. By the outbreak of the French Revolution it is estimated that the Greeks controlled half of the commerce between the Levant and western Europe.[93] This story is well known and is usually described as the rise of Greek commerce. It is understood as the culmination of a unique long-term development that had its obscure beginnings sometime in the seventeenth century. I would argue that we can also see it as the re-internationalization of the Greek community, a process that drew on the same two main factors that created the Greek moment in the sixteenth century. Once again, great-power conflict and the ambitions of a state that lacked a maritime class (Russia) created opportunities for the Greeks.

European rivalry returned to the Mediterranean in the second half of the eighteenth century and with it the need for maritime labor. The Greeks were there to supply it. In the Seven Years' War (1756–63) Britain used Greek privateers in its attempt to destroy French commerce. Greeks were very active under the Russian flag during the Russo-Turkish wars of 1768–74 and 1787–92. Finally the Anglo-French wars of the late eighteenth and early nineteenth century also extensively employed Greek mariners. Memoirs of those who participated in the Greek Revolution of 1821 make it clear just how common this experience was for the Greeks of that generation.[94]

In the case of the Russians, the opportunities extended beyond wartime. Like the Italian city-states of the sixteenth century, Russia wanted to extend its commercial influence into the eastern Mediterranean but lacked the sailors, the ships, and the merchants to do so. It turned to the Greeks, offering them protection under the Russian flag, and soon Greek commerce had penetrated southern Russia and the Ukraine.[95] Development continued apace to the point, mentioned above, where Greek shipping came to control much of the international commerce of the Mediterranean.

Although the external factors that stimulated this development were remarkably similar to those in the sixteenth century, the areas of the Greek world which responded were rather different from those that had been so prominent in the sixteenth century. For example, despite its long and sophisticated commercial history, Crete is entirely absent from the eighteenth-century moment. The Cycladic islands, on the other hand, which had been unimportant in the earlier age, were now at the forefront of Greek commerce. The reasons for this geographical variation cannot be explored in this article; only the question can be posed.

Beginnings and endings, a rise and then a fall, are popular concepts with historians. An awareness of the similarities between the Greek moment of the sixteenth century and the much better-known Greek moment two centuries later suggests that, in this case at least, we would do better to think in terms of a cyclical process of expansion, contraction, and then re-expansion. The dynamics of this cycle are still poorly understood. Nevertheless, it does seem clear that certain structural features persisted throughout the early modern Mediterranean and well into the eighteenth century and that the expansion or the contraction of the Greek world moved quite reliably in tandem with them. Greek maritime and commercial power was not so much rising or falling, in other words, but was rather a permanent feature of the early modern Mediterranean.

NOTES

1. Avigdor Levy speaks of a "golden age." A. Levy, *The Sephardim in the Ottoman Empire* (Princeton, N.J.: Darwin Press, 1992), p. 75.
2. Benjamin Ravid, "A Tale of Three Cities and Their Raison d'Etat: Venice, Ancona and Livorno and the Competition for Jewish Merchants in the Sixteenth Century," *Mediterranean Historical Review*, 6(2), 1991, pp. 138–162.
3. Peter Earle, "The Commercial Development of Ancona 1479–1551," *Economic History Review*, New Series, 22(1), 1969, p. 40.
4. St. Spanakes, "Relazione del Nobil Huomo Zuanne Mocenigo ritornato provveditore generale del regno di Candia presentata nell'eccellentissimo consillio 17 Aprile 1589," *Mnemeia tes Kretikes Istorias* [Monuments of Cretan History] (Herakleion, Greece), 1, 1940, p. 171.
5. A. Panopoulou, "Oi Technites Naupegeion tou Chandaka kai ton Chanion kata to 16 kai 17 aiona" [The Shipyard Workers of Chandaka and Chania in the Sixteenth and Seventeenth Centuries], *Kretike Estia*, 4(3), 1989–90, p. 182.

6. Lucia Frattarelli Fischer, "Alle Radici di Una Identita Composita. La 'Nazione' Greca a Livorno," in *Le Iconostasi di Livorno: Patrimonio iconografico post-bizantino*, ed. Gaetano Passarelli (Livorno: Comune di Livorno, 2001), p. 49. Individual Greeks served in Livorno as early as the 1540s but their numbers only grew substantially with Cosimo's invitation.

7. Ibid., pp. 51–52.

8. Ibid., p. 49.

9. "alli greci li quali habitano di presente in Livorno familiarmente et a quelli che verranno per l'avvenire ad habitarvi." Ibid., p. 49

10. "capo bombardiere della galera Capitana." Ibid., p. 50.

11. Marie-Christine Engels, *Merchants, Interlopers, Seamen and Corsairs: The Flemish Community in Livorno and Genoa (1615–1635)* (Hilversum, The Netherlands: Verloren, 1997), p. 22.

12. Franco Angiolini, *I Cavalieri e Il Principe* (Florence: Edifir, 1996), p. 17.

13. Engels, *Merchants, Interlopers*, p. 42. This number is based on the number of hearths, which were counted for fiscal purposes. In general, sailors and slaves were excluded from the calculations, so the numbers actually living in the city at any one time were certainly higher.

14. S. Camerani, "Contributo alla storia dei trattati commerciali fra la Toscana e I Turchi," *Archivio Storico Italiano*, 97(2), 1939, p. 88.

15. A Venetian admiral, writing about 1550, spoke of Ottoman raids on the Greek islands to obtain rowers for the galleys. He said that if watch towers were not built along the coasts of Crete to permit warning of such raids, then Crete would soon be as short of manpower as Dalmatia. F. Lane, *Venice: A Maritime Republic* (Baltimore: Johns Hopkins University Press, 1973), p. 368.

16. M. I. Manousakas, "Episkopese tes Istorias tes Ellenikes Orthodokses Afelfotetas tes Venetias (1498–1953)" [An Overview of the History of the Greek Fraternity in Venice 1498–1953], *Ta Historika*, 6(11), 1989, p. 251; Giorgio Plumides, "Considerazioni sulla popolazione greca a Venezia nella seconda meta del '500,'" *Studi Veneziani*, 14, 1972, p. 221.

17. F. Mavroeide, *Symvole sten Historia tes Hellenikes Adelphotetas Venetias sto 16th Aiona* [Contribution to the History of the Greek Fraternity of Venice in the Sixteenth Century] (Athens: Vivliopoleion Note Karavia, 1976), p. 117.

18. Ibid., p. 118.

19. Lane, *Venice*, pp. 361–362.

20. Ibid.

21. Ibid.

22. Ibid., p. 368. The Ottomans, too, preferred the Greeks to the Dalmatians. V. Sfyroeras, *Ta Hellenika Plyromata tou Tourkikou Stolou* (Athens, 1968), p. 117.

23. Lane, *Venice*, p. 346.

24. Ibid.

25. In his pioneering work on Greeks in the service of the Ottoman navy, Sfyroeras speaks of "the tragedy of the Nation, whose seafaring blood is spilled out first drop by drop, then in larger quantities, but always with a view toward bolstering the seapower of a conqueror who lacked any maritime knowledge." Sfyroeras, *Ta Hellenika Plyromata*, p. 8.

26. St. Spanakes, "1610 a 9 Genaro, Relation de s. Doflin Venier ritornato di duca di Candia," *Kretika Chronika*, 4, 1950, p. 339.

27. St. Spanakes, "Relazione Pietro Giustiniano capitan generale de Resmo 1630," *Mnemeia tes Kretikes Istorias*, 5, 1969, p. 233; idem, "Relazione de sr. Isepo Civran tornato di Prov. R. Gen.l di Candia 1639," *Kretika Chronika*, 21, 1969, p. 371.
28. Sfyroeras, *Ta Hellenika Plyromata*, p. 26.
29. Lane, *Venice*, p. 381 (reckoning by total tonnage).
30. Ibid., p. 380.
31. Sfyroeras, *Ta Hellenika Plyromata*, p. 28.
32. See ibid., passim, for recruitment methods.
33. Ibid., p. 21.
34. Ibid., p. 22
35. Ibid., p. 26.
36. Ibid.
37. Ibid., p. 99.
38. In some places, such as Istanbul, they were welcomed.
39. Benjamin Ravid, "A Tale of Three Cities and Their Raison d'Etat: Venice, Ancona and Livorno and the Competition for Jewish Merchants in the Sixteenth Century," *Mediterranean Historical Review*, 6(2), 1991, p. 139. "Many Italian authorities hoped that by attracting both Levantine Jews from the Ottoman Empire and judaizing New Christians from the Iberian Peninsula ... they could greatly enhance their maritime commerce and consequently also their general prosperity."
40. Quite possibly the Greeks were not perceived to be as powerful as their Jewish counterparts. See Benjamin Braude, "The Myth of the Sefardi Economic Superman," in *Trading Cultures: The Worlds of Western Merchants: Essays on Authority, Objectivity and Evidence*, ed. Jeremy Adelman and Stephen Aron (Turnhout, Belgium: Brepols, 2001), pp. 165–191.
41. Cemal Kafadar, "A Death in Venice: Anatolian Muslim Merchants Trading in the Serenissima," *Journal of Turkish Studies*, 10, 1987, p. 192.
42. Ravid, "A Tale of Three Cities," pp. 140–141. The Venetian diarist Mario Sanudo refers to "li subditi nostri da parte da mar, et li subditi del Signor turcho." Everyone else was a *forestiero* and the *forestieri* were explicitly barred from these privileges. Mario Sanudo, *I Diarii* (Venice: F. Visentini, 1897–1903), vol. 36, p. 240.
43. Kafadar, "A Death in Venice," p. 199.
44. Maria Pia Pedani, *In Nome del Gran Signore: inviati ottomani a Venezia dalla caduta di Constantinopoli alla Guerra di Candia* (Venice: Deputazione editrice, 1994). Although Pia Pedani's work concentrates on diplomatic missions to Venice, the Ottoman mercantile presence in the city is obvious throughout. Some diplomatic missions took up commercial disputes as well.
45. See M. I. Manousakes, "Episkopese tes Istorias tes Ellenikes Orthodokses Afelfotetas tes Venetias (1498–1953)" [An Overview of the History of the Greek Fraternity in Venice 1498–1953], *Ta Historika*, 6(11), 1989, pp. 243–265, for a succinct review of the Fraternity's history.
46. Mavroeide, *Symvole sten Historia tes Hellenikes Adelphotetas*, p. 120.
47. This tax was lifted after ten years. See Manousakas, "Episkopese," p. 249; and Mavroeide, *Symvole*, p. 120. Once again, the merchant community stepped in and provided funds.
48. Mavroeide, *Symvole*, pp. 64–65. Cypriots were also well represented.

49. The Ottomans conquered the island in 1479; this was followed by a period of instability. Ottoman rule was not solidified until 1503. Mavroeide, *Symvole*, p. 65.
50. As the most prominent Greek community outside the Ottoman Empire in the early modern period, known not only for their wealth but also for their scholarship and cultural achievements, the Greeks of Venice have received an enormous amount of attention.
51. Mavroeide, *Symvole*, p. 119.
52. St. Kaklamanes, "Markos Defaranas (1503–1575)," *Thesaurismata*, 21, 1991, p. 219.
53. Mavroeide, *Symvole*, pp. 124–125; N. St. Vlassopoulos, *Ionioi Emboroi kai Karavokyrides ste Mesogeio 16–18th Aionas* [Ionian Merchants and Shipowners in the Mediterranean 16th to 18th Centuries] (Athens: Finatec-Multimedia, 2001), p. 43.
54. Vlassopoulos, *Ionioi Emboroi*, pp. 35–37. This Matthew was probably the grandson of the first Matthew Vergis. The *botte* (plural *botti*) was the wine cask used at Venice in estimating the size of ships. Nine hundred *botti* was about 720 deadweight tons. Lane, *Venice*, pp. 479–480. Also see Mavroeide, *Symvole*, p. 139, for more information on Matthew Vergis.
55. Lane, *Venice*, p. 379.
56. With very few exceptions, most notably Maria Fusaro, "Les Anglais et les Grecs. Un réseau de coopération commerciale en Méditerranée vénitienne," *Annales*, 58(3), 2003, pp. 605–626.
57. The fact that the Venetians never formally struck down the laws prohibiting the participation of their subjects in international trade may be one reason why this phenomenon has been so widely overlooked. Thiriet writes that the Venetians chose to close their eyes instead. F. Thiriet, *La romaine venitienne au Moyen Age* (Paris: De Boccard, 1959), p. 420.
58. Ibid., p. 280.
59. Fusaro, "Les Anglais et les Grecs," p. 14. "Nel 1545 veniva segnalato a Zante un notevole aumento del traffico di transito in mano a 'forestieri,' che si svolgeva quindi non su navi di veneziani o di sudditi della Repubblica." The Senate made this distinction over and over again. A petition submitted to the authorities in 1578 defined foreigners as simply "mercanti non sudditi di Vostra Serenita" without bothering to distinguish between Venetians and subjects of Venice. Ibid., p. 29.
60. Ch. Maltezou, "The Historical and Social Context," in *Literature and Society in Renaissance Crete*, ed. D. Holton (Cambridge, England: Cambridge University Press, 1991), p. 29.
61. Frattarelli Fischer, "Alle Radici," p. 60.
62. Mavroeide, *Symvole*, pp. 64–66.
63. Thiriet, *La romaine venitienne*, p. 426. From the beginning of the sixteenth century an English consul was resident in Candia for the sole purpose of ensuring the wine supply to his country. Chr. Maltezou, "E Krete ste diarkeia tes periodou tes venetokratias" [Crete during the Period of Venetian Rule], in *Krete: Istoria kai Politismos* [Crete: History and Civilization], ed. N. Panayiotakes (Herakleion, Greece: Vikelaia, 1988), p. 139.
64. Fernand Braudel, *The Mediterranean and the Mediterranean World in the Age of Philip II* (New York: 1973), vol. 1, p. 156. "Malmsey" was the English term for *malvasia*.

65. St. Alexiou, *E Kretike Logotechneia kai e Epoche tes* [Cretan Literature and Its Era] (Athens: Stegme, 1985), p. 65.
66. "Molti ne vanno in Costantinopoli et nel mar maggiore, et assai in Alessandria dove non si consumano altri vini che di Candia." Robert Pashley, *Travels in Crete*, vol. 2 (Athens: Dion N. Karavias, 1989) p. 56.
67. A. Pippidi, "Le portrait d'un homme d'affaires Cretois au XVI siecle," in *Pepragmena tou G 'Diethnous Krētologikou Synedriou, Rethymnon, 18–23 Septembriou 1971* (Athens, 1973–75), pp. 266–273.
68. Ibid., p. 269.
69. Ibid., p. 270.
70. Ch. G. Patrineli, "Kretikoi Emboroi ste Moldavia kai ten Polonia kata ton 16 Aiona" [Cretan Merchants in Moldavia and Poland during the Sixteenth Century], in *Pepragmena tou G'Diethnous Krētologikou Synedriou*, p. 252.
71. Molly Greene, *A Shared World: Christians and Muslims in the Early Modern Mediterranean* (Princeton, N.J.: Princeton University Press, 2000), especially chapters 4–5.
72. F. Mavroeide, *O Hellenismos sto Galata (1453–1600)* (Ioannina, Greece: Panepistemio Ioanninon, 1992), p. 74.
73. Mavroeide says that most Greeks in Galata were members of the Venetian nation. Ibid., p. 24.
74. Ibid., p. 85.
75. E. Dursteler, *Venetians in Constantinople: Nation, Identity and Coexistence in the Early Modern Mediterranean* (Baltimore: Johns Hopkins University Press, 2006), p. 161.
76. In 1615, at the request of the Bailo, the Sultan commanded the Kadi of Gallipoli to ensure that Cretan ships leaving Constantinople for Venetian territories paid their ten-ducat duty to the Consul of Gallipoli. Ibid., p. 168.
77. Mavroeide, *O Hellenismos*, p. 41.
78. In 1477 the population of Galata was 535 Muslim households versus 592 Orthodox Greek households. H. Inalcik, "Ottoman Galata 1453–1553," in *Premiere Recontre Internationale sur l'Empire ottoman et la Turquie moderne: Institut national des langues et civilisations orientales, Maison des sciences de l'homme, 18–22 janvier 1985*, ed. Edhem Eldem (Istanbul: Editions ISIS, 1991), p. 247.
79. So much so that Greek sources of the time spoke of the "archontes of the City and of Galata." Ibid., p. 70.
80. For just one example of this see the classic article by T. Stoianovich, "The Conquering Balkan Orthodox Merchant," *Journal of Economic History*, 20(2), 1960, pp. 234–313. He writes, "The victory of the Ottoman Empire symbolized in the sphere of economics, a victory of Greeks, Turks, renegade Christians, Armenians, Ragusans and Jews over the two century old commercial hegemony of Venice and Genoa" (p. 6).
81. Mavroeide, *O Hellenismos*, pp. 69–70.
82. Mavroeide, *Symvole*, p. 130. This must have had the potential to expose the Galata branch of the family to great danger, but Mavroeide does not comment on this.
83. Mavroeide, *O Hellenismos*, pp. 69–70.
84. Ibid., p. 137.
85. Mavroeide, *Symvole*, p. 131.

148 *A Faithful Sea*

86. This is Mavroeide's suggestion in *O Hellenismos*, p. 135.
87. Ibid.
88. Mavroeide, *Symvole*, p. 121; M. I. Manousakas, "Grammata Patriarchon kai Metropoliton tou 16 Aiona ek tou Archeiou tes en Venetia Ellenikes Adelfotetas," *Thesaurismata*, 5, 1968, p. 12.
89. Greene, *A Shared World*, chapter 4.
90. Molly Greene, 'Resurgent Islam (1500–1700),' in *The Mediterranean in History*, ed. David Abulafia (London: Thames & Hudson, 2003).
91. See Greene, *A Shared World*; idem, "Beyond the Northern Invasions: The Mediterranean in the Seventeenth Century," *Past and Present*, 174, February 2002, pp. 40–72.
92. D. Panzac, *La caravane maritime: Marins Europeens et Marchands Ottomans en Mediterranee (1680–1830)* (Paris: C.R.N.S., 2004), p. 142.
93. G. Leon, "The Greek Merchant Marine 1453–1850," in *The Greek Merchant Marine*, ed. Stelios Papadopoulos (Athens: National Bank of Greece, 1972), p. 32.
94. Ibid., p. 27.
95. Ibid.

7

A TRAVELOGUE MANQUÉ?

THE ACCIDENTAL ITINERARY OF A MALTESE PRIEST IN THE SEVENTEENTH-CENTURY MEDITERRANEAN

Ariel Salzmann

I, Fra Alfonso Son of Claudio Moscati of Malta, cleric, professed in the Order of the Friars Minor Reformed Observants of Saint Francis, and whose age is 33, have composed this in person as [final] judgment & on my knees before this Sacred Tribunal of the Inquisition of Venice. Having before my own eyes the Sacred Book, which I hold with my own hands, I swear that I have always believed and still believe and with the help of God will in the future forever believe in all it contains and which the Holy Catholic & Apostolic Roman Church believes, preaches, & instructs. By this Holy Office [i.e. the Inquisition] and because of the accusations contained in this Trial formed against me, I have been judged *vehemently* suspect of Apostasy from the Holy Christian Faith, the Roman Catholic one, to the impious and false sect of Mohammed and of having believed and held this Mohammedan [sic] sect to be good.

Wanting to lift from my mind [and that] of the Faithful of Christ this *vehement* suspicion and its just causes, I abjure and curse and detest *the above sect and heresy* & error and in general any other *sect, heresy* & error that contradict the aforementioned Holy Catholic & Apostolic Roman Church. And I swear that in the future I will neither do nor say anything that may appear to confirm that suspicion, nor will I contact or converse with Heretics or those suspected of heresy. And if I know of such a person or act, I will denounce them to the Inquisition or to the authority of the Place where I am found. I swear additionally and promise to submit to and offer myself entirely to all the penalties and penitence that are assigned to me, as they will be imposed by this Holy Office if I would contravene any of these promises and oaths of mine (may God forbid it!), and I submit to all the pains and chastisement that are in the Sacred Canon & other General Constitutions & are specifically imposed and promulgated against similar violators. And thus may God and his Holy Gospels, which he touched with his own hands, save me.

I, *Fra Alfonso da Malta*, am he who abjured, swore, promised, and obligated himself as stated above. Faithful to the truth, I have signed below with my own hand on this printed form [*cedula*] of my adjuration and recited it word for word on this the *6th* Day *of April 1692*.

— I, f. Alfonso di Malta

Apart from his habit, soiled from months in the prison of the Sant'Ufficio and torn from bouts of torture, the man who repeatedly signed his name as "Fra Alfonso *of* Malta" – and not "Alfonso *from* Malta," as the scribe entered into the *cedula* – betrayed no distinguishing features. Eyewitnesses who had encountered him in Alexandria, Rosetta, and Nicosia described "a tall cleric, with a black beard, about the age of thirty," with "a long face, black hair and black eyes;" because his brothers in the Order of Saint Bonaventure had not been able to provide for his needs properly while in the public jail he no longer carried the paunch that had made one witness comment that he had been "a bit plump, that is, fatter than leaner." Any and all of these descriptions could have been applied to a Spaniard, an Italian, a Greek, a Turk, a Muslim, a Christian, or a Jew. Some three hundred years later, his individuality rests on the details of his trial found in the transcripts preserved in the Venetian State Archive and in the violations of cult and religious law specified in the handwritten entries (italicized above) in the standard printed form (*cedula*) to which he affixed his signature.[1]

The voice of the defendant comes to us in the form of depositions he made before the tribunal. In them, he provided the bare outlines of an autobiography and the narrative of a journey. Before his accusers, Alfonso Moscati held stubbornly to his contention that his infractions were not deliberate: his was an accidental itinerary, one that carried him unwittingly from one religious shore to another. A priest and scholar of civil and canon law, he had left the City of the Lagunes in 1689. For some reason, instead of returning immediately to his native Malta, he crossed the Mediterranean into Ottoman Egypt and the Muslim world. Three years later, the offices of the Venetian

Inquisition would reclaim him for Christendom. During his peregrinations, according to his own testimony, he committed acts unimaginable for a Catholic cleric. Shortly after his arrival in Alexandria, under the pressure exerted by new Muslim acquaintances and under the influence of the coffee they offered him, he accepted Islam and submitted to circumcision.

Whether or not this initial act of conversion was voluntary or coerced cannot be established; however, all witnesses concur that he quickly repented. Eventually, his coreligionists in Lower Egypt were able to extricate him from his predicament, sending him for penance to Cyprus. Yet his journey into the Muslim world had only begun. A second, more compromising detour took place several months later, on 30 March 1690 in the city of Nicosia. This time, his declaration of being Muslim took place before many witnesses, Muslim officials, and Christian merchants. It was this flight from Christendom together with several other compromising acts that determined his fate. The Inquisitioners added "vehemently" to the charge of suspicion of apostasy on the printed confession that was posted for all to see.

If Alfonso Moscati's story sounds more like fiction than fact, it is because early modern literature abounds in such picaresque tales. European writers, from Cervantes to Voltaire and Swift, wove yarns of shifting identities, confessional changelings, and abrupt reversals of fortunes, as individuals were carried off in unanticipated directions. Yet the inspiration for these tales owed to the realities of the sixteenth- and seventeenth-century Mediterranean: corsairs who changed religion as they abandoned one ship for another, Muslim frontier raiders in the Balkans who took vows in blood to protect their Christian counterparts, a false messiah who with his entire Jewish flock embraced Islam at the order of the Sultan,[2] and the thousands of Christians who out of conviction, fear, hope, or despair made themselves "Turks." The picaresque was not a trope but an expression of the Mediterranean zeitgeist. The Armenian-Turkish narrative poem entitled "The Jewish Bride," composed by Eremya Komurjian (1637–95), recounts in a satirical tone an Albanian Catholic's seduction of a Jewish girl in Istanbul and their elopement to Venice, the portal to the Occident.[3]

Despite the literary trope of the renegade, Alfonso's story remains unique, although it too, given the constraints of the Inquisition narrative, must straddle the line between fact and fiction, or, as he would insist to his accusers, between rationality and insanity.[4] Although this

is not the first time the case of this friar has been examined by a contemporary scholar,[5] the historical questions surrounding these
"singular events" have not been exhausted. Many pieces of the puzzle
of his life are still missing. Above all, what remains to be determined is
where the friar's self-determined voyage began and where it ended. It
remains to be seen whether conversion was at all central to his quest or
whether his intellectual curiosity and ambivalence toward the Church
and its hierarchy played the dominant role in his many detours away
from Christendom. The trial transcripts reflect an individual determined to defer and mitigate a judgment and his tale purposefully
deletes many details, particularly the most incriminating. The missing points in his itinerary are, however, as compelling for the modern
reader as they were for his interrogators three centuries ago: how
is it that a man of undeniable scholarship, certainly polyglot, may
have slipped, repeatedly, by accident or intention through the
Mediterranean's religious frontier?

In answering such questions, however, we must be sure not to take
the part of the tribunal. Rather, if we take a cue from the picaresque,
Alfonso Moscati's multiple conversions might better be understood
as one of the real stories behind the yarns spun by writers and symptomatic of the perils of travel within a shared but contested sea. The
Inquisition transcript is thus not a deposition or an interrogation
concerning the trespasses of a wayward Catholic, but a type of travelogue manqué, the story of a flight from Malta into the Muslim world
which was aborted by fear, a sudden crisis of conscience, and circumstances beyond the man's control.

Certainly, it is difficult to classify such a travelogue.[6] Alfonso's visit
to the Muslim world did not constitute an official visit or a mission
sanctioned by his ecclesiastical superiors; nor did he seek the release of
captives of war like his Moroccan contemporary, Mohammad bin Abd
al-Wahab al-Ghassani, who left his own perspectives on the culture of
Christendom, including the Inquisition, in the diary of his travels in
Spain.[7] Perhaps he sought to follow in the footsteps of his brother, a
Jesuit missionary in the Pacific, to taste the exotic lifestyle of the other.
Or perhaps it was to find enlightenment and self-discovery in the mys-
teries of the Orient, which may explain his eagerness to enter into a dia-
logue with knowledgeable Muslims, such as the Kadi of Alexandria.
Had circumstances permitted him to regain his own direction when
things went awry and to return on his own, he might well have committed these adventures to paper. Yet events and people pre-empted his

travelogue: it would be the Venetian Inquisition, the Sant'Ufficio, who finished the tale and determined the traveler's final destination.

THE FLIGHT FROM MALTA

Alfonso Moscati's tale began at the very periphery of Christendom, in an archipelago of islands between North Africa and Italy. If the young Franciscan did repeatedly knock at the door of the Islamic world, it was in no small part because of a deep-seated urge to escape his native land, the "sterile rock" of Malta. Malta's ancient, Arab capital of M'dina had largely been abandoned with the arrival of new immigrants from Rhodes. In the third decade of the sixteenth century, the knights were given safe passage from their Aegean home by Sultan Suleiman the Lawgiver and a new center for their activities in the middle of the Mediterranean by the princes of Christendom. The knights built the Renaissance and Baroque port city of La Valletta which served as base of operations for a perpetual war against Islam. Although Mediterranean commerce was declining in the face of the rising Atlantic commerce, owing in no small part to the piracy that was their chief occupation, the knights prospered. They continued to receive subsidies from the papacy alongside their considerable earnings from plunder.[8]

Alfonso was born in this port in 1659. As the son of the Grand Master's personal physician, he was thoroughly indoctrinated by the island's militant culture and its hatred of all things Muslim. Small-scale violence plagued this area of the Mediterranean and remained a constant irritant to maritime trade and to relationships between the Ottomans and Christian powers. It had been a Maltese sea attack that provoked the long Venetian–Ottoman war over Crete which ended when Alfonso was ten years old. In the 1680s, the Most Christian King Louis XIV, an ally of the Ottomans, attempted to suppress piracy generally, attacking the North African cities and putting greater restraints on Maltese activities. During the years 1683–99, the years of Alfonso's travels, however, the main theater of East–West conflict was the eastern Mediterranean, where the Hapsburgs and their Holy League partners, the armies of Poland and Venice, fought the Ottoman armies and armada in southeastern Europe and the Aegean.

Although the threat of a full-scale assault by the Ottoman armada receded, the peoples of the coastal areas and travelers in this region of the Mediterranean continued to live in dread of violence. Christians of the frontier, innocent bystanders as well as combatants, feared the possibility of kidnap by Muslim pirates who scoured the northern coastline and Mediterranean islands.[9] So, too, many Muslims, and not an inconsiderable number of Orthodox Christians and Jews, found themselves enslaved captives of Christian privateers and corsairs whose sorties from the *presidios* in North Africa and La Valletta claimed many men, women, and children.[10] Servile labor was the linchpin of the maritime system. Muslim slaves powered the galleys of the Maltese, Genoese, and papal fleets while Christians were the drudges in the warships of the Maghribi deys. Although we have yet to gain an accurate census of the numbers of individuals trapped in the Mediterranean trade in human beings, recent studies have shown that there were significant differences in the status of slaves in each realm. Whereas many Englishmen, Spaniards, and Italians chose conversion to Islam as a means of escaping a lifetime of drudgery in the *bagnios* of Algiers or Tunis, an act that often offered them a passport into a new society, Catholic authorities encouraged few Muslim galley slaves to defect from their faith, whether for reasons of general mistrust or of racism.

One of the rare exceptions to this rule, a man of legendary accomplishments in Malta during Alfonso's childhood, was the Dominican monk known as the "Padre Ottomano."[11] As a babe, Ahmed had been the child of one of the noble ladies aboard the *Sultana*, the Ottoman vessel whose seizure by the Knights of Saint John in 1644 provoked the War of Candia. The knights baptized the child with the name Domenico Tommaso and entrusted his upbringing to the Church. Upon reaching his majority, he joined the Dominican order. Considered a potential pretender to the sultanate, Father Ahmed/ Domenico was enlisted by the Pope to raise support for the war. Before embarking on his overseas mission, he toured the Italian courts. Despite his failure to rouse Anatolian Muslims and Christians to revolt and to incite the population of the Morea, at his death in Malta in 1676 the ex-Muslim was greatly revered.

Other than such rare individuals, it is doubtful that the ordinary Christians of Malta would have had the opportunity to speak at length with the Muslim captives on the island. Yet, as Malta had one of the foremost slave markets of the Mediterranean, the numbers of such captives were considerable, so large that even the pious Order of Saint John was forced to concede them places to conduct prayer and for proper burial.[12] As the miserable base of the social pyramid of La Valetta, they symbolized the moral and social rigidity of a polity based on holy war and the absence of social mobility for natives within the ruling order. The island and its peasants and resources were hostages to the political dictates of European princes, the pope, and the administration of Sicily. The knights constituted a ruling class whose ranks were refilled by the second sons of the European aristocracy, particularly members of the French nobility, who came to seek their fortune.[13] Only a trickle of Maltese natives had begun to infiltrate their ranks in the later seventeenth century.

La Valletta's intellectual horizons were similarly limited. The Christian population were themselves subject to the oversight of the Sicilian hierarchy and one of the most violent inquisitions under Spanish rule.[14] Although such an atmosphere might suit the ascetic or militant cleric,[15] it provided limited options for a man of intelligence and curiosity. As a son of a noted physician, Alfonso had some training in medicine (or so it would seem from the high demand for his services in Egypt after his first conversion) and he continued to show interest in the sciences thereafter. But medicine would not take him far. Only the Church furnished an outlet for his intellectual ambitions and a ticket to more sophisticated and cosmopolitan centers in Italy where he could pursue his studies. His superiors, because they were either impressed by his abilities or pressured by his well-placed relatives, provided the means and motive for him to venture beyond the island. They sent him to first to Sicily, to Palermo, for studies in canon and civil law. He joined the "reformed order" of the Franciscans at the age of twenty-five. A subsequent trip was allowed him to accompany his brother to Naples, whence the young Jesuit missionary would set sail for the Philippines.

Had Alfonso himself remained in Malta, he might have taken his place among the brothers of the famous Monastery of Saint Mary of Jesus, of the Friars Minor of the Observance of Saint Francis (Convento di Santa Maria di Gesu de Frati Minori dell'Osservanza di San Francis). Instead, he sought at every opportunity to flee his place of birth. New studies took Fra Alfonso to Turin at the age of twenty-six. He stayed in the city close to the French border for seven months. We have no means of reconstructing his extracurricular reading. Perhaps in this period when Protestants were fleeing France, he might have had some contact with Reformed theology. He certainly read secular literature and might have pondered the import of the "Tale of

Three Rings" in Boccaccio's *Decameron*, which gives equal weight to the three Abrahamic faiths. His research into law would have taken him toward Grotius's writings on the international system or toward the political theory of Machiavelli, Bottero, and Bodin, all of whom devoted attention not only to the organization of the monarchies of Europe, but also to Ottoman state and society.

Already a man of considerable learning, Fra Alfonso fled to Egypt at the end of another period of scholarship in northern Italy. He spent several months between 1687 and 1688 in Bologna, a center of the sciences, especially of cartography and medicine. There his reading might have included travelogues of those who had ventured to the Indies and the Americas as well as to Ottoman and Safavid lands. He would have certainly learned about coffee, a new beverage that was already the rage in Venice and Paris. He might have also delved into the occult, astrology,[16] or developed a Neoplatonic bent, one that drew him toward the Orient. Which impulse or combination of ideas piqued his curiosity and brought him toward his next decision is not known. However, rather than returning home overland and then via ship to Palermo and La Valletta, the young priest chose another direction: in Venice he booked passage on a Flemish vessel bound for Candia, whence he boarded a French tartan heading toward Alexandria; destinations he would later claim were only accidental.

THE PASSAGE TO EGYPT

The dockworkers in Herakleion, the old port of Crete, might have gawked at Alfonso when he stepped ashore. It would have been strange to see a Maltese of any station or profession, much less a Catholic cleric, a generation from the devasting war in 1669. In 1644 a Maltese raid triggered a conflict that would ultimately force Venice to cede Crete to the Sultan. The knights trapped an Ottoman vessel laden with riches and transporting many high-ranking officials *en route* to join the *hajj* caravan departing from Cairo.[17] Recognizing the status of many of the passengers, the knights took many hostages. However, they slew the Sultan's favorite, the Chief Eunuch of the Harem, Sünbül Ağa.[18] Ottoman retaliation followed, particularly against Venice, which had protected the Maltese ship.

Perhaps it is not strange that Crete does not merit a place in Alfonso's transcripts. Although this interlude might have figured in a personal travelogue, the friar did not devote any details to it in his deposition before the court, because the Inquisition could not call his movements and motives there into question. In any event, there had been few Catholics on the island since the war. If the priest noted that the town still bore the scars of the Grand Vizier Köprülü Fazīl Ahmet's bombardment, he might have been less informed about its rural economy. Under Ottoman rule the olive oil economy rebounded, but much of its latifundia remained unproductive because of peasant flight. Those civilians who had survived the conflict crowded into the cities and not a few of them were recent converts to Islam.[19] Despite such changes, Crete provided a deceptive portal into the Muslim world for the Maltese visitor. Only recently integrated into the empire, the island's population remained predominately Christian.

It would take days at sea, sailing aboard a French ship, and finally disembarkation in Egypt to appreciate fully the distance he had placed between himself and Christendom. Not even Venice could be compared to Alexandria in the diversity of its population. Next to Istanbul and Salonika, Alexandria was one of the most cosmopolitan cities in the Mediterranean. Its markets bustled with commerce: silk, cotton, and woolen cloth, glassware, spices, fragrances, and a booming commerce in coffee. Merchants from many lands, including Protestants and Catholics from Europe, made it their base of operations. Jewish brokers controlled its customs station; with their Muslim partners in Cairo, they organized trans-shipments of goods to and from Christendom as well as to Mecca and Medina.[20] Along with the other Egyptian ports of Rosetta (Rushīd) and Damietta (Dimyāt), Alexandria provided the relay between the Mediterranean, the Red Sea, and the Indian Ocean bearing not only goods, but every year hundreds of Muslim pilgrims who during the month of Dhu' l-Hijja joined the caravans that proceeded up the Nile.

For the Vatican, Alexandria meant far more than commerce. It was one of the key points of entry into the Muslim world and a nerve center for Catholic missions to Africa and the Middle East.[21] To better "promote the faith," a new missionary offensive from Levantine ports led to the foundation of monasteries and churches by Franciscans, Jesuits, Dominicans, and Capuchins. The French King, who declined an invitation to join the Holy League of 1684, played an important diplomatic role in advancing Catholicism during these years. Louis XIV's good relations with Istanbul furnished Catholic missionaries with unprecedented privileges and access in Palestine and even, in 1690, the keys to the Holy Sepulcher.[22] Nonetheless mission and commerce went hand in hand. Catholic clerics and lay brothers created a cultural medium and founded new outposts, including in such Muslim cities as Damascus, Diyarbekir, and Basra; orders like the Carmelites brought the Catholic frontier into the Caucasus and Iran.

Given the risks in preaching to Muslims, the Roman Church's immediate goals were to proselytize to Middle Eastern Christians and coax their clergy toward the union. During the seventeenth century, the Catholic missionaries made overtures to the Melkites of Damascus and Sidon, the Copts of Egypt, the Nestorians of Mosul and Diyarbekir, and in East Africa the Ethiopic Church. However, these churches did not simply surrender their authority to Rome. Coptic and Greek Orthodox ecclesiastics vied for adherents to their sects and used their superior understanding and long association with the Ottoman authorities to regain access to Christian holy sites.[23] Thus, although Rome found an enthusiastic advocate in the likes of Mekhitar of Sivas (1676–1749), who spread Catholicism among Armenians, the Gregorian Church appealed to the Sultan to enforce Orthodoxy. Catholic Armenians were sent into exile or punished with galley slavery.[24]

The Father President, a native of the Piedmont, who received the uninvited Maltese friar was angry: he was keenly aware of these challenges and difficulties. He rejected Alfonso's excuses and called him a "vagabond." While the Maltese scholar took umbrage at the hostility of his reception in the Alexandrine convent, he clearly did not understand that the Catholic mission in the Levant was both offensive and defensive.[25] If promotion of the Roman Church's hegemony in the Middle East and East Africa was the first charge of the missionary orders, the second was protection of its flock from the temptations of Ottoman society. In a religiously mixed society, missionaries inveighed, often in vain, against intermarriage with Orthodox Christians and recourse to the Ottoman courts to obtain divorces, as much as to prevent participation in "heretical" or "schismatic" rites and rituals. Moreover, in a state where Catholicism had no distinct status and where Catholic churches and convents were dependent on the political agreements struck by European states with Muslim authorities, the missionaries could do little to keep their parishioners, including the clergy, away from the appeal of Islam itself, or "Turcism" as it was often called.[26]

The appearance of this friar before the convent doors made the senior cleric immediately suspect the worst. Instead of believing Alfonso's excuse that he had "landed in this place by accident and not by intent," he accused him of flirting with apostasy, pointing out that he was heading in the wrong direction if his intention had been to return to his convent in Malta. In describing this heated exchange at the trial, Alfonso would have the Inquisitors believe that much of the animus toward him owed to competition between orders, quoting the superior's accusation that "it is because you Reformists [referring to Alfonso's order of Friars Minor] are not worth anything, that we Observants will not deal well with you." However, the gravity of the accusations and threat to have the Maltese priest "sent back to the Province of Sicily" (and perhaps for investigation before a tribunal of the Spanish Inquisition), for insubordination or worse, struck an acutely sensitive nerve. Alfonso fled the convent and headed into the marketplace nearby.

CONVERSION BY COFFEE

The members of the Inquisition tribunal who would later ponder Alfonso Moscati's offenses might have weighed the friar's disobedience and insolence against the Alessandrine superior's ill-considered reaction. By chasing him away, the missionaries sent an unworldly cleric into a society of great cultural complexity and many temptations. In an Ottoman city during wartime, an inadvertent act or injudicious word might have serious consequences for the Catholic community as a whole. As the new arrival wandered the streets of the bazaar aimlessly, it must have been easy to read the signs of distress on his face: he had no place to go and no community to turn to. He was soon spotted by a man whom he would later describe as a "Turco," probably a convert and possibly a sailor or janissary. Finding a sympathetic audience, Alfonso volunteered information about his altercation with his superior. Little was required for the "Turco" to reinforce his mounting paranoia over the possibility that his coreligionists were plotting "to send him back to Christendom in chains."

While it is unlikely the Maltese friar's receptivity to these overtures owed to a premeditated desire to change cults, he began to worry about the repercussions of his unauthorized journey. Perhaps it was not only fear but also the underlying intellectual curiosity that had brought him to Egypt that induced Alfonso to accept the stranger's hospitality. As if to emphasize the callousness of his treatment at the hands of his coreligionists, he would later relate to the Inquisitioners that his new Muslim acquaintance convinced him that the Egyptians were hospitable folk and "do not act cruelly [*selvaggi*] to strangers."

In order to prove his point, Alfonso's acquaintance led him to the office of Alexandria's judge (kadi). Obviously, Alfonso hoped to find a civil remedy for his problem with the monastery. The kadi assured him that he would be able to resolve his dilemma: "Have no fear," he promised; "I will fix everything for you." In the meantime, Alfonso took his place in the judge's chambers alongside other men. These "Turchi," meaning in this case Muslims in a generic sense, formed the local gendarmerie ["tutti li Aga, o Officiali di quella citta"] of the city as well as being members of the janissary corps.

Initially, the rapport between friar, judge, and janissaries appears to have been friendly and even jocular. In his depositions, we have, at best, a telegraphic account of the events that transpired that evening. It seems that over the course of many hours the group conversed on many non-religious topics. Although the eating and drinking continued until bedtime, at some point the conversation took a more serious turn. From an innocent meeting across cultures, a drama suddenly took place which left the Maltese cleric feeling extremely compromised. Having accepted their hospitality and kindnesses, he did not know what to when "they told me that I must become a Turk" ("mi dissero che bisognava mi facesi Turco ..."). In the company of heavily armed police, there was little he could do. It was out of fear of physical harm, as he would tell the judges of the Sant'Ufficio, that he accepted his hosts' proposal, albeit insincerely, without ever intending to "apostate myself from my law [*mia legge*]."

As a specialist in law, Fra Alfonso knew well that a charge of apostasy hinged not on a single act but on many incriminating details that demonstrated an individual's spiritual intention. Moreover, because the witnesses to his conversion were Muslim, there would be no Inquisition record of his utterances or oaths. He did admit that the janissaries provided him with new clothes and that he dressed as a Muslim; perhaps in the knowledge that this in itself did not constitute more than a minor infraction in the eyes of his Catholic superiors.[27] But he evaded other more serious admissions, such as whether he had repeated the Muslim profession of faith or in what other manner he might have demonstrated his sincerity as a convert. Nonetheless, the single most important and indelible proof of his transition from Christendom to Islam was not expressed in words or thoughts, but inscribed on his body: during the course of the night he was circumcised.

Here, Alfonso's story makes a clever detour. In order to deflect the charge of personal guilt and responsibility, he assigns culpability to his Muslim companions who carried out the operation without his consent and to a beverage they offered him. As bedtime approached, the janissaries gave him a coffee-like substance ("something, I don't know what, some type of black coffee"). Despite its novelty in the West, both Alfonso and his interrogators must have known that coffee was a stimulant and therefore could not have been the cause of his deep sleep. By referring to "some type of black coffee," the friar also suggested that his cup had been laced with some drug. This is not entirely farfetched, being an accusation frequent enough among the detractors of coffee in the Muslim world as to have some merit.[28] Thus, sedated, he fell into a deep, insensible sleep and was unable to prevent his companions from carrying out the deed.

Alfonso's ascription of blame for his conversion to the drinking of coffee may seem to be only a clever ploy. However, it may also illustrate a widespread cultural anxiety before new substances and social manners in western European society. Coffee appealed to the demand for the exotic and reflected an age in which the fear and revulsion toward Islam were coupled with an almost insatiable demand for Oriental goods. The first *bottega del caffe* opened in Venice in 1683, but a year before the formation of a new crusade against the Ottomans. Consumption of coffee in Europe and the number of coffee houses where men would gather would grow explosively over the next half-century. Yet from its inception in European society, coffee's charms remained infused with medicinal claims and associations with high status and martial prowess. In his book on the beverage, published in Bologna in 1691 at the height of the Venetian–Ottoman campaigns, Angelo Rambaldi pitched its benefits in the following terms: "the modern Arabs [*li Arabi moderni*], Pashas, Muslims [*Turchi*], Grandees of the East [*Grandi d'Oriente*], [and] everyone who is traveling or who follows the army, drinks coffee for a variety of problems, including weight loss and stomach problems."[29]

Although we may doubt whether Alfonso fully disclosed what transpired during these hours, his exchange with his new Muslim friends the morning after his operation suggests their conversation had less to do with theological debates or religious transgression than with mutual curiosity over cultural mores, scientific information, and recipes for health. To Alfonso's demand to know why his Muslim acquaintances had circumcised him without his consent, they responded, half in jest no doubt, that they had done it because "it was good for the health" ["ricercai essi Turchi per qual causa m'havessero circonciso, mi risposero, che cio era buona per la salute"].[30] Physically transformed in a strange land, the cleric, now a convert to a new religion, contemplated the next leg of his journey.

A PRODIGAL RETURNS

In his deposition before the courts, Fra Alfonso would repeatedly insist that this initial incident was completely unintentional. He would reason successfully with the fathers of the Sant'Ufficio about this point and point out that if he had truly desired to convert to Islam and migrate permanently to the Muslim world, he would have done so in Egypt.[31] The Catholic Church had no political power to stop him and his notoriety had already earned him special treatment by the Ottoman authorities. As for why he did not immediately leave the kadi's house, he explained that it was not out of moral confusion but purely because he was unable to get free of his armed companions. When he did flee from the kadi's house, he realized that his conversion was already the talk of the city. To evade his former hosts, as much as to avoid facing the wrath of the missionaries who had already treated him so harshly upon arrival, he traveled to Rashīd/Rosetta. There, his testimony and that of his confessor concur: the Maltese friar threw himself at the mercy of the convent of the Capellan monks and asked to be "liberated and to be reconciled with the Christian faith" ["per liberarmi e riconciliarmi all Fede Christiana"]. However, given the close communications between merchants and members of the *ocak* (military establishment), the sensational news that a Latin cleric had "made himself a Turk" had already reached the Ottoman governor in Cairo. The missionaries were forced to surrender Alfonso to the two guards sent by the Ottoman Pasha.

In a period of war against the Holy League and the Pope, no Ottoman official would have missed the opportunity to celebrate such a spiritual victory. For the governor of Egypt, it was an opportunity to burnish his administration's credentials in the eyes of the people of Cairo, the scholars of the University of Al-Azhar, and the sheikhs of the many Sufi convents. Such symbolic acts enhanced a legitimacy that was challenged by the local Muslim authorities who controlled much of Egypt's government, finances, and military. Istanbul had long tried to rein in the Egyptian beys, with varied success.[32] Some were co-opted into the official Ottoman hierarchy and sent as governors to other provinces. Fierce competition between branches of these local military clans took care of others, including the once powerful members of the Fiqariyya. Under the governorship of Ibrahim Pasha (1661–64), Ottoman control reached its highpoint and receipts from the Egyptian treasury which were sent to Istanbul doubled.

Although during the Maltese friar's sojourn in Egypt, the pendulum of power had swung again in favor of local elites (the leader of the janissary *ocak*, Küçük Mehmet, who died in 1694, built his empire on the basis of the revenues from agriculture and the receipts from the customs station at Suez), in matters concerning the foreign communities, particularly the Catholic, the governor retained special authority. To celebrate the new convert to Islam, he might have presented a spectacle, perhaps organizing an afternoon of festivities and celebrations, including the presentation of a robe to the former priest, who would then be paraded before the palaces lining the shores of Birkat al-Fīl or directly on horseback to the Bāb-i 'Alī in the northern part of the city near the markets of Nahhasin and Sagha.[33] The Pasha's eagerness to summon Alfonso contained a personal interest: rumors of the new convert's medical skills had preceded him in Cairo. The guards who had been sent to bring the new convert to "Gran Cairo" had specific instructions to lodge him in the quarters of the governor's chief physician.

As guest in the Pasha's palace, the man who straddled Islam and Christendom had another week to contemplate the strange twists and turns in his fortune and to reconsider his decision to return to the Church. Yet after eight days he fled again into one of the largest cities of the Ottoman Empire. Along the route to the Franciscan mission in Cairo, he was seen by a merchant from Livorno plying the trade of Tripoli in Syria; the merchant saw the Catholic cleric "dressed as a Turk, with a turban on his head." When he reached the convent, Alfonso related, "I threw myself at their [the missionaries'] feet with the intention of showing them that my transgression did not occur because of my choice but that I was menaced ... by the Turks." His brothers granted him absolution and redressed him in Christian garb.

To make sure the Pasha would lose his trail as much as to assure the friar's change of heart, the missionaries hid the Maltese for forty days within the convent. From Cairo, they sent him to the port of Damietta/Dimyāt with, as his deposition stated, "The absolution signed by all of the apostolic missionaries in order that, from Damietta, they carry me to Cyprus, [and from there] find me transport toward Christendom."

A HALFWAY HOUSE FOR WAYWARD CATHOLICS

The idea that a renegade priest would be sent from Muslim Cairo to the Ottoman eastern Mediterranean for reconciliation to the Catholic faith seems contradictory. However, Cyprus had earned an important role in the Catholic network of missions that had been established during the second half the seventeenth century. It was this web of missions which advanced Rome's plans for gaining new Christian souls. It also served as a firewall against defections in the other direction: to prevent conversion to Islam and to recapture wayward and prodigal souls who had inadvertently slipped into the Muslim world.[34]

Prior to Crete, Cyprus had once been one of the jewels in the crown of the Venetian empire, a source of one of the medieval world's most costly agricultural goods, cane sugar. The bitter conflict that ousted the Venetians in 1571 decimated the island's Catholic population. Yet not long after the Ottoman conquest churchmen began to return. Within a year, the Franciscans were granted permission to build a new church.[35] From the early seventeenth century onward, Catholic momentum accelerated: there was a new wave of missions, including a hospice founded in 1662 by the Capuchin monks at Larnaca.[36]

These monks and lay brothers preached to the "heretical and schismatic" Christians – Greek, Armenian, and Maronite Christians on the island itself. They also made the island famous as a safe haven and halfway house for wayward Catholics. In 1650, the Prefect in charge of the "Missions in the Reign of Cyprus and Karaman," Batista da Todi, claimed a specialty in this area. In his correspondence with his superiors, he boasted of having rehabilitated many renegades. The Franciscan gave the names of men from Lucca, Palermo, Paris, Marseilles, Tuscany, Vicenzo, Ferrara, Milano, Bressano, and Bergamo all of whom he had recovered for the Church and afterward dispatched to Christendom.[37]

Cyprus's relative autonomy from Istanbul contributed to its utility to the Church and allowed European merchants greater leverage in their transactions and shipments.[38] After its seizure, Cyprus and its resources had been awarded as an appanage with its income accruing to one of the leading officers of the state. On an everyday basis, the Pasha's agents or entrepreneurs would collect revenues; over time, many members of the janissary corps who were garrisoned on the island came into possession of these revenue contracts, which they exploited for personal profit or in lieu of salary. As in Egypt, these fiscal privileges allowed local leaders greater control over the politics of the island. In the midst of a long war and the dynastic instability that followed the death of Sultan Mehmet IV in 1687, the janissaries also grew restive. As in Istanbul itself, a rebellion broke out. In Cyprus, the janissary captain, Boyaçioglu Mehmed Aga, seized control of the administration.

Alfonso's arrival in Cyprus in early 1690 coincided with a moment in which European influence was strong, because of the rebel captain's acute dependence on foreign trade. However, that does not mean that Cyprus was free from tension, sectarian and political. Quite the opposite: the Aegean region was roiling with conflict. Venetian forces occupied Athens and invested many of the Morean ports that year. As the crusade that began seven years earlier dragged on, the Republic grew increasingly bold, attempting to retake Crete in 1693. A year later, Venetian soldiers occupied the island of Chios, directly off the coast of Izmir. It is precisely because the Greek Orthodox and Armenians of Chios had not forgotten the bitterness of Latin rule that a general uprising in favor of the Sultan would drive the Venetian Admiral Zeno into the sea in 1695.

Given these concerns and the pervasive mistrust and resentments between Catholics and Cyprus's Christian Orthodox majority, the renegade cleric's reception was no warmer there than it had been in Alexandria. Against the backdrop of rival Christian sects, what Paolo Preto calls the "double scandal" of clerical conversion to Islam delivered a stunning blow to the prestige and authority of the Catholic Church. Not only did it signfy the loss of another one of the flock to what Christians generally considered to be "error," "heresy," and a "profane rite," but the act also entailed the betrayal of one of its ecclesiastical shepherds. Yet Fra Alfonso's case was hardly unique. Many clerics had "turned Turk" over the centuries. In 1650 a Capuchin monk in Aleppo took full advantage of the cosmopolitan environment provided by the Ottoman system: after months of contemplation and learned disputation with Muslim and Christian theologians, he decided to leave his order for the religion of the Prophet Muhammed.[39]

In his testimony before the Inquisition in Venice, Alfonso seems still oblivious to these cultural dimensions of the problem. He complained that the monks went to extraordinary lengths to humiliate him and torment him. They exposed him, while garbed in his letter "A," to the ridicule of visiting merchants and clerics. He tolerated the treatment as long as he could. Finally tempers flared: in a particularly violent confrontation he threatened his superior with a knife; a Greek layman knocked him down with a stone. After regaining consciousness, he fled the convent and, according to the testimony submitted by another cleric, Father Francesco Maria of Malaga, the Padre Guardino ran after him in tears, fearing that Alfonso would once again be tempted by apostasy.

Although Alfonso denied any such intention, events got the better of him. He journeyed to Nicosia, where he hoped to find redress and more respectful treatment among his fellow Franciscans. Although he remained longer in the Nicosian monastery, his superior rejected his demand to leave the island aboard a ship bound for Livorno. In late March 1690, he decided that he needed to seek the mediation of civil authorities. He left the monastery to petition the French consul, the chief political authority for both lay and clerical Catholics on the island.

On the most tormented day of his travels in the Muslim world, 30 March 1690, his deposition and the contrasting testimony given by many witnesses bring us no closer to understanding Alfonso's intentions. Somewhere en route, he had found a curious piece of paper to which he and the Inquisitioners would refer as a "carta magica," a magic paper. The document is still extant: it was a single sheet of paper upon which were written two tables composed of Arabic letters and numbers, one of which seems to be merely a mnemonic device for remembering the ninety-nine attributes of Allah.[40] This sheet of paper was in Alfonso's possession when he proceeded to the house of the merchant Andrea Santamente, where he hoped to speak directly with the French consul, Baltazar Savran.

What if any relationship this paper had to the events that followed is unclear. On his first attempt to meet with Savran, Alfonso was rebuffed. Returning for a second visit, he forced his way into the house while the consul, his interpreter, and the members of the European merchant community were meeting with the rebel captain of the island. The Maltese friar was in a state of extreme agitation; he was barefoot and wearing the habit of the Franciscan order when he burst into the audience. Many witnesses testified that the cleric threw himself at the janissary captain's feet and declared himself to be a Muslim ("while we sat with all of the nation in an audience with the rebel governor of the Regno he arrived before the divan, saying that he wished to again be a Muslim, having once converted"). Through his interpreter, the consul and the merchants attempted to deny Alfonso's assertions. Enraged by their words, Alfonso was determined to make a point: he hoisted his habit to display his circumcision. In the confusion, he divulged information about other renegades, specifically, two of the captain's own Christian slaves, whom the Larnaca monastery had hidden until such time as they could find a secure means of transporting them to Venice.

The spectacle of a Catholic friar publicly embracing Islam and betraying his coreligionists realized the worst fears of the Europeans living in the Ottoman Empire. It jeopardized commercial interests and agreements, undermined personal and political alliances, and again made a mockery of the Catholic hierarchy. Yet Alfonso's desperate resort to exposing his private parts also made it easier for Consul Savran and the merchants to convince the janissary that the friar was truly a madman.

Money proved the salve for other problems.[41] The French consul, who also represented the commercial interests of Dutch and English Protestant traders, was able to convince the janissary to turn Alfonso Moscati over to them. In exchange for a hefty gift, collected from the merchants on the island and with the promise of their continuing support for his administration, the Cypriot leader was willing to overlook the matter of the Christian slaves as well.

Once Fra Alfonso had been taken into custody by the French consul, churchmen on the island initiated the Inquisition process. In Larnaca, Father Antonio Lepori, "Reverend Guardian and Commissary of the Sainted Office and a Deputy of their Excellence, the Fathers of the Inquisition of the Venetian Republic," who was entrusted with the interests of Christendom in the "Reign of Cyprus," gathered testimony and existing documentation surrounding the friar's time on the island and details of the final incident. Baltazar Savran secured the prisoner, writing to the Inquisition tribunal in Venice that "we have held him in our custody from that instant until now, and we dispatched him on this tartan, the Saint Giovanni which is captained by Patron Desiderio Pellegrin whose orders are to consign him to [you] by the Reverend Guardian."

THE FINAL CHAPTER

It took many months for the Sant'Ufficio to compile its case against Alfonso Moscati. Letters to and from the Venetian Inquisition crisscrossed the Mediterranean between 1690 and 1691. Testimony arrived from merchants and monks, from La Valletta, Alexandria, Cairo, Damietta, Larnaca, and Nicosia. Until the spring of 1692, the Inquisitioners interrogated the prisoner in many sessions, attempting to ascertain what they considered to be an elusive truth lost in concealed details and motives.

The interrogation did not tarry over the first detour into Islam that occurred in Egypt in 1689. In addition to the accused's own strong defense – that if he truly had intended to become a Muslim he would have done so in Egypt – Alfonso's tale was a stock account; one of many similar Levantine stories, product of a moment of doubt or weakness so common among the uninitiated in the baffling world of the Ottoman sultan. With the war raging, the Inquisition dockets were filled with accidental travelers who needed to be processed to rejoin Christendom.[42]

But there were no satisfactory answers for Alfonso's defiance of the ecclesiastical hierarchy, beginning with his outward journey. As time passed, he stood by his story without resolving its many contradictions. The members of the tribunal were particularly concerned about the reason for the friar's having retained the "magic paper" that, they reminded him, he claimed to have found while walking in Cyprus. They pressed him for an answer: why had he held on to that piece of paper? Was it for "superstition, magic, love potion, protection or another purpose?" When he insisted that it was nothing, they recommended further torture.

In a strange half-admission of intent and desire to retain his dignity and intellectual authority, Alfonso begged the court in 31 May 1691 not to:

deny the possibility that someone blind with anger might also speak in a balanced fashion; for it is like a wise man, who when he goes mad may at times, in the very act of insanity, appear to speak wisely ... that is because it [the substance of this speech] derives from the great accumulation of knowledge, albeit distorted by fantasy even when he was wise.

Lucia Rostagno considers Alfonso's insanity plea "a brilliant self-defense."[43] But could it not also be more than a legal technicality? Was not the plea of insanity a traveler's final surrender to the tide of events that had swallowed him up like Jonah, overwhelming his journey and taking his narrative beyond his control? Or, as he stated on 7 June 1691:

I don't deny being guilty; I reject being guilty voluntarily. I don't deny having committed a crime. I deny having committed it consciously. I don't deny knowing the infraction was committed; I deny knowing of it through my own cognition, because, as I have already said, I know it through the mouth of others.

In the end, however, the fathers of the Inquisition tribunal were unable to reconcile erudition with madness or personal travel with an accidental itinerary across the religious frontier. They held the Maltese friar accountable for his speech regardless of his intentions or presence of mind; they condemned him for serious political offenses including revealing the presence of captives hidden in the convent, which endangered the entire Catholic community on Cyprus. Finally, they remained unconvinced of his intellectual motives concerning the "magic paper" in question. Never satisfied that they had arrived at the "truth," the Inquisition simply had no legal language for his true crime: his repeated attempts to reclaim both his personal autonomy and the authorship of his travelogue.

The tribunal ended the travels of Alfonso Moscati. He was sentenced to another two-year term in the public jail, to be followed by six months of repentance in the monastery of Saint Bonaventure. Yet he would not serve out his entire sentence in the public jail. His brothers succeeded in gaining his early release to their custody; a year later they petitioned that they believed in his spiritual transformation, and that all the monks had accepted his sincere and total repentance. On 21 June 1693, at the age of thirty-five, the cleric-scholar-traveler who had visited Palermo, Naples, Turin, Bologna, Venice, Egypt, and Cyprus was sent back to his native Malta.

NOTES

1. The printed announcement of the verdict of the trial and the Inquisition transcripts are located in the Archivio di Stato di Venezia (Fondo Santo Ufficio,
Busta 126); all quotations are from the trial transcriptions; translations are by
the author.

2. For the latest work on the followers of Shabetai Zevi, see Cengiz Şişman,
"Sabetayciliğin Osmanli ve Türkiye Serüveni," *Tarih ve Toplum*, 223, 2002,
pp. 4–6.

3. See Eremya Chelebi Komurjian's Armeno-Turkish poem *The Jewish Bride*, ed.
Avedis K. Sanjian and Andreas Tietze (Wiesbaden: Harrassowitz, 1981).

4. Compare Bartolomé Bennassar, "Conversion ou Reniement? Modalitiés d'un
Adhesion Ambiguë des Chrétiens a L'Islam (XVIe–XVIIe siècles)," *Annales
ESC*, 6, 1988, pp. 1349–1366. For the use of the Inquisition as a soapbox for an
idiosyncratic philosopher, see Carlo Ginzburg, *The Cheese and the Worms: The
Cosmos of a Sixteenth Century Miller* (Baltimore: Johns Hopkins University
Press, 1992).

5. For other accounts, see Lucia Rostagno's reconstruction of the trial, "Apostasia
all'Islam e Santo Ufficio in un Processo dell'Inquisizione Veneziana," *Il Veltro*,
23(2–4), 1979, pp. 293–314; Ariel Salzmann, *Vita e Avventure di un Rinnegato*
(Venice: Centro Internazionale della Grafica, 1992); idem, "Notes from Rome:
Islam, Italy's Internal Frontier," in *Views from the Edge: Essays in Honor of
Richard W. Bulliet*, ed. Neguin Yavari, Lawrence G. Potter, and Jean-Marc Ran
Oppenheim (New York: Columbia University Press/Middle East Institute,
2004), pp. 240–254. Paolo Preto was the first to call attention to the case of
Alfonso di Malta in his *Venezia e il Turco* (Florence: G. C. Sansoni, 1975).

6. For some thoughts on the subject of the Western travelogue into the Muslim
world, see Jean-Claude Vatin, "Le Voyage: Elements pour Une Taxonomie," in
La Fuite en Egypte: Supplement aux voyages europeens en Orient, ed. Claude Vatin
(Cairo: C.E.D.E.J., 1989), pp. 9–50.

7. See his "Rihlat al-Wazir fi Iftikak al-Asir," in *In the Lands of the Christians, Arabic
Travel Writing in the Seventeenth Century*, ed. Nabil Matar (London: Routledge,
2003), pp. 113–196.

8. Michel Fontenay," La Place de la course dans l'économie portuaire: l'example de
Malte et des Ports Barbaresques," *Annales ESC*, 6, 1988, pp. 1321–1347. For an
overview of the period, see Dorothy M. Vaughan, *Europe and the Turk: A Pattern
of Alliances 1350–1700* (Liverpool: Liverpool University Press, 1954).

9. Robert C. Davis concentrates on the Christian side of this equation: "Counting
European Slaves on the Barbary Coast," *Past & Present*, 172, 2001, pp. 87–124;
idem, *Christian Slaves, Muslim Masters: White Slavery in the Mediterranean, the
Barbary Coast, and Italy, 1500–1800* (Basingstoke, England: Palgrave
Macmillan, 2003).

10. Salvatore Bono, *Schiavi musulmani nell'Italia moderna. Galeotti, vu'cumpra',
domestici* (Naples: Edizioni Scientifiche Italiane, 1999), pp. 41–45; for a personal
account see Frederic Hitzel, "Osman Aga, captif ottoman dans l'empire des
Habsbourg a la fin du XVIIe siecle," *Turcica*, 33, 2001, pp.191–212.

11. Bono, *Schiavi musulmani*, pp. 301–302. See also Marko Jacov, *Le missioni cattoliche nei Balcani tra le due grandi guerre: Candia (1645 1669), Vienna e Morea
(1683 1699)* (Vatican City: Biblioteca apostolica vaticana, 1998).

12. Michel Fontenay, "L'empire ottoman et le risque corsaire au XVIIeme siècle," *Revue d'histoire moderne et contemporaine*, 32, 1985, p. 195; Bono, *Schiavi musulmani*, p. 245.

13. Mohammad bin Abd al-Wahab al-Ghassani (1690–91) ("Rihlat al-Wazir fi Iftikak al-Asir," in Matar, *In the Lands of the Christians*, p. 169), who transited Spain in these years, realized that the crusade against Muslims was the ticket to improved status.

14. Henry Charles Lea, *The Inquisition in the Spanish Dependencies: Sicily - Naples - Sardinia - Milan - the Canaries - Mexico - Peru - New Granada* (New York/ London: Macmillan, 1908), p. 39. For more recent work on the Maltese Inquisition itself, see Alexander Bonnici, *A Trial in Front of an Inquisitor of Malta: 1562–1798* (Rabat, Malta: Religjon u Hajja, 1998).

15. Fr. Gio Francesco Abela (1582–1655), *Malta illustrata, ovvero Descrizione di Malta isola del mare Siciliano e Adriatico: con le sue antichità, ed altre notizie* (Malta: Nella Stamperia del Palazzo di S.A.S., 1772–80), paints a more appealing picture of Malta in the seventeenth century. For another account, see Joe Zammit Ciantar (ed.), *A Benedictine's Notes on Seventeenth-Century Malta* (Hal Tarxien, Malta: Gutenberg Press, 1998).

16. For earlier debates over the legitimacy of astrology with respect to religion, see Eugenio Garin, *Lo Zodiaco Della Vita: La Polemica sull'Astrologia dal Trecento al Cinquecento* (Rome: Laterza, 1982).

17. See K. M. Setton, *Venice, Austria and the Turks in the Seventeenth Century* (Philadelphia: American Philosophical Society, 1991); Molly Greene, *A Shared World: Christians and Muslims in the Early Modern Mediterranean* (Princeton, N.J.: Princeton University Press, 2000), pp. 94–95.

18. On the life of this eunuch, see Ahmed Resmi Efendi, *Hamiletü'l Kübera ed. Ahmed Nezihi Turan* (Istanbul: Kitabevi, 2000), pp. 50–51.

19. Greene, *A Shared World*, p. 69.

20. See Nelly Hanna, *Making Big Money in 1600: The Life and Times of Isma'il Abu Taqqiya, Egyptian Merchant* (Syracuse, N.Y.: Syracuse University Press, 1998).

21. Bernard Heyberger, *Les Chrétiens du Proche Orient au Temps de la Réforme Catholique (Syrie, Liban, Palestine, XVIIe–XVIIIe siècles)* (Rome: École Françaises, 1994), p. 268.

22. Jean Berenger, "La politique ottomane de la France dans les années 1680," in *I Turchi, il Mediterraneo e l'Europa*, ed. Giovanna Motta (Milan: FrancoAngeli. 1998), pp. 269–275.

23. André Raymond, *Les commerçants au Caire au XVIIIe siècle* (Damascus, Institut Français de Damas, 1973–74), vol. 2, p. 454; Heyberger, *Les Chrétiens du Proche Orient*, pp.166, 178, 222; see also Lucette Valensi, "Inter-communal Relations and Changes in Religious Affiliation in the Middle East (Seventeenth to Nineteenth Centuries), *Comparative Study of Society and History*, 39, 1997, pp. 251–269.

24. Uriel Heyd, *Studies in Old Ottoman Criminal Law* (Oxford: Oxford University Press, 1973), p. 306.

25. On the concept of missions as firewalls against conversion, see Salzmann, "Notes from Rome," pp. 252–254.

26. Lucia Rostagno, *Mi Faccio Turco: Esperienze ed immagini dell'Islam nell'Italia moderna* (Rome: Instituto per l'Oriente C. A. Nallino, 1983), p. 13.

27. Brian S. Pullan, *The Jews of Europe and the Inquisition of Venice, 1550–1670* (Totowa, N.J.: Barnes & Noble, 1983), p. 69; see also Suraiya Faroqhi,

"Introduction, or Why and How One Might Want to Study Ottoman Clothes," in *Ottoman Costumes: From Textile to Identity*, ed. Suraiya Faroqhi and Christoph K. Neumann (Istanbul: Eren, 2004), pp.15–48.

28. Ralph S. Hattox, *Coffee and Coffeehouses: The Origins of a Social Beverage in the Medieval Near East* (Seattle: University of Washington Press, 1988), p. 111.

29. Angelo Rambaldi, *Ambrosia Arabica overo Dealla Salutare Bevanda Cafe* (Bologna: Longhi, 1691), p. 23.

30. Compare James A. Boon, "Circumscribing Circumcision/Uncircumcision: An Essay amid the History of Difficult Description," in *Implicit Understandings: Observing, Reporting, and Reflecting on the Encounters between Europeans and Other Peoples in the Early Modern Era*, ed. Stuart B. Schwartz (Cambridge, England: Cambridge University Press,1994), p. 564.

31. "I never had the intention to [adhere] to the Mahometan Law, because in fact, I returned spontaneously to the Church while in the Land of the Turks and if I had had this intention, I would not have returned, as in fact I have returned."

32. See Jane Hathaway, *The Politics of Households in Ottoman Egypt: The Rise of the Qazdaglis* (Cambridge, England: Cambridge University Press, 1997); Robert Mantran (ed.), *Histoire de l'Empire Ottoman* (Paris: Fayard, 1989) pp. 398–399.

33. Paul Rycault, *The Present State of the Ottoman Empire* (London: John Starkey & Henry Brome, 1668), p. 157.

34. Salzmann, "Notes from Rome," pp. 252–254.

35. Frazee, *Catholics and Sultans*, p. 111.

36. Heyberger, *Les Chrétiens du Proche Orient*, p. 322.

37. Zacharias N. Tsirpanle (ed.) *Anekdota engrapha ek ton Archeion tou Vatikanou (1625–67)* (Nicosia, Cyprus: Kentrou Epistemonikon Evevnon, 1973), pp. 152–158, 178.

38. Ronald C. Jennings, *Christians and Muslims in Ottoman Cyprus and the Mediterranean World, 1571–1640* (New York: New York University Press, 1993), pp.137–143.

39. Many cases of clerical conversions are recorded in the *Chronicles and Annals of the Holy Land* (Pietro Verniero di Montepiloso (ed.), *Croniche ovvero annali di Terra Santa ...: Pubblicate per la prima volta con note e schiarimenti dal P. Girolamo Golubovich* [Florence: Quaracchi presso Firenze, Collegio di S. Bonaventura, 1929–36]), which was cited in Salvatore Bono, "Conversioni all'islam e riconciliazioni in Levante nella prima meta del Seicento," in *I Turchi, il Mediterraneo e l'Europa*, ed. Giovanna Motta (Milan: FrancoAngeli, 1998), pp. 325–339. For other examples, see Charles Frazee, *Catholics and Sultans*, vol. 2, p. 136; Heyberger, *Les Chrétiens du Proche Orient*, pp. 76, 166, 174–178, 322; and Preto, *Venezia e i turchi*, pp. 223–225.

40. Rostagno, ("Apostasia all'Islam e Santo Ufficio," p. 311) has reproduced a copy of the infamous "carta magica."

41. There is a record of "Mehemet Aga's" debts to the French nation, in Anna Pouradier Duteil-Loizidou, *Consulat de France à Larnaca (1600–1696)* (Nicosia: Centre de Recherche Scientifique: Source et Étude de L'Histoire de Chypre, 1991), vol. 1, pp. 169–170.

42. Salzmann, "Notes from Rome," pp. 249–250.

43. Rostagno, "Apostasia all'Islam e Santo Ufficio," p. 302.

8

APOLOGY FOR S. D. GOITEIN: AN ESSAY[1]

Steven M. Wasserstrom

Michel de Montaigne (1533–92) begins his classic essay, "Apology for Raymond Sebond," in praise of scholarship. "Truly, learning is a most useful accomplishment and a great one."[2] Truly, great scholars themselves require the closest study.[3] I write as a working historian of religions whose career began beholden to the massive accomplishments of Shlomo Dov (Fritz) Goitein (1900–85). My questions, pursued here in retrospect, concern notions of religion and the framing assumptions about humanism that he brought to his oceanic researches.[4] I do so not because he was "great," although I am constrained to confess my OTSOG-ian deference toward him.[5] Rather, I see floating in the sea-change of civilizational conflict breaking around us the shards of Goitein's wishful edifice, which we perhaps cannot put back together again.

The Orientalism culture wars were getting underway when I entered graduate school in 1978 – Patricia Crone and Michael Cook published *Hagarism* in 1977, Edward Said published his *Orientalism* in 1978. Territory I was entering was contested, intimidating. It hardly helped that my primary inspiration was Goitein – his reputation as an arch-Orientalist and true believer in the civilizing humanism of the philological vocation seemingly rendered him vulnerable from both flanks. Nevertheless, directly following his scholarly lead, I chose the "creative symbiosis" between Muslim and Jew as subject of my research.[6] He died in 1985, just as I was writing the last pages of my dissertation. In other words, I set forth fully under the sign of Goitein.[7] And so, answering an invitation from the editors to write an essay on the Mediterranean, I thought immediately of Goitein's valediction, delivered in the last year of his long life.[8] In 1987, taking my academic post, I was at once perplexed and impressed by this heartbreakingly optimistic talk. Its title faced me as a challenge: "The Humanistic Aspects of Oriental Studies."

Montaigne's *Apology for Raymond Sebond* (1580) sheds an odd light slantwise on my encounter with Goitein. A kind of irreligious defense of religion written under the bloodstained insignia of the Wars of Religion, Montaigne's innovative essay shares with Goitein's "sociography" a resolute aversion to abstraction. In the spirit, I hope, underwritten by Montaigne and Goitein, I too seek to see a person whole. In the case of Goitein, seeing the whole person is dauntingly difficult indeed. Goitein's constellation of accomplishments is rare in the history of scholarship.[9] Nor was he a mere energetic pedagogue – he took understandable umbrage when Gershom Scholem denigrated him as a "born Schulmeister." Eric Ormsby, a student of Goitein who reported his teacher's hurt feelings, captured his rainbow of attainment.

> Goitein was a very great scholar and historian, an Islamicist by formation but also a biblical expert and commentator, an editor of texts, a paleographer, an ethnologist whose fieldwork on the Jews of Yemen remains fundamental, a linguist, a medievalist and economic historian, a pedagogue, a professor at Hebrew University in Jerusalem from its inception, and, not least, a Hebrew poet and playwright. A polyglot, the list of his over six hundred works in Hebrew, English, German, and French fills an entire book.[10]

Ormsby recently asked of Maimonides, "How write the life of such a polymath?"[11] Like Maimonides the polymath, Goitein's stature as polyglot, universal scholar resists the essayist, who is by definition a miniaturist. How embrace a subject as big as a sea in the intimate terms of the personal essay? The intimacy of the genre Montaigne invented would seem antipodes away from the five oceanic volumes of *A Mediterranean Society: The Jewish Communities of the Arab World as Portrayed in the Documents of the Cairo Geniza*.[12] But first, back to the *Heimat*.

GOITEIN IN GERMANY

Fritz Goitein was proudly descended from Moravian-Hungarian Rabbi Baruch Goitein, the author of *Kesef Nivhar*.[13]

My own great-great-grandfather's *Kesef Nivhar*, which is still popular with the Talmudists and has often been reprinted, also in [the U.S.], appeared first in Prague 1827 [sic], preceded by a long list of sponsors (including, incidentally, the grandfather of Theodor Herzl, the founder of Zionism).[14]

Kojetin (also known as Gojetein or Goitein) produced a line of rabbis that included his own father, who raised him in Burgkunstadt, Bavaria.[15] The young scholar made a daring leap from orthodox practice of Judaism to the philological study of Islam. In the opening remarks at the inaugural conference of the Society of Judaeo-Arabic Studies in 1984, Goitein recalled that, when he entered Islamic studies sixty-six years before, less than half a dozen universities even offered such studies.[16] He wrote his thesis, on prayer in the Qur'an, under Josef Horowitz (1874–1931).[17] His work in this regard descended directly from the co-founder of the Reform movement, Abraham Geiger. Geiger's 1833 *Was hat Mohammed aus dem Judenthum aufgenommen?* began a line of inquiry to which Goitein now centrally returned. Goitein, furthermore, remained animated by this fundamental question, developing it again in his 1958 essay "Muhammad's Inspiration by Judaism."[18] While he began his career with Syriac influence on the Qur'an, Goitein was never inimical to Muhammad or his revelation.[19]

In any case, Goitein happily, for him and for us, emerged out of the intense Jewish renaissance of Weimar Germany.[20] As he recalled it nostalgically, "the real formative years of my life were the years 1914 to 1923 which I spent in Frankfurt and partly also in Berlin. It gave me inspiration, knowledge and friendship. It was a time of great enthusiasm."[21] Such enthusiasm was an earmark of the circle around Rabbi Nehemias Anton Nobel (1871–1922). Goitein was only twenty-two years old when he published his eulogy for Nobel alongside those by senior luminaries Leo Baeck and Franz Rosenzweig, among other leaders of German Jewry.[22] He characterized Nobel in terms one associates with the contemporaneous Stefan George circle. "The phenomenon of Nobel's notion of personality is thoroughly that of the artistically organized human being" ("Das Phänomen der Nobelschen Persönlichkeit ist das eines durchaus künstlerisch organisierten Menschen").[23] Goitein, it would seem, epitomized the ideal he attributed to his cousin, the distinguished philologian of Islam, D. Z. H. Baneth.[24] With Baneth "one was always in the presence of creative thought based on the sound foundation of profound scholarship."[25]

Young Jewish Orientalists were in some serious sense in love with Islam, a love perhaps not inconsistent with the Orientalist depredations attributed to it by Edward Said and others.[26] Some – including al-Raschid Bey, Essad Bey, and Muhammad Asad – "converted" to Islam, in one form or another.[27] A circle of unusually talented Jewish Islamicists formed around their teacher, Hans Heinrich Schaeder. These so-called "puppies" flourished in social proximity to Goitein, although, tellingly, he was not one of them.[28] Several of these Jewish Islamicist students clustered around Carl Heinrich Becker (1876–1933), the teacher both of Goitein and Schaeder.[29] Goitein still praised Becker as late as 1987.[30] It should be said that while Becker was properly lauded as a minister of culture during the Weimar Republic, responsible for visionary innovations in university life, he was also actively devoted to the German colonial project.[31] He was not infected, however, with race-hatred, and indeed when he abandoned Islamic studies to serve as minister of culture in the Weimar Republic, he became patron to leading liberal intellectuals.[32]

Goitein left aside Becker's colonialism, even when the loyal student returned to his teacher decades later. Writing in the poignantly retrospective epilogue to *A Mediterranean Society*, Goitein paid homage a final time: "My model in Islamic history was Carl Heinrich Becker (d.1933), whose lectures I attended in Berlin. He taught Islam as a civilization (and not merely as a religion), at that time a revolutionary attitude (for which a professor at Cairo University lost his post)."[33] Goitein himself retained that "revolutionary attitude." Based squarely on this civilizational imperative, he even coined a new world-age, "the Intermediate Civilization."[34] Becker's formulation is explicitly his point of departure. "Did they grasp the spirit of Hellas? ... For C. H. Becker, one of the most competent students of our problem, Islam is Hellenism, to be sure an Islamicized Hellenism."[35] As Becker influentially put it, "Islamic civilization is naught but a fusion of ancient Greek intellectuality with Oriental contemplativeness."[36] Goitein seemed to demur in favor of a somewhat more nuanced periodization, but otherwise embraced this civilizational ideal.

While devoted to his German teachers, the young Zionist determined that, on receiving his doctorate, he would emigrate to Palestine. In a moving recollection, he recalled his prayers at the home of Franz Rosenzweig, on Rosh Hashana 1923, the day before he boarded the boat with Scholem.[37]

I did not have to "look" into the Scriptures; I was in them. It happened on September 11, 1923, when Erich Fromm (to become renowned for his psychoanalytical writings) and I officiated as cantors at the Jewish New Year's service in the house of the philosopher Franz Rosenzweig ... When I recited Genesis 21:12, "God hears the voice of the boy wherever he might be," I was to leave the next day for Palestine ... [t]hat the boy in the biblical story was Ishmael seemed to be altogether appropriate for a fledgling Arabist.[38]

Goitein then sailed the Mediterranean Sea, together with Gerhard (Gershom) Scholem. Even now I imagine them dividing their worlds down the middle of that sea – Goitein relishing his eastbound journey both to a new home and to a scholarly mastery of an ancient "Orient" while Scholem gazes forward toward Zion even as he remains rooted in the spiritual history of European Jews.[39] Goitein implied that his emigration coincided with his disillusionment with orthodoxy. Thus, the elderly scholar reminisced about German Jewry with a sardonic edge. "In the magnificent, *hyperorthodox* synagogue of Frankfurt am Main (now destroyed, of course) [the service immediately following conclusion of Sabbath] did not take more than twenty minutes at most, but endless rows of cars waited outside to take busy executives to their offices."[40] Subsequently he would identify with Abraham Maimonides, who "went so far as to accuse the *hyperorthodox* of their disregard for the laws of nature and of the sciences that studied them."[41]

GOITEIN IN PALESTINE AND ISRAEL

I too was once a medieval man; now, I am a medievalist, which is, of course, quite a different matter.[42]

Like the similarly disillusioned medievalist Scholem, Goitein carried compensatory ambitions with him in his emigration.[43] It is not surprising that Goitein, like many of his cohort, identified with the twelfth-century Andalusian emigration generation.[44] Jews of his generation in Germany thrived on the wish-fulfillment of reliving the Golden Age of the Jews of Spain. More generally, German Jews identified with the Jews of Islam, in the now well-known romantic myth of Sepharad.[45] But only some could recognize that the myth of German–Jewish symbiosis was disintegrating and that they needed therefore to find a national homeland of their own.

The young emigrant was especially enamored of the poet laureate of the Andalusian emigration, Yehuda Halevi.[46] This affection was consistent with the German–Jewish love affair with this great poet, whose devotees included Moses Mendelssohn, Moses Hess, Heinrich Heine, and Rosenzweig.[47] One of Goitein's first publications was a passionate 1924 review of Rosenzweig's translations of Halevi's poetry.[48] Goitein made major contributions to the study of Halevi, including the identification of autograph letters found in the Genizah.[49] "From Biblical times down to modern Hebrew literature, there has certainly been no Hebrew poet, as *perfect in form* and as true an intepreter of the spirit of the age as Judah ha-Levi ... [whose *Kuzari*] is perhaps the most authentic exposition of Judaism in existence."[50] He made the point slightly differently in the last pages of *A Mediterranean Society*, to the effect that in "the combination of his *perfection in form* and the elementary power of religious conviction ha-Levi seems to have been unique."[51]

Goitein became a founder of so-called "Oriental studies" in the new Jewish state.[52] He did so in part by continuing projects connected with his graduate school mentors. Milson notes that "According to Goitein, in his introduction to his edition of volume V of *Ansāb al-ashrāf*, it was Weil who originally suggested this project to Horowitz, and Carl Becker, the famous German Islamicist who discovered the manuscript, warmly agreed."[53] Goitein's view of "symbiosis" thus was fully formed rather early. A good example is his 1937 Hebrew essay "Some Comparative Notes on the History of Israel and the Arabs."[54]

His major contributions from this period of his career were collected in *Studies in Islamic History and Institutions.*[55] At the end of his forty-year Islamics career, he publicly changed some positions he had long espoused.

> There is no subject of Islamic social history on which the present writer had to modify his views so radically while passing from literary to documentary sources, i.e., from the study of Muslim books to that of the records of the Cairo Geniza as the *jizya* or the poll tax to be paid by non-Muslims. It was of course, evident that the tax represented a discrimination and was intended, according to the Koran's own words, to emphasize the inferior status of the non-believers. It seemed, however, that from the economic point of view, it did not constitute a heavy imposition, since it was on a sliding scale, approximately one, two, and four dinars, and thus adjusted to the financial

capacity of the taxpayer. This impression proved to be entirely falla-
cious, for it did not take into consideration the immense extent of
poverty and privation experienced by the masses, and in particular,
their persistent lack of cash, which turned the 'season of the tax' into
one of horror, dread, and misery.[56]

Turning away from sustained success as a major Islamicist, Goitein
then largely left the field, on retirement, to pursue Geniza studies.

GOITEIN'S GENIZAH

The *de rigueur* comparison with the socio-historical project of
Ferdinand Braudel is not as flattering as it was just a few years ago.[57]
Goitein was aware of the Annales project and contributed to its
flagship journal in 1958.[58] His preferred self-designation was practi-
tioner of "Oriental studies."[59] Of all the forms he had practiced –
philology, history, literary criticism, *Religionswissenschaft* – he ultimately chose "sociography" for his life work. His was perhaps the
largest and most influential application of Clifford Geertz's "thick
description," whose influence he cited.[60] Perhaps Goitein's closest
sociographic forerunner to *A Mediterranean Society* was his 1937
ethnography, *Von den Juden Jemens. Eine Anthologie.*[61]

It is no longer agreed that "Mediterranean society" is the best designation for his object of study.[62] In fact, it seems clearly superseded
today. But it was based on human realities that will not go out of style:
documentary sources for real life, social life, lived practices, intimate
letters, all aspects of social existence. In short, Goitein studied people.
He was not the only one to find romance in the Geniza, which has
given rise to such novels as Amitav Ghosh's *In an Antique Land* and
A. B. Yehoshua's *A Journey to the End of the Millennium.*[63]

Late life was laden with honors.[64] These included, in 1983, the third
year of the John D. and Catherine T. Macarthur "genius" grant,
given to the "doyen of Genizologists." Goitein's mastery of the Cairo
Geniza, arguably the most significant horde of medieval manuscripts
discovered anywhere, was thus properly recognized as a colossal
accomplishment.[65] Even more impressive is the range of other
scholarly areas in which he had a broad impact. These include popu-
larizations;[66] advances in Geniza research;[67] studies on poverty and
charity,[68] messianic movements,[69] and marriage.[70] In all this work,
he sustained an old-fashioned, straightforward, head-held-high

Orientalism that inevitably drew some fair critiques.[71] Shlomo Goitein passed away in 1988, as the anti-Orientalism controversies were reaching their peak.

GOITEIN'S JUDAISM

Among his numerous contributions to Jewish studies, including a substantial body of scholarship on the Bible, were significant studies in the history of Jewish religious practice.[72] He noted, for example, the utter absence of significant Bar Mitzvah practice in the Geniza society and thus could write "Bar Talmud – an Initiation Rite at Sixteen," in which he proposed a new ritual.[73] Nor was he averse to announcing his own religious suggestions. "If we can learn anything from Jewish family life as revealed by the Genizah records it is this: the renowned cohesiveness of the Jewish family has nothing to do with the non-existent Jewish race. It is the fruit of religious education. If we wish our children should love us, we must teach them to love mitsvot [religious commandments]."[74]

In a 1970 obituary for his friend the Nobel-Prize-winning Israeli novelist, Shmuel Yosef Agnon, Goitein spoke with remarkable directness. Goitein knew Agnon well, having met and become familiar with Agnon's future wife Esther Marx in 1918, two years before she married Agnon, and having delivered the first lecture on Agnon's work.[75] Goitein experienced a time out of joint with these friends, literally strolling with Agnon, whom he considered a kind of Ha-Levi *redivivus*. The scholar sketched his encounter with the novelist with an exquisitely dialectical ambivalence:

> As rightly expressed in the bestowal of the Nobel Prize, Agnon is the representative Hebrew writer of our age. Since Biblical times there has not been in Hebrew language a corpus of narrative prose of the magnitude, dignity, and meaningfulness of Agnon's creation. He has done for Hebrew prose what Yehuda Halevy has achieved in religious poetry. Halevy wrote in the forms and the spirit of the 12th century. Agnon expressed the mood and the refinement of the 20th. But both are the mouth-pieces of genuine and integral Judaism.
>
> For my taste, both Yehuda Halevy and Agnon are a little bit too Jewish. I mean, in both the mere human element is too often subordinated to the specifically Jewish aspect. But this cannot be helped. This is the way in which a comparatively small religious community, which had played a very particular role in world history looked upon

itself. Yehuda Halevy in religious poetry and Shumel Yosef Agnon in narrative prose are the most genuine and *most perfect exponents* of post-Biblical Judaism.[76]

From his passionate obituary for Rabbi Nobel, written at age twenty-two, to his dispassionate eulogy for Agnon at age seventy, Goitein remained a religiously engaged though no longer orthoprax Jew. While he could acknowledge that Agnon's practice of traditional Judaism was central to understanding his fiction, Goitein remained consistently wary of orthodoxy. His subsequent words, applied to Islam, spoke equally to his sense of his own humanistic Judaism – as only appropriate for the author of "The Humanistic Aspects of Oriental Studies."[77]

> There is nothing wrong with a man's conviction that his religion is the best (at least for himself), as long as this belief does not make him blind to the virtues of others and as long as the supreme values of morality and mercy are not sacrificed to confessional fanaticism.[78]

Goitein expressed his conflicted nostalgia most intimately in his 1983 poem "Midnight Watch (Reflections after the Holocaust)."[79] It was no accident that the lover of Yehuda Ha-Levi published this most intimate expression in verse. I find it rather remarkable to compare this intimate verse with that of Gershom Scholem. A number of themes seem saliently shared, including the fall from tradition; the power of the Holy Name; the decline of commentary; the darkness of the hour; and the conviction that "The people of Israel are Your witnesses ... / Witnesses each in their own way." This poignant confession addressed the past, the beloved lost world to which Goitein devoted his life work. "A world of Order was there / In spite of everything / *Perfection within perfection* / A great world of Order."[80] While the poem presumed cultural degeneration, and in spite of the fact that he framed it in terms of the Holocaust, the immediate referent was Goitein's beloved "Intermediate Civilization," his model of a world in order. His Mediterranean society was a "an orderly and harmonious world, complete in itself. Whether we read the sublime concluding chapter of the *Guide for the Perplexed* of Moses Maimonides or the day-to-day correspondence of his humble contemporaries, we feel that the ideals of a world at peace and *a perfect man* did not appear to them to be out of reach, of course, if God decreed so."[81]

GOITEIN'S MIDDLE AGES AND THE PERFECT MAN

> The idea common to the three monotheistic religions, that *man is bound above all to work on his own moral and spiritual perfection*, while serving the community, could become a new base for the development of a healthy individualism, as opposed to the ideals of conformity, recommended as leading to success, and to that of following the party line as a means to strengthen a monolithic state.[82]

Goitein saw himself as originally a medieval man. For the truly medieval man, nothing less than perfection itself was the goal and *"a perfect man did not appear to them to be out of reach*, of course, if God decreed so."[83]

Montaigne and Goitein started out as such medieval men. They subsequently devoted careers to study what they were undergoing, to study medieval society in order better to grasp their respectively rapid detachment from that past. Their science of the human, their cleaving so closely to what we can know about people, had more than a little poetic touch to it, but remained first and last committed to the object of knowledge, to people themselves.

They were in fact especially occupied with the imperfect, with the plight of those undergoing terrible demands of historical change, the imperfection and the pain of which they sought to describe in detail and with compassion. Montaigne and Goitein were humanists skilled in disparate modes of expression but equally humane in the subtlest precisions of detail, of attention to the truly human. Both loved familiarities of "humanity," the wideness with the microscopic; both were humanists who confront us with life-worlds of other human beings, while holding no illusions about That Noble Dream of objectivity. Montaigne and Goitein meant the people whom they observed to be nothing more and nothing less than themselves, themselves as such. Montaigne and Goitein, artists as much as they were scientists, sought, as best they could see, both the beauty and the truth of human lives seen as they lived.

Goitein loved the imperfect – but he idealized perfection. On the basis of a humanistic idealization of *Kultur*, he romanticized two figures in particular, Yehuda Ha-Levi and Abraham Maimonides. He leaned not toward the rational Moses Maimonides but rather to Abraham Maimonides, his mystical son, a longstanding hero to whom Goitein dedicated the elegiac concluding lines of *A Mediterranean Society* under the rubric *"A perfect man with a tragic fate.*[84] Goitein "fell in love" with Abraham Maimonides in 1936 and soon thereafter expressed it in print. "The work before us is a religious testament of the greatest interest. It demonstrates that Abraham Maimonides was not satisfied with the Judaism which he found before him. Seeking a new form of expression suitable to his religious outlook, he found it – in Muslim Sufism."[85] The young scholar then translated Abraham Maimonides' *Responsa*, published in 1937. Nevertheless, he could also, rather curiously, later call him "A Jewish Addict to Sufism."[86] While it lies beyond my scope here, it must be noted that the scholarly consensus concerning Abraham is shifting, with Paul Fenton at the lead.[87]

Still, Goitein sought humanity in the round, in a capacious appreciation for all things human that was Montaignean in scale. And, like his French predecessor, he admired the fully integrated personality, in his case as epitomized by Abraham Maimonides. "For Abraham united in one person three spiritual trends which were mostly opposed to each other: strict legalistic orthodoxy, ecstatic pietism, and Greek science – sober, secular humanism. He represented all the best found in medieval Judaism as it developed within Islamic civilization."[88] "The question is whether this entire intellectual and spiritual endeavor forms an integrated, organic unit behind which stands a strong, single-minded personality. Such was indeed the case."[89] The question is whether this was Goitein's own ideal. Such, I submit, was indeed the case.

When he addressed Maimonides *père*, to whose study he made major contributions, he returned to the possibility of perfection. On Goitein's reading, Maimonides "impresses on the reader that the *ultimate purpose of life was the perfection of one's own individuality*, consisting, according to him, in the right knowledge of God, and in permanent consciousness of His presence. This insistence on *incessant striving for one's own perfection is an ideal valid for all times*."[90] Goitein gives readers this advice directly. With proper irony, the road to perfection runs through the acknowledgment of the limits of human knowledge.[91] "The reader who wishes to attempt the study of the Guide without additional help is advised to start, after the reading of the introductions, with Book I, Chapter 32, and then to read wherever he is attracted by the subject matter. He will be richly rewarded."[92] Goitein himself held perfection as a personal ideal. The words he applied to his cousin Baneth can thus be read to be self-reflexive: "Baneth had always the totality of a text in mind, that is, together with its language, its content and the social and spiritual ambiance in which it was written ... However, only a man possessed of the universal knowledge and the penetrating critical mind of Baneth could do full justice to such demands."[93]

But such men are rare. Goitein concluded that the "thirteenth century witnessed the definite turn for the worst. With the fourteenth, the night of the Middle Ages had become total."[94]

GOITEIN'S RELIGION

As a religious man, Goitein described a religious society, ironically from the outside, but precisely the better to see inside as well. This double position might be the definition of a certain sort of humanism, pioneered, he repeatedly noted, by Muslims – and, I add, by Montaigne too.[95] With regard to the goal of my discipline, that of understanding religion, I certainly agree with his observation that "when we compare Shahrastani's detailed, well-informed and remarkably unbiased accounts with the Greek and Latin texts related to Judaism, we have to confess that between Tacitus and Shahrastani, humanity has made a great step forward."[96] I cannot resist the unpopular parallel, that is, that, between Montaigne and Goitein, religious studies made a great step forward. Goitein made much the same comment in 1971. "A particular title of honor of Islamic civilization is the creation of the science of comparative religion ... [Shahrastani's] objective and valuable survey of human belief is one of the finest expressions of the concept of mankind in Islam."[97]

In 1973 he stressed that the monotheisms "shared one basic concept of the world" which constituted their "great common spiritual heritage."[98]

Writing as a historian of the history of religions, I am constrained to note some features of Goitein's characterization of "religion" that are no longer generally operative for working scholars. These include his claim that there was in Genizah Judaism "a total absence of intermediaries."[99] The same may be said of his conventional distinction between magic and religion.[100] Thus of an abjuration he says that this "formulary belongs to the world of magic rather than of religion."[101] Montaigne made the same distinction, contrasting "real" religion with "jiggery-pokery, enchantments, magic spells producing impotence, communication with the spirits of the dead, prognostications, casting horoscopes and even that absurd hunt for the philosopher's stone."[102] Goitein programmatically disregarded the vast reservoir of literary sources found in the Genizah, in favor of those "documentary" sources of which he was the undisputed supreme master. One consequence of this choice, on my observation, is that he did not confront the anthropological breadth and depth of religious expression of this Mediterranean society.

He once observed that "it lies in the very nature of religion, as Plato had it, that there are many who carry the thyrsus, and only a few that are entheoi or 'enthusiasts' that is, 'filled with God.' "[103] Given his descriptions of his own experience, it seems clear that he met at least two such *entheoi*, Rabbi Nobel and Franz Rosenzweig, both of whom he characterized in terms of their *Gefühl* (religious feeling).[104] His more distant heroes, Yehuda Ha-Levi and Abraham Maimonides, were historic examples of *entheoi* for him. It is rather less certain, though I think likely, that Goitein excluded himself from the ranks of the *entheoi*. Given his various autobiographical statements, it would seem that he considered himself, as Max Weber did, as "religiously unmusical."

If, finally, we seek the Judaism of Goitein, we should recall that his vast resurrection of the Geniza people, and of previous generations more generally, was an expression of a characteristically Jewish dilemma. It would not be irresponsibly misleading to consider him as a type of the historically self-conscious modern Jew, tragically constrained from but hopelessly nostalgic for an "unhaddable" history. Goitein literally walked with legends of the modern Jewish predicament: Agnon, Scholem, Rosenzweig, among many others. With them, Goitein felt achingly out of synch with the times, and recognized that ache as constitutive of his people's misadventure with the modern. In his writings, the ache and the self-recognition are equally unmistakable.

GOITEIN'S HUMANISM

In the spirit of apology, and in spite of current polarization, I submit that this man was even-handed. His 1958 lecture "Muhammad's Inspiration by Judaism" might seem an insult to the uniqueness and authenticity of the Islamic revelation.[105] However, this was a man who could proudly pronounce the honorific that accompanies the name of the Prophet Muhammad.

> When the present author studied *hadīth* with the late Sheikh Sa'ud al-'Uri in Jerusalem, the master always succeeded in preceding the disciple by the split of second in pronouncing the eulogy over the Prophet whenever his name was mentioned. It took me some time to understand that the saying of that blessing by a non-Muslim, notwithstanding the good intention, was bad form.[106]

Goitein even stated flatly that "Muhammad was one of the great men of all time."[107] In any case, he was just as willing to turn the tables, to utilize the Arabic language to interrogate the sources of Torah too.[108] He taught Arabic in Jewish schools and Hebrew in Palestinian schools.[109] Indeed, he saw them as part of a larger whole. For example, see his 1937 "Some Comparative Notes on the History of Israel and the Arabs." For Goitein, the very essence of symbiosis is that this road ran both directions. He was tolerant, dialectically and continuously, capable of saying that "Islam rested on Judaism" but also that "it was Islam that saved Judaism."[110]

Montaigne, of course, was hardly "enlightened" with regard to Islam: "When Mohammed promises his followers a paradise tapestried, adorned with gold and precious stones, peopled with wenches of surpassing beauty, with rare wines and foods, I can easily see that they are mockers stooping to our folly to honey us and attract us by these ideas and hopes appropriate to our moral appetites." In this regard, certainly, he resembled such "enlightened" contemporaries as Francis Bacon, for whom "The religion of the heathen had no constant belief or confession; and the religion of Mahomet on the other side interdicts argument altogether; so that the one has the very face of vague and manifold error, the other of crafty and cautious imposture."

Goitein's humanism began far from the freshly minted and therefore defensibly under-informed essayism of Montaigne. It was formed in the "culturally advanced" Weimar Republic, with its characteristics of philological purism, *Kultur*, and world-spanning erudition. His teacher Becker specified these features in the opening pages of the inaugural issue of *Der Islam*. It was a humanism, in any case, and it was explicitly a humanism predicated on "the Intermediate Civilization." In one of the final sentences of *A Mediterranean Society* he made this point directly, one more time: "the centuries between, say, 850 and 1250 could be described as 'humanistic Islam' with all the facets of meaning – *mutatis mutandis* – included in the 'humanism.' "[111]

Goitein summarized his scholarly self-understanding in the 1952 Hebrew University jubilee symposium. "The study in Israel of the Ancient East, or of Medieval Islam, or of folk life in the contemporary Orient, is therefore part and parcel of that search for self-knowledge which is one of the main aims of humanistic studies."[112] Goitein gave a talk entitled "The Life Story of a Scholar" to the assembled faculty and students of the Department of Oriental Studies on 30 April 1970 in which he reiterated this creed. He did so yet again in the 1980s when eventually he reflected on his mission in "the Humanistic Aspects of Oriental Studies."[113] He consistently believed that humanistic scholarship, in Montaigne's phrase, "is a most useful accomplishment and a great one." Finally, the oceans of ink in *A Mediterranean Society* washed ashore in its final section, bearing the noble title "The Prestige of Scholarship."[114]

That being said, it is also the case that this great scholar did not countenance the dark side of "Oriental studies." He neglected to inform readers that his revered teacher Carl H. Becker was an architect of German colonial policy. He also did not want to see or at least to express the less pleasant implications of his imperial if not prophetic notion of his Orientalism. In this sense and not only in this sense, Goitein's Judaism is considerably Cohenian in temper. Noting that Hermann Cohen, citing Psalm 73, "defines nearness to God as the absolute good," Goitein insisted that "the Geniza people were not theologians, but, as far as they were thinking at all, *their basic attitude was consonant with Cohen's concept.*"[115] His longstanding and often repeated emphasis on the sobriety, rationalism, and secularism of the Geniza world express what was emphatically an identification he originally made in Germany.

Religion of the Mediterranean "person," as reflected in the Geniza, was proto-bourgeois:[116]

a stern, straightforward, Talmudic type of piety, concerned with the strict fulfillment of the commandments and with the pursuit of the study required for their knowledge. This somewhat jejune character of their religiosity was enhanced by the rigorous rationalism embraced by Jewish orthodoxy in the wake of centuries of sectarian and theological controversies.[117]

He stressed this point even on the very last page of *A Mediterranean Society*. "With the exception of the few really pious and God-possessed, religion formed the frame, rather than the content of the daily existence."[118] "Supernatural men seem not to have belonged to the spiritual climate of that society."[119] He did not forget his rabbinic experience, "medieval" as it was. Indeed, he confessed that "the inside experience gained by me in a previous life might serve as a corrective, a Socratic *daimon*, a restraining inner voice."[120] By contrast to his shipmate Scholem, whose focus was on the extraordinary, Goitein's Mediterranean world, like that of Montaigne, was everyday, presenting us with "a fairly regular type of humanity."[121]

From Athens to Jerusalem, or was it vice versa? That being said, he was still filled with the messianic neo-Kantianism of Hermann Cohen when he penned a final astonishing fugue on humanistic scholarship:

"The breath entered them; they came to life and stood upon their feet, a very large host" (Ezekiel 37:10). "The dry bones," the dispersed Geniza fragments, had to be brought together, "bone matching bone," to form skeletons; "sinew, flesh, and skin" grew over these, philological and historical comments making them viable; finally, a breath or "wind," the contact with the other resurrected, let them come to life as members of "a vast multitude," a flourishing society.[122]

Cohen's student, Ernst Cassirer, citing Friedrich Schlegel, had identified the historian in just this way, that is, as "*einen ruckwarts gekehrten Propheten*, a retrospective prophet. There is a prophecy of the past, a revelation of its hidden life."[123]

One glance back he saw as piercing, and that was the rightful place of the Islamicate era in Jewish history. "Every aspect of what we regard today as Judaism – the synagogue service and prayer book, law and ritual, theology and ethics, the text of the Bible, the grammar and vocabulary of the Hebrew language – was consolidated, formulated and canonized in [the first centuries of Islamicate civilization]."[124]

In fact, he said, "It was Islam that saved Judaism."[125] On the other hand – and there seems always to be another hand for Goitein –

most of the Jewish authors of the Middle Ages who wrote in Arabic never had the slightest doubt about the absolute superiority of Judaism. I emphasize this fact not because I believe that such an attitude should be adopted in our times, but simply as an indication that Judaism inside Islam was an autonomous culture sure of itself despite, *and possibly because of,* its intimate connection with its environment.[126]

CONCLUSIONS

> Then compare our behaviour with a Moslem's or a pagan's: you always remain lower than they are.[127]

Michel de Montaigne apologized for Raymond Sebond but Goitein hardly needs my puny defense. Still, the greatest scholars require the closest study and Goitein is no exception. Montaigne defended Sebond not because he, Montaigne, was a "Sebondist." Montaigne defended Sebond in the sense that I submit an apology for Goitein, that is, not as an "Orientalist" and certainly not as a "Goiteinist" but simply as a humanist. Both were humanists because they opposed unreality in honoring the limits of human knowledge. Both humanists loved what is available to human knowledge, with its delectable details and deliciously sensory particulars. Montaigne wrote of cannibals, coaches, thumbs, a monster-child, and the armor of the Parthians; Goitein detailed slave girls, piracy, druggists, surnames, dowry, polygyny. Montaigne wrote an essay on war horses and Goitein a chapter on the riding animal as status symbol.

But Goitein looked equally hard at the large scale. Uncharacteristically, but not inappropriately, he boasted at the end of *A Mediterranean Society* that "A distinguished reviewer wrote with regard to Volume I of this book: 'Now that we have access to such data, *Islam studies will never be the same again.*' "[128] The poignancy in this pride and irony in this confidence remind me of Herman Cohen's now bathetic pamphlet *Deutschtum und Judentum*, published in 1915.[129] In fact – and this twist makes him rather more compellingly interesting – Goitein could also venture bold geopolitical opinion, world-historical periodizations, and contemporary political journalism.[130] Even in his journalism, Goitein looked to the larger ideals. His propensity for geopolitical generalization about the Middle East is most pointed in his 1957 "Eurafrasia."[131]

These, however, are not the impulses for an apology for S. D. Goitein. I do not apologize for Orientalism – though it appeals to me, I confess, no more than a fork appeals to my appetite. Orientalism is with us, it comprises our usable heritage, however discomfiting; there is no other way to the past but through it. That's the OTSOG-ian way and, however unsteadily, I stand by it. In any case, an apology for S. D. Goitein is not an apology for Orientalism, Zionism, philology. It is a tribute to a complex man and a great scholar in complicated times. While the ideal of perfection appealed to him, Goitein was not perfect. Goitein's frequent pronouncements on perfection and the perfect man notwithstanding, he stood by the ordinary man and woman, Muslim and Jew, each seen in an appropriately concrete social life-world.

"There is no sign that he ever disguised anything through hatred, favour or vanity."[132] Montaigne preferred a person who saw straight and spoke straight, and so do I. Part of that seeing straight, I hope, is acknowledging that I will always remain far, far from being a Montaigne or a Goitein. I can, however, emulate their example of studying religions. Once this was rare, in the day of Montaigne's Wars of Religion, when "only the highest category of men can stop to take a pure look at the phenomenon itself, reflecting on it and judging."[133] This is still an ideal worth emulating, as is the Montaignean dispassionate attitude toward religions more generally, an attitude so strenuously sustained by Shlomo Dov Goitein. "All this is a clear sign that we accept our religion only as we would fashion it, only from our own hands – no differently from the way other religions gain acceptance."[134]

NOTES

1. The research and composition of this article was made possible by the Paid Leave Award, the Stillman Drake Fund, and Dean's Research Funds at Reed College. I could not have completed the present work without the dedicated labors of Vahid Brown.
2. The first line of "An Apology for Raymond Sebond," in Michel De Montaigne, *Complete Essays*, trans. M. A. Screech (New York: Penguin, 1993), p. 491.
3. Steven M. Wasserstrom, *Religion after Religion: Gershom Scholem, Mircea Eliade, and Henry Corbin at Eranos* (Princeton, N.J.: Princeton University Press, 1999).
4. His humanism may be compared, in philosophical terms, to that articulated by Lenn Evan Goodman, *Islamic Humanism* (Oxford: Oxford University Press, 2003) and, in historical terms, to the medieval Islamic world described by Joel L. Kraemer in *Humanism in the Renaissance of Islam: The Cultural Revival during the Buyid Age* (Leiden, The Netherlands: Brill, 1992).
5. Robert K. Merton, *On the Shoulders of Giants: A Shandean Postscript* (New York: Free Press, 1965).
6. This is not the place to review the arguments for and against such "symbiosis." I have tried to summarize the issues in Steven M. Wasserstrom, "Recent Works on the 'Creative Symbiosis' of Judaism and Islam," *Religious Studies Review*, 16, 1990, pp. 42–47, and idem, *Between Muslim and Jew: The Problem of Symbiosis under Early Islam* (Princeton, N.J.: Princeton University Press, 1995).
7. For a partial bibliography, see Robert Attal, *A Bibliography of the Writings of Prof. Shelomo Dov Goitein* (Jerusalem: Israel Oriental Society/Institute of Asian and African Studies, Hebrew University of Jerusalem, 1975).

8. S. D. Goitein, "The Humanistic Aspects of Oriental Studies," *Jerusalem Studies in Arabic and Islam*, 9, 1987, pp. 1–13. This was one of the very last things from Goitein's pen.

9. For some overviews see the eulogy by Mark R. Cohen, "Goitein, the Geniza, and Muslim History," Moshe Dayan Center for Middle Eastern and African Studies, <http://www.tau.ac.il/dayancenter/mel/cohen.htm>; Gideon Libson, "Hidden Worlds and Open Shutters: S. D. Goitein between Judaism and Islam," in *The Jewish Past Revisited: Reflections on Modern Jewish Historians*, ed. David N. Myers and David B. Ruderman (New Haven: Yale University Press, 1998), pp. 163–198.

10. Eric Ormsby, "The "Born Schulmeister," *New Criterion*, 22(1), 2003, <http://www.newcriterion.com/archive/22/sep03/goitein.htm>.

11. *New York Sun*, 10 October 2005.

12. S. D. Goitein, *A Mediterranean Society: The Jewish Communities of the Arab World as Portrayed in the Documents of the Cairo Geniza*, 5 vols (Los Angeles: University of California, 1967–88). In paperback: *A Mediterranean Society: An Abridgment in One Volume* (Los Angeles: University of California Press, 1999).

13. Baruch Bendit Goitein, *Kesef Nivhar* (Prague: Baruch Bendit, 1826).

14. Review of *Guide for the Perplexed*, in the *Jewish Exponent*, 6 December 1963, p. 22.

15. See "History of the Jews in Kojetin (Kojetein) Prepared by Arthur Steiner, Engineer, in Brno (Brunn), 1929," <http://members.tripod.com/~A30s/gold1a.html>.

16. He was honored as the patron of the event.

17. "Josef Horowitz was an Orthodox Jew, the son of the Rabbi of Frankfurt. An accomplished scholar in Arabic and Islamic studies, between 1907 and 1914 he taught in the Anglo-Mohammedan Oriental College in Aligarh in India, and worked for the Indian government as director of the Islamic Inscriptions Department. From 1920 he was Professor of Semitic Languages in Frankfurt. He became one of Europe's best known Orientalists, famous particularly for his critical editions of Arabic historical texts and his research on the Koran. It was Horowitz who determined the research program of the School of Oriental Studies [of the Hebrew University] when it was established in 1926." Menahem Milson, "The Beginnings of Arabic and Islamic Studies at the Hebrew University of Jerusalem," *Judaism*, 45, 1996, pp 168–183.

18. S. D. Goitein, "Muhammad's Inspiration by Judaism," *Journal of Jewish Studies*, 9, 1958, pp. 149–162.

19. The Syriac theory has been revived by pseudonymous "Luxenberg." See Christoph Luxenberg, *Die syro-aramäische Lesart des Koran – Ein Beitrag zur Entschlüsselung der Koransprache* (Berlin: Verlag Hans Schiler, 2004).

20. Michael Brenner: *The Renaissance of Jewish Culture in Weimar Germany* (New Haven/London: Yale University Press, 1996).

21. Cited by Abraham Udovich, "Foreword," in Goitein, *A Mediterranean Society*, vol. 5, p. x.

22. Israelitische Gemeinde zu Frankfurt am Main. Vorstand, *Nachrufe auf Rabbiner N.A. Nobel, geb. 6. November 1871, gest. 24. Januar 1922* (Frankfurt am Main, 1923). He is identified as "Cand. phil. Fritz Goitein" (p. 40). Goitein refers to Rabbi Nobel as "Der Meister" (p. 42). For his role in the Jewish renaissance, see Rachel Heuberger: *Rabbiner Nehemias Anton Nobel. Die jüdische Renaissance in*

Deutschland (Frankfurt am Main: Societät, 2005). See the striking memories of the Nobel circle from Leo Lowenthal in *An Unmastered Past* (Berkeley: University of California Press, 1987), pp. 19–22.

23. *Nachrufe auf Rabbiner N.A. Nobel, geb. 6. November 1871, gest. 24. Januar 1922,* p. 43.

24. b. 1893, Krotoschin, Germany; d. 1973.

25. S. D. Goitein, "David Hartwig (Zvi) Baneth 1893–1973)," in *Studia Orientalia Memoriae D. H. Baneth Dedicata,* ed. Joseph L. Blau (Jerusalem: Magnes Press, 1979), pp. 1–5 at p. 4.

26. Martin Kramer (ed.), *The Jewish Discovery of Islam: Studies in Honor of Bernard Lewis* (Tel Aviv: Moshe Dayan Center/Syracuse University Press, 1999).

27. For al-Raschid Bey, see Paul Mendes-Flohr, "Fin-de-Siecle Orientalism, the Ostjuden and the Aesthetics of Jewish Affirmation," *Studies in Contemporary Jewry,* 1, 1984, pp. 96–139. For Essad Bey, see Tom Reiss, *The Orientalist: Solving the Mystery of a Strange and Dangerous Life* (Prince Frederick, Md.: R.B. Large Print, 2005). Ruchama Johnston-Bloom wrote her thesis at Reed College on Asad, and continues this research at the graduate level.

28. "Concubines and Puppies: Philologies of Esotericism in Jerusalem between the Wars," forthcoming in a Festschrift for Joel Kraemer to be edited by Ilai Alon and Tzvi Langermann.

29. Becker was a professor at Hamburg, Bonn, and Berlin before becoming minister of cultural affairs for the state of Prussia.

30. "The Humanistic Aspects of Oriental Studies," *Jerusalem Studies in Arabic and Islam,* 9, 1987, pp. 1–13 at p. 6.

31. For his reforms see Guido Müller, *Weltpolitische Bildung und akademische Reform. Carl Heinrich Beckers Wissenschafts- und Hochschulpolitik 1908–1930* (Cologne: Böhlau, 1991). For his colonial views and activities see Carl Heinrich Becker, *Deutsch–türkische Interessengemeinschaft* (Bonn: F. Cohen, 1914); idem, *Das türkische Bildungsproblem* (Bonn, 1916); "Der Islam und die Kolonisierung Afrikas," *Internationale Wochenschrift,* 4, 1910, pp. 227–252; idem, "Staat und Mision in der Islampolitik," *Islamstudien,* 2, 1932, pp. 211–230; idem, "Die Araber als Kolonisatoren," *Jahrbuch der deutschen Kolonien,* 7, 1914, pp. 197–206; idem, "Ist der Islam eine Gefahr für unsere Kolonien," *Koloniale Rundschau,* 1, 1909, pp. 266–293. In 1910 Becker wrote *L'Islam et la colonisation de l'Afrique: conférence faite sous le patronage de l'Union Coloniale Française le 22 janvier 1910* (Paris: Union Coloniale Française, 1910). For his work in China, see Susanne Kuß (ed.), *Carl Heinrich Becker in China. Reisebriefe des ehemaligen preußischen Kultusministers 1931/32* (Berliner China-Studien/Quellen und Dokumente Bd. 4, 2004).

32. I detail these relations in Steven M. Wasserstrom, "Hans Jonas in Marburg, 1928," in *Judaism and the Phenomenon of Life: The Legacy of Hans Jonas,* ed. Hava Samuelson and Christian Wiese (Leiden, The Netherlands: E. J. Brill, forthcoming).

33. Goitein, *A Mediterranean Society,* vol. 5, p. 497.

34. S. D. Goitein, "The Rise of the Near Eastern Bourgeoisie in Early Islamic Times," *Journal of World History,* 32, 1956– 57, pp. 583–604; idem, "Between Hellenism and Renaissance: Islam, the Intermediate Civilization," *Islamic Studies,* 2, 1963, pp. 217–233.

35. Goitein, "Between Hellenism and Renaissance," p. 228.

36. C. H. Becker, "The Origin and Character of Islamic Civilization," in *Contributions to the History of Islamic Civilization*, vol. 2, trans. S. Kuda Bukhsh (Lahore), p. 8. I deal with Becker somewhat more fully in Wasserstrom, "Hans Jonas at Marburg, 1928," in *Judaism and the Phenomenon of Life: The Legacy of Hans Jonas, Historical and Philosophical Studies*, eds. Hava Tirosh-Samuelson and Christian Wiese (Boston: Brill Academic, forthcoming).

37. See the reminiscence in the foreword to Goitein, *A Mediterranean Society*, vol. 5, p. xiv.

38. Goitein, *A Mediterranean Society*, vol. 5, p. 597, n. 49.

39. As already implicitly evoked by Arnaldo Momigliano. I once asked a student of Goitein's and he told me the following anecdote. On the boat Goitein asked Scholem, "So what is all this kabbalistic stuff about?" and Scholem replied, "I'll tell you in fifty years."

40. Goitein, *A Mediterranean Society*, vol. 5, p. 632, n. 123.

41. Ibid., p. 475.

42. S. D. Goitein, *Religion in a Religious Age* (Cambridge, Mass.: Association for Jewish Studies, 1974), p. 4.

43. Arnaldo Momigliano observed the contrast. "In September 1923 two young German Jews embarked together at Trieste on their way to settle in Palestine. One, Gerhard (Gershom) Scholem, born in 1897, was soon to become the greatest Jewish historian of our century. The other, Fritz (Shlomo Dov) Goitein, born in 1900, was perhaps slower in developing, from a conventional Arabist into a student of the Jewish–Arabic symbiosis of the Middle Ages and beyond. Yet the volumes of *A Mediterranean Society*, which Goitein started to publish in 1967, amount to a revolutionary picture founded upon new sources (mainly from the repository of documents of the old synagogue of Cairo) that bears comparison with Scholem's achievements." Arnaldo Momigliano, *On Pagans, Jews, and Christians* (Wesleyan University Press/University Press of New England, 1987), pp. 254–264.

44. See Steven M. Wasserstrom, "Jewish–Muslim Relations in the Context of Andalusian Emigration," in *Christians, Muslims and Jews in Medieval and Early Modern Spain*, ed. Mark D. Meyerson and Edward D. English (Notre Dame, Ind.: University of Notre Dame Press, 1999), pp. 69–91.

45. Ismar Schorsh, "The Myth of Sephardic Supremacy," *Leo Baeck Institute Yearbook*, 34, 1989, pp. 47–66.

46. See his telling, touching review of Rosenzweig's Halevi, in S. D. Goitein, "Franz Rosenzweig: Jehuda Halevi deutsch," *Der Jude*, 9, 1924, pp. 751–752. Even in his last years Goitein held *Der Jude* in high esteem. "This controversial but highly artistic work, with its epilogue and notes full of ideas, is recommended to everyone interested in the subject and in full command of the German language" (Goitein, *A Mediterranean Society*, vol. 5, p. 635, n. 168). In the *Der Jude* review, Goitein emphasizes Rosenzweig's *Gefühl*, the same characterization he applied to Nobel the preceding year.

47. Adam Shear describes the *Kuzari* as popular for those in transition between *yeshiva* and *maskil*. See "Judah Halevi's *Kuzari* in the Haskalah: The Reinterpretation and Re-imagining of a Medieval Work," in *Renewing the Past, Reconfiguring Jewish Culture from al-Andalus to the Haskalah*, ed. Ross Brann and Adam Sutcliffe (University Park: University of Pennsylvania Press, 2004).

48. Goitein, "Franz Rosenzweig: Jehuda Halevi deutsch", pp. 751–752.

49. S. D. Goitein, "What Would Jewish and General History Benefit by a Systematic Publication of the Documentary Geniza Papers?" *Proceedings of the American Academy for Jewish Research*, 23, 1954, pp. 29–39. For the autograph letters see S. D. Goitein, "Judaeo-Arabic Letters from Spain (Early Twelfth Century)," in *Orientalia Hispanica, sive studia F.M. Pareja octogenario dicata*, vol. 1, ed. Pareja Casanas and J. M. Barral (Leiden, The Netherlands: Brill, 1974), pp. 331–350.

50. "The Biography of Rabbi Judah Ha-Levi in the Light of the Cairo Geniza Documents," *Proceedings of the American Academy for Jewish Research*, 28, 1959, p. 42, emphasis added.

51. Goitein, *A Mediterranean Society*, p. 448, emphasis added.

52. See Milson, "The Beginnings of Arabic and Islamic Studies." For Goitein's own view, see his "Oriental Studies in Israel," in *Hebrew University Garland; a Silver Jubilee Symposium*, ed. Norman Bentwich (London: Constellation Books, 1952), pp. 96–11. See also S. D. Goitein, "The School of Oriental Studies: A Memoir," *Like All the Nations? The Life and Legacy of Judah L. Magnes*, ed. William M. Brinner and Moses Rischin (Albany: State University of New York Press, 1987), pp. 167–175.

53. Milson, "The Beginnings of Arabic and Islamic Studies," p. 5, referring to Ahmad b. Yahyâ al-Balâdhurî (d. 892), *Ansâb al-Ashrâf*, vol. 5, ed. S. D. Goitein (Jerusalem: Hebrew University Press, 1936).

54. Goitein, "Some Comparative Notes on the History of Israel and the Arabs," *Zion*, 3(2), 1937, pp. 97–117 (in Hebrew).

55. S. D. Goitein, *Studies in Islamic History and Institutions* (Leiden, The Netherlands: Brill, 1966).

56. S. D. Goitein, "Evidence on the Muslim Poll Tax from Non-Muslim Sources," *Journal of the Economic and Social History of the Orient*, 6, 1963, pp. 278–279.

57. On this comparison, see Kate Fleet, "The Mediterranean," *Journal of Early Modern History*, 6(1), 2002, pp. 63–72.

58. S. D. Goitein, "Le culte du Vendredi musulman: son arrière-plan social et économique," *Revue Annales*, 13, 1958, pp. 488–501.

59. A usage retained by the American Oriental Society and its journal, *Journal of the American Oriental Society*.

60. Goitein, *A Mediterranean Society*, vol. 5, p. 500.

61. S. D. Goitein (trans.), *Von den Juden Jemens; eine Anthologie* (Berlin: Schocken, 1934).

62. He never developed a defense of the category. "This study is called *A Mediterranean Society* because the people described in it are to a certain extent representative of their class in the Mediterranean world in general and its Arabic section in particular." Goitein, *A Mediterranean Society*, vol. 1, p. viii. W. V. Harris would seem to articulate the consensus, that Goitein's notion of a "Mediterranean society" does not "represent what scholars currently think about the history of the ancient or medieval Mediterranean – a subject that has inevitably passed into other hands." "The Mediterranean and Ancient History: in favour of a wider ethnography," in W. V. Harris, *Rethinking the Mediterranean*, ed. W. V. Harris (Oxford: Oxford University Press, 2005), pp. 38–45 at p. 30.

63. Amitav Ghosh, *In an Antique Land* (London: Granta/Penguin, 1994); and A. B. Yehoshua, *A Journey to the End of the Millennium* [*Masah El Sof Ha-Elef*] (New York: Doubleday, 1999).

64. Note the several collections of essays honoring or dedicated to S. D. Goitein: Amin Banani and Speros Vryonis, Jr. (eds.), *Individualism and Conformity in Classical Islam* (Wiesbaden: Harrassowitz, 1977); S. Morag and I. Ben-Ami (eds.), *Studies in Geniza and Sepharadi Heritage* (Jerusalem: Magnes Press, 1981); S. Morag, I. Ben-Ami, and N. A. Stillman (eds.), *Studies in Judaism and Islam* (Jerusalem: Magnes Press, 1981), both dedicated to Goitein, on the occasion of his eightieth birthday, by Misgav Yerushalayim (the Center for Research and Study of Sephardi and Oriental Jewish Heritage); R. Ahroni, *Biblical and Other Studies in Memory of S. D. Goitein* (Columbus: Ohio State University Press, 1986).

65. Stefan C Reif, *A Guide to the Taylor-Schechter Genizah Collection*, 2nd edn. (Cambridge, England: Cambridge University Library, 1979); Stefan C. Reif, *A Jewish Archive from Old Cairo* (Richmond, England: Curzon Press, 2000).

66. S. D. Goitein, "Jewish Society and Institutions under Islam," in *Jewish Society through the Ages*, ed. H. Ben-Sasson and S. Ettinger (New York: Schocken, 1975), pp. 170–185; *Jews and Arabs: Their Contacts through the Ages*, 3rd edn. (New York: Schocken, 1974).

67. Stefan C. Reif (ed.), *The Cambridge Genizah Collections: Their Contents and Significance*, vol. 1 (Cambridge, England/New York: Cambridge University Press, 2002).

68. Mark R. Cohen, *Poverty and Charity in the Jewish Community of Medieval Egypt* (Princeton, N.J.: Princeton University Press, 2005); and idem, *The Voice of the Poor in the Middle Ages: An Anthology of Documents from the Cairo Geniza* (Princeton, N.J.: Princeton University Press, 2005).

69. Mordechai Akiva Friedman, *ha-Rambam, ha-mashiah be-Teman veha-shemad* (Jerusalem: Rubin Mass, 2002) (in Hebrew).

70. Mordechai Akiva Friedman, *Jewish Marriage in Palestine: A Cairo Geniza Study* (Tel-Aviv/New York: Jewish Theological Seminary of America, 1980); idem, *Jewish Polygyny in the Middle Ages: New Documents from the Cairo Geniza* (Tel-Aviv: Bialik Institute, 1986) (in Hebrew).

71. Kathleen Biddick, "Translating the Foreskin," in *Queering the Middle Ages*, ed. Glenn Burger and Steven Kruger (Minneapolis: University of Minnesota Press, 2001), pp. 193–212.

72. His biblical studies written in Hebrew are collected in S. D. Goitein, *Studies in the Bible* (Tel Aviv: Yavneh Press, 1957). Some were translated and published posthumously. See S. D. Goitein, "The Song of Songs: A Female Composition," in *Feminist Companion to the Song of Songs*, ed. Athalya Brenner (Sheffield: Sheffield Academic Press, 1993), pp. 58–66 (originally in *Studies in the Bible*, pp. 301–307); and idem, "Women as Creators of Biblical Genres," *Prooftexts*, 8, 1988, pp. 1–33.

73. S. D. Goitein, "*Bar Talmud* – An Initiation Rite at Sixteen," *Conservative Judaism*, 15(2), 1961, pp. 28–32.

74. S. D. Goitein, "The Jewish Family in the Days of Moses Maimonides," *Conservative Judaism*, 29(1), 1974, pp. 25–35 at p. 35. Note that he says "love mitsvot," and not "practice mitsvot." That he published in *Conservative Judaism* may presumably be taken as an indicator of his own position in the matter of practice.

75. S. D. Goitein, "S. Y. Agnon: A Personal Account," in *A Memorial Tribute to Dr. Shmuel Yosef Agnon Presented by Dropsie University and the Consulate General*

of Israel, Sunday, March 29, 1970 (Philadelphia: Dropsie University, 1970), pp. 9–12.

76. Ibid., p. 12, emphasis added.

77. S. D. Goitein, "The Humanistic Aspects of Oriental Studies," *Jerusalem Studies in Arabic and Islam*, 9, 1987, pp. 1–13.

78. S. D. Goitein, "The Concept of Mankind in Islam," in *History and the Idea of Mankind*, ed. W. Warren Wager (Albquerque: University of New Mexico Press, 1971), pp. 72–91 at p. 84.

79. S. D. Goitein, "Midnight Watch (Reflections after the Holocaust)," trans. Marganit Weinberger-Rotman, *Jewish Spectator*, 48, 1983, p. 14. It was a fairly common practice among German Jews to compose verse for public and private occasions. I address this phenomenon with regard to Goitein's emigration shipmate, Gershom Scholem, in Steven M. Wasserstrom, "The Fullness of Time: Thoughts on the Poetry of Gershom Scholem," *The Fullness of Time: Poems by Gershom Scholem*, trans. Richard Sieburth (Jerusalem: Ibis Editions, 2003), pp. 13–41.

80. Ibid., p. 14, emphasis added.

81. S. D. Goitein, "Religion in Everyday Life as Reflected in the Documents of the Cairo Geniza," in *Religion in a Religious Age*, ed. S. D. Goitein (Association for Jewish Studies, 1974), pp. 3–17 at p. 17, emphasis added.

82. S. D. Goitein, "M.E.'s [sic] Future in 'Eurafrasia': Third World Power Might Extend from France to Persia," *Jerusalem Post*, 33(8737), 1957, pp. 50–52, emphasis added.

83. Goitein, "Religion in Everyday Life," p. 17, emphasis added.

84. Goitein, *A Mediterranean Society*, vol. 5, p. 502.

85. S. D. Goitein, *Kirjath Sepher*, 15, 1938–39, p. 442 (in Hebrew). As cited and translated by Daniel Frank, *Journal of Jewish Studies*, 39, 1988, p. 273.

86. S. D. Goitein, "A Jewish Addict to Sufism," *Jewish Quarterly Review*, 44, 1953, pp. 37–49.

87. P. Fenton, *The Treatise of the Pool* (London: Octagon Press, 1981); idem, "Some Judaeo-Arabic Fragments by Rabbi Abraham He-Hasid, the Jewish Sufi," *Journal of Semitic Studies*, 26, 1981, pp. 47–72; idem, "More on Rabbi Hananel, the Master of the Hasidim," *Tarbiz*, 55, 1986, pp. 77–107 (in Hebrew); idem, *Al-Murshid ila al-Tafarrud* (Jerusalem: Mekizei Nirdamim, 1987); idem, *Deux traités de mystique juive* (Paris: Verdier, 1987); reviewed by D. Frank, *Journal of Jewish Studies*, 39(2), 1988, pp. 273–276; idem, "La 'Hitbodedut' chez les premiers Qabbalistes en Orient et chez les Soufis," in *Priere, Mystique, et Judaisme*, ed. R. Goetschel (Paris: Presses Universitaires de France, 1987), pp. 133–158; idem, "Deux traités musulmans d'amour mystique en transmission judéo-arabe," *Arabica*, 37, 1990, pp. 47–55; idem, "A Judeo-Arabic Commentary on the Haftarot by Hanan'el ben Shmu'el, Abraham Maimonides' Father-in-Law," *Maimonidean Studies*, 1, 1990, pp. 27–56; idem, "The Hierarchy of the Saints in Jewish and Islamic Mysticism," *Journal of the Muhiyddin Ibn Arabi* Society, 10, 1991, pp. 12–33; idem, " 'La tête entre les genoux': Contribution à l'étude d'une posture méditative dans la mystique juive et islamique," *Revue d'histoire et de philosophie religieuses*, 72, 1992, pp. 413–426; idem, "A Mystical Treatise on Prayer and the Spiritual Quest from the Pietist Circle," *Jerusalem Studies in Arabic and Islam*, 16, 1993, pp. 137–175; idem, "A Mystical Treatise on Perfection, Providence, and Prophecy from the Jewish Sufi Circle," *The Jews of Medieval Islam*, ed. D. Frank (Leiden, The Netherlands: Brill, 1995), pp. 301–334; idem, "Solitary

Meditation in Jewish and Islamic Mysticism in the Light of a Recent Archaelogical Discovery," *Medieval Encounters,* 1(2), 1995, pp. 271–296; idem, "New Light on R. Abraham Maimonides' Doctrine of Mystical Experience," *Daat,* 50/52, 2003, pp. 107–119 (in Hebrew).

88. S. D. Goitein, "Abraham Maimonides and His Pietist Circle," *Jewish Medieval and Renaissance Studies,* ed. A. Altmann (Cambridge, Mass.: Harvard University Press, 1967), pp. 145–164 at p. 151.

89. Goitein, *A Mediterranean Society,* vol. 5, p. 476.

90. S. D. Goitein, "A New Translation of Maimonides' '*Guide for the Perplexed,*' " *Jewish Exponent,* 6 December 1963, p. 54, emphasis added.

91. Ibid., p. 75. The limitations of human knowledge is the subject of this chapter.

92. Ibid., p. 75.

93. D. H. Baneth and Joshua Blau, *Studia Orientalia memoriae D. H. Baneth dedicata* (Jerusalem: Magnes Press/Hebrew University, 1979), p. 4.

94. Goitein, "Muhammad's Inspiration by Judaism," p. 404.

95. See the now standard discussion by Joel Kraemer, *Humanism in the Renaissance of Islam: The Cultural Revial during the Buyid Age* (Leiden, The Netherlands: Brill, 1986).

96. Goitein, "Between Hellenism and Renaissance," pp. 229–230.

97. S. D. Goitein, "The Concept of Mankind in Islam," in *History and the Idea of Mankind,* ed. W. Warren Wager (Albquerque: University of New Mexico Press, 1971), pp. 72–91 at p. 89.

98. S. D. Goitein, "The Mediterranean Mind in the High Middle Ages (950–1250), As Reflected in the Cairo Geniza Documents," in *Amalfi nel medioevo: convegno internazionale, 14–16 giugno 1973* (Salerno: Centro Raffaele Guariglia di studi salernitani, 1977), pp. 179, 185.

99. Goitein, *A Mediterranean Society,* vol. 5, p. 336.

100. Steven M. Wasserstrom, "The Magical Texts in the Cairo Genizah," in *Genizah Research after Ninety Years, the Case of Judaeo-Arabic: Papers Read at the Third Congress of the Society for Judaeo-Arabic Studies,* ed. Stefan Reif and Joshua Blau (Cambridge, England/New York: Cambridge University Press, 1992), pp. 160–166; idem, "The Unwritten Chapter: Notes towards A Social and Religious History of Geniza Magic," in *Officina Magica: Essays on the Practice of Magic in Antiquity,* ed. Shaul Shaked (Leiden, The Netherlands: Brill, 2005), pp. 269–295.

101. Goitein, *A Mediterranean Society,* vol. 5, p. 599, n. 33.

102. Montaigne, "An Apology for Raymond Sebond," p. 631.

103. Goitein, "*Bar Talmud* – An Initiation Rite at Sixteen," p. 32.

104. This description from the then student Goitein was certainly an allusion to Schleiermacher. See Julia A. Lamm, "The Early Philosophical Roots of Schleiermacher's Notion of *Gefühl,* 1788–1794," *Harvard Theological Review,* 87(1), 1994, pp. 67–105.

105. Goitein, "Muhammad's Inspiration by Judaism," *Journal of Jewish Studies,* 9, 1958, pp. 149–62.

106. Goitein, *Studies in Islamic History and Institutions,* p. 78, n. 6.

107. Goitein, "Muhammad's Inspiration by Judaism," p. 152.

108. S. D. Goitein, "YHWH the Passionate: The Monotheistic Meaning and Origin of the Name YHWH," *Vetus Testamentum,* 6, 1956, pp. 1–9.

109. S. D. Goitein, *Horaat ha-'Ivrit: darkhe ha-limud ba-miktso'ot ha-'Ivriyim* (Tel-Aviv: Yavneh, 1967).
110. Goitein, "Some Comparative Notes", *Zion*, 3(2), 1937, pp. 97–117 (in Hebrew) citing English summary, pp. i–ii.
111. Goitein, *A Mediterranean Society*, vol. 5, p. 495.
112. S. D. Goitein, "Oriental Studies in Israel," in *Hebrew University Garland; a Silver Jubilee Symposium*, ed. Norman De Mattos Bentwich (London: Constellation Books, 1952), pp. 96–111 at p. 97.
113. S. D. Goitein, "The Humanistic Aspects of Oriental Studies," *Jerusalem Studies in Arabic and Islam*, 9, 1987, pp. 1–13.
114. Goitein, *A Mediterranean Society*, vol. 5, pp. 415–496.
115. Ibid., p. 498, n. 3.
116. He was not uninterested in this social type. See S. D. Goitein, "The Rise of the Near Eastern Bourgeoisie in Early Islamic Times," *Journal of World History*, 32, 1956–57, pp. 583–604.
117. Goitein, "Religion in Everyday Life," p. 8. I address this charactrization in my introduction to Wasserstrom, *Between Muslim and Jew*.
118. Goitein, *A Mediterranean Society*, vol. 5, p. 503.
119. Ibid., p. 337.
120. Goitein, "Religion in Everyday Life," p. 4.
121. Goitein, *A Mediterranean Society*, vol. 5, p. 501.
122. Ibid., p. 501.
123. Cited in Steven M. Wasserstrom, *Religion after Religion: Gershom Scholem, Mircea Eliade, and Henry Corbin at Eranos* (Princeton, N.J.: Princeton University Press, 1999), p. 114.
124. S. D. Goitein, "Political Conflict and the Use of Power in the World of the Geniza," in *Kinship and Consent: The Jewish Political Tradition and Its Contemporary Uses*, ed. Daniel J. Elazar (Washington: University Press of America, 1983), pp. 169–181 at p. 169.
125. Goitein, "Muhammad's Inspiration by Judaism," p. 162.
126. S. D. Goitein, *Jews and Arabs. Their Contacts through the Ages* (New York: Schocken Books, 1955), p. 130, emphasis added.
127. Montaigne, "Apology for Raymond Sebond," p. 493
128. Goitein, *A Mediterranean Society*, vol. 5, p. 501, emphasis added.
129. The range of this lugubrious controversy is conveniently documented in Christoph Schulte (ed.), *Deutschtum und Judentum* (Stuttgart: Reclam, 1993).
130. See S. D Goitein, "Between Hellenism and Renaissance – Islam, the Intermediate Civilization," *Islamic Studies*, 2, 1963, pp. 217–233; and, for the journalism, Goitein, "M.E.'s [sic] Future in 'Eurafrasia.' "
131. Goitein, "M.E.'s [sic] Future in 'Eurafrasia.' "
132. Michel De Montaigne, "On books," in *Complete Essays*, p. 470, in reference to Guicciardini.
133. Michel De Montaigne, "On diversion," in *Complete Essays*, p. 938.
134. Montaigne, "Apology for Raymond Sebond," p. 497.

BIBLIOGRAPHY

'Abbas, Ihsan (ed.). *A Biographical Dictionary of Sicilian Learned Men and Poets.* Beirut, Dar al-Gharb al-Islami, 1994.

Abela, Giovanfrancesco, and Giovannantonio Ciantar. *Malta illustrata, ovvero Descrizione di Malta isola del mare Siciliano e Adriatico: con le sue antichita', ed altre notizie, divisa in quattro libri.* Malta, Nella Stamperia del Palazzo di S.A.S.: Per F. Giovanni Mallia suo stampatore, 1772.

Abou-El-Haj, Rifa'at Ali. "The Formal Closure of the Ottoman Frontier in Europe," *Journal of the American Oriental Society,* 89(3), 1969, pp. 467–475.

Abraham ben Moses ben Maimon. *Sefer ha-Maspik le-ovde ha-Shem: hu Kitab kifayat al-abidin: (ha-kerekh ha-sheni mi-tokh ha-helek ha-sheni),* ed. Nissim Dana. Ramat-Gan, Israel, Universitat Bar-Ilan, 1989.

Abulafia, David. "Mediterraneans," in *Rethinking the Mediterranean,* ed. W. V. Harris. Oxford, Oxford University Press, 2005, pp. 64–93.

Ahmet Resmi, Efendi, and Ahmet Nezihi Turan. *Hamiletü'l-küberâ: Darüssaade agalar, Osmanl i tarih kaynaklar.* Istanbul, Kitabevi, 2000.

Ahroni, Reuben. *Biblical and Other Studies in Memory of S. D. Goitein, Hebrew Annual Review,* vol. 9. Columbus, Dept. of Judaic and Near Eastern Languages and Literatures, Ohio State University, 1986.

Akbari, Suzanne. "From Due East to True North: Orientalism and Orientation," in *The Postcolonial Middle Ages,* ed. Jeffrey Jerome Cohen. New York, St. Martin's Press, 2000, pp. 19–34.

Alberigo, Giuseppe, and Jacques Mignon. *Les conciles oecuméniques: les décrets. Tome II-2:Trente à Vatican II.* Paris, Ed. du Cerf, 1994.

St. Alexiou, *E Kretike Logotechneia kai e Epoche tes* [Cretan Literature and Its Era]. Athens, Stegme, 1985.

Al-Idrisi. *L'Italia descritta nel "Libro del re Ruggero,"* ed. M. Amari and C. Schiaparelli. Rome, Salviucci, 1883.

———. *Opus Geographicum*, ed. E. Cerulli. Leiden, The Netherlands, Brill, 1970.

Almosnino, Moses, and Jacob Cansino. *Extremos y grandezas de Constantinopla*. Madrid, Francisco Martinez, 1638.

Almosnino, Moses ben Baruch. *Crónica de los Reyes Otomanos, Fuente clara*, vol. 1, trans. Pilar Romeu Ferré. Barcelona, Tirocinio S.L., 1998.

Angiolini, Franco. *I Cavalieri e Il Principe*. Florence, Edifir, 1996.

Arkoun, Mohammed. "Thinking the Mediterranean Arena Today," *Diogenes*, 52(2), 2005, pp. 99–121.

Attal, Robert. *A Bibliography of the Writings of Prof. Shelomo Dov Goitein*. Jerusalem, Israel Oriental Society and the Institute of Asian and African Studies, Hebrew University of Jerusalem, 1975.

Bakhtin, M. M., and Michael Holquist. *The Dialogic Imagination: Four Essays*. Austin, University of Texas Press, 1981.

Baladhuri, Ahmad ibn Yahya. *Ansab al-ashraf li-Ahmad ibn Yahyá ibn Jabir al-Baladhuri: The ansab al- ashraf of al-Baladhuri*, ed. Max Schloessinger and S. D. Goitein. Jerusalem, Magnes Press, 1936.

Banani, Amin, and Speros Vryonis. *Individualism and Conformity in Classical Islam*. Wiesbaden, Harrassowitz, 1977.

Basset, René. "Les sources arabes de Floire et Blanchefleur," *Revue des Traditions Populaires*, 22, 1907, pp. 241–45.

Battaglia, Salvatore, and Giorgio Bàrberi Squarotti. *Grande dizionario della lingua italiana*. Turin, Unione tipografico-editrice torinese, 1961.

Becker, Carl Heinrich. *Das türkische Bildungsproblem; akademische Rede, gehalten am Geburtstag Sr. Majestät des Kaisers in der Aula der Rheinischen Friedrich-Wilhelms-Universität*. Bonn, F. Cohen, 1916.

———. "Der Islam und die Kolonisierung Afrikas," *Internationale Wochenschrift*, 4, 1910, pp. 227–252.

———. *Deutsch–türkische interessengemeinschaft, Bonner vaterländische reden u. vorträge während des krieges*, vol. 2. Bonn, F. Cohen, 1914.

———. "Die Araber als Kolonisatoren," *Jahrbuch der deutschen Kolonien*, 7, 1914, pp. 197–206.

———. "Ist der Islam eine Gefahr für unsere Kolonien," *Koloniale Rundschau*, 1, 1909, pp. 266–293.

———. "The Origin and Character of Islamic Civilization," in *Contributions to the History of Islamic Civilization*, vol. 2, trans. S. Kuda Bukhsh. Lahore.

———. "Staat und Mision in der Islampolitik," *Islamstudien*, 2, 1932, pp. 211–230.

Bel Bravo, Maria. "The Expulsion of the Spanish Jews as Seen by Christian and Jewish Chroniclers," in *The Jewish Communities of Southeastern Europe. From the Fifteenth Century to the End of World War II*, ed. I. K. Hassiotis. Thessaloniki, Institute for Balkan Studies, 1997, pp. 55–73.

Benayahu, Meir. *Rabi Eliyahu Kapsali, ish Kandiah: rav, manhig ve-historyon, Pirsume ha-Makhon le-heker ha-tefutsot; sefer 56.* Tel-Aviv, University of Tel-Aviv, 1983.

Benbassa, Esther, and Aron Rodrigue. *Sephardi Jewry: A History of the Judeo-Spanish Community, 14th–20th Centuries.* Berkeley, University of California Press, 2000.

Bennassar, Bartolomé. "Conversion ou Reniement? Modalitiés d'un Adhesion Ambiguë des Chrétiens a L'Islam (XVIe–XVIIe siècles)," *Annales ESC,* 1988, 6, pp. 1349–1366.

Berenger, Jean. "La politique ottomane de la France dans les années 1680," in *I Turchi, il Mediterraneo e l'Europa,* ed. Giovanna Motta. Milan, FrancoAngeli, 1998, pp. 269–275.

Berenson, Bernard. "Ugolino-Lorenzetti," *Art in America,* 5, 1916–17, pp. 259–275; 6, 1917–18, pp. 25–52.

Biddick, Kathleen. "Translating the Foreskin," in *Queering the Middle Ages,* ed. Glenn Burger and Steven Kruger. Minneapolis, University of Minnesota Press, 2001, pp. 193–212.

Bisaha, Nancy. "Petrarch's Vision of the Muslims and Byzantine East," *Speculum,* 76(2), 2001, pp. 284–314.

Blau, Joshua (ed.). *Studia Orientalia memoriae D. H. Baneth dedicata.* Jerusalem, Magnes Press, 1979.

Blundell, Sue, and Margaret Williamson. *The Sacred and the Feminine in Ancient Greece.* London/New York, Routledge, 1998.

Bnaya, Meir Zvi. *Mosheh Almosnino, ish Saloniki: fealav vi-yetsirato, Pirsume ha-Makhon le-heker ha-tefutsot; sefer 114.* Ramat-Aviv, Israel, University of Tel-Aviv, 1996.

Boccaccio, Giovanni. *Il Filocolo,* trans. Donald Cheney. New York, Garland, 1985.

Bonnici, Alexander. *A Trial in Front of an Inquisitor of Malta, 1562–1798.* Rabat, Malta, Religjon u Hajja, 1998.

Bono, Salvatore. "Achat d'Esclaves Turcs pour les Galeres Pontificales (XVI–XVIII siecle)," *Revue d'Occident Musulman et de la Mediterranée,* 39, 1985, pp. 79–92.

——. "Conversioni all'islam e riconciliazioni in Levante nella prima meta del Seicento," in *I Turchi, il Mediterraneo e l'Europa,* ed. Giovanna Motta. Milan, FrancoAngeli, 1998, pp. 325–339.

——. *Schiavi musulmani nell'Italia moderna: galeotti, vu' cumpra', domestici.* Naples, Edizioni scientifiche italiane, 1999.

Boon, James A. "Circumscribing Circumcision/Uncircumcision: An Essay amid the History of Difficult Description," in *Implicit Understandings: Observing. Reporting, and Reflecting on the Encounters between Europeans and Other Peoples in the Early Modern Era,* ed. Stuart B. Schwartz. Cambridge, England, Cambridge University Press, 1994, pp. 556–585.

Boussel, Patrice. *Des reliques et de leur bon usage*. Paris, Balland, 1971.

Bracciolini, Poggio, and Riccardo Fubini. *Opera omnia*. Turin, Bottega d'Erasmo, 1963.

Braude, Benjamin, "The Myth of the Sefardi Economic Superman," in *Trading Cultures: The Worlds of Western Merchants: Essays on Authority, Objectivity and Evidence*, ed. Jeremy Adelman and Stephen Aron. Turnhout, Belgium, Brepols, 2001, pp. 165–191.

Braudel, Fernand. *The Mediterranean and the Mediterranean World in the Age of Philip II*, trans. Sian Reynolds. Berkeley, University of California Press, 1972.

Brenner, Michael. *The Renaissance of Jewish Culture in Weimar Germany*. New Haven/London, Yale University Press, 1996.

Brown, Peter. "*Mohammed and Charlemagne* by Henri Pirenne," *Society and the Holy in Late Antiquity*. Berkeley, University of California Press, 1982, pp. 63–79.

Brunschvig, Robert. *La Berbérie orientale sous les Hafsides: des origines à la fin du XVe siècle*. Paris, Adrien-Maisonneuve, 1982.

Bruzelius, Caroline. "Charles I, Charles II, and the Development of an Angevin Style in the Kingdom of Sicily," in *L'État Angevin: Pouvoir, culture et société entre XIIIe et XIVe siècle*. Rome, École Française de Rome, Palais Farnèse, 1998, pp. 99–114.

Brydone, Patrick, and William Beckford. *Tour through Sicily and Malta: In a Series of Letters to William Beckford, Esq. of Somerly in Suffolk*. London, Strahan & Cadell, 1773.

Bukhsh, S. K. *Contributions to the History of Islamic Civilization*, 2nd edn. Calcutta, 1929 (reprinted Lahore, Accurate Printers, n.d.).

Bulliet, Richard. *The Case for Islamo-Christian Civilization*. New York, Columbia University Press, 2004.

Bynum, Caroline Walker. *Holy Feast and Holy Fast: The Religious Significance of Food to Medieval Women*. Berkeley, University of California Press, 1988.

Cahen, Claude. *Orient et Occident au temps des Croisades, Collection historique*. Paris, Aubier Montaigne, 1983.

Camerani, S. "Contributo alla storia dei trattati commerciali fra la Toscana e I Turchi," *Archivio Storico Italiano*, 97(2), 1939, pp. 83–101.

Capsali, Elijah, and Sultan Sultan-Bohbot. *Chronique de l'expulsion: Seder Eliahou zouta, Toledot-Judaïsmes*. Paris, Editions du Cerf, 1994.

Cassidy, Brendan. "A Relic, Some Pictures, and the Mothers of Florence in the Late Fourteenth Century," *Gesta*, 30, 1991, pp. 91–99.

——. "The Assumption of the Virgin on the Tabernacle of Orsanmichele," *Journal of the Warburg and Courtauld Institutes*, 51, 1988, pp. 174–180.

Chapoutot-Remadi, Mounira. "Tunis," in *Grandes villes méditerranéennes du monde musulman médiéval*, ed. Jean-Claude Garcin. Rome, Ecole française de Rome, 2000, pp. 235–362.

Cioni, Alfredo. *Bibliografia delle sacre rappresentazioni*. Florence, Sansoni, 1961.

Cohen, Mark R. "Goitein, the Geniza, and Muslim History," Moshe Dayan Center for Middle Eastern and African Studies, <http://www.tau.ac.il/dayancenter/mel/cohen.htm>.

——. *Poverty and Charity in the Jewish Community of Medieval Egypt: Jews, Christians, and Muslims from the Ancient to the Modern World*. Princeton, N.J., Princeton University Press, 2005.

——. *The Voice of the Poor in the Middle Ages: An Anthology of Documents from the Cairo Geniza*. Princeton, N.J., Princeton University Press, 2005.

Cohn, Samuel Kline. *The Cult of Remembrance and the Black Death: Six Renaissance Cities in Central Italy*. Baltimore, Johns Hopkins University Press, 1997.

Cole, Bruce, and Adelheid Medicus Gealt. "A New Triptych by Niccolò and a Problem," *Burlington Magazine*, 119, 1977, pp. 184–187.

Constable, Olivia Remie. *Housing the Stranger in the Mediterranean World: Lodging, Trade, and Travel in Late Antiquity and the Middle Ages*. Cambridge, England, Cambridge University Press, 2003.

Cutler, Anthony. "From Loot to Scholarship: Changing Modes in the Italian Response to Byzantine Artifacts, ca. 1200–1750," *Dumbarton Oaks Papers*, 49, 1995, pp. 237–267.

D'Ancona, Alessandro. *La legenda della reina Rosanna e di Rosana, sua figlivola*. Livorno, Pei tipi di F. Vigo, 1871.

——. *Sacre rappresentazioni dei secoli XIV, XV e XVI*. Florence, Successori Le Monnier, 1872.

D'Ascia, Luca. *Il corano e la tiara: l'epistola a Maometto di Enea Silvio Piccolomini (papa Pio II): introduzione ed edizione*. Bologna, Pendragon, 2001.

Davis, Robert C. *Christian Slaves, Muslim Masters: White Slavery in the Mediterranean, the Barbary Coast, and Italy, 1500–1800*. Basingstoke, England/New York, Palgrave Macmillan, 2003.

——. "Counting European Slaves on the Barbary Coast," *Past & Present*, 172, 2001, pp. 87–124.

Delehaye, Hippolyte, and Paul Peeters. *The Legends of the Saints*. London, G. Chapman, 1962.

Dennett, Daniel C., Jr. "Pirenne and Muhammad," *Speculum*, 23, 1948, pp. 165–190.

Derenzini, Giovanna. "Esama paleografico del Codice X.IV.1 della Biblioteca Communale degli Intronati e Contributo Documentale alla Storia del 'Tesoro' dello Spedale de Santa Maria della Scala," *Annali della Facoltà di lettere e filosofia – Università di Siena*, 8, 1978, pp. 41–76.

——. "Il codice X.IV.1 della Biblioteca Communale degli Intronati di Siena," *Milion*, 1, 1988, pp. 307–325.

204 *A Faithful Sea*

————. "Le reliquie da Constantinopoli a Siena, " *L'Oro di Siena: Il Tesoro di Santa Maria della Scala*. Milano, Skira, 1996.

Di Clari, Robert. "The History of Them that Took Constantinople," ch. 81, in *Three Old French Chronicles of the Crusades*, ed. and trans. Edward N. Stone (Seattle, University of Washington Press, 1939).

Doumerc, Bernard. *Venise et l'émirat hafside de Tunis (1231–1535)*. Paris, L'Harmattan, 1999.

Dufourcq, Charles Emmanuel. *L'Espagne catalane et le Maghrib aux XIIIe et XIVe siècles, de la bataille de Las Navas de Tolosa (1212) à l'avènement du sultan merinide Abou-l-Hazzan (1331)*. Paris, Presses universitaires de France, 1966.

Dursteler, E. *Venetians in Constantinople: Nation, Identity and Coexistence in the Early Modern Mediterranean*. Baltimore, Johns Hopkins University Press, 2006.

Earle, Peter. "The Commercial Development of Ancona, 1479–1551," *Economic History Review*, 22(1), 1969, pp. 28–44.

Egidi, Pietro. *La colonia saracena di Lucera e la sua distruzione*. Naples, Pierro, 1915.

Eickhoff, Ekkehard, and Rudolf Eickhoff. *Venedig, Wien und die Osmanen: Umbruch in Südosteuropa 1645–1700*, 2nd edn. Munich, Callwey, 1973.

Elliott, J. K. *The Apocryphal New Testament: A Collection Of Apocryphal Christian Literature in an English Translation*. Oxford, Clarendon Press, 1993.

Emmanuel, Isaac Samuel. *Histoire des Israélites de Salonique: T. 1. (140 av. J.-C. à 1640): histoire sociale, économique et littéraire de la Ville Mère en Israel ... contenant un supplément ... l'Histoire de l'industrie des tissus des Israélites de Salonique*. Thonon, France, Lipschutz, 1936.

Engels, Marie-Christine, *Merchants, Interlopers, Seamen and Corsairs: The Flemish Community in Livorno and Genoa (1615–1635)*. Hilversum, Verleron, 1997.

Ettinger, Samuel, and Haim Hillel Ben-Sasson. *Jewish Society through the Ages*. New York, Schocken Books, 1971.

Evans, Helen C., and Metropolitan Museum of Art. *Byzantium: Faith and Power (1261–1557)*. New York, Metropolitan Museum of Art, 2004.

Faroqhi, Suraiya. "Introduction, or Why and How One Might Want to Study Ottoman Clothes," in *Ottoman Costumes: From Textile to Identity*, ed. Suraiya Faroqhi and Christoph K. Neumann. Istanbul, Eren, 2004, pp. 15–48.

Fenton, Paul. "A Judeo-Arabic Commentary on the Haftarot by Hanan'el ben Shmu'el, Abraham Maimonides' Father-in-Law," *Maimonidean Studies*, 1, 1990, pp. 27–56.

——. "A Mystical Treatise on Perfection, Providence, and Prophecy from the Jewish Sufi Circle," in *The Jews of Medieval Islam*, ed. D. Frank. Leiden, The Netherlands, Brill, 1995, pp. 301–334.

——. "A Mystical Treatise on Prayer and the Spiritual Quest from the Pietist Circle," *Jerusalem Studies in Arabic and Islam*, 16, 1993, pp. 137–175.

——. *Deux traités de mystique juive*. Paris, Verdier, 1987.

——. "Deux traités musulmans d'amour mystique en transmission judéo-arabe," *Arabica*, 37, 1990, pp. 47–55.

——. "The Hierarchy of the Saints in Jewish and Islamic Mysticism," *Journal of the Muhyiddin Ibn Arabi Society*, 10, 1991, pp. 12–33.

——. "La 'Hitbodedut' chez les premiers Qabbalistes en Orient et chez les Soufis," *Priere, Mystique, et Judaisme*, ed. R. Goetschel. Paris, Presses Universitaires de France, 1987, pp. 133–158.

——. "'La tête entre les genoux': Contribution à l'étude d'une posture méditative dans la mystique juive et islamique, *Revue d'histoire et de philosophie religieuses*, 72, 1992, pp. 413–426.

——. "More on Rabbi Hananel, the Master of the Hasidim," *Tarbiz*, 55, 1986, pp. 77–107 (in Hebrew).

——. "New Light on R. Abraham Maimonides' Doctrine of Mystical Experience," *Daat*, 50/52, 2003, pp. 107–119 (in Hebrew).

——. "Solitary Meditation in Jewish and Islamic Mysticism in the Light of a Recent Archaelogical Discovery," *Medieval Encounters*, 1–2, 1995, pp. 271–296.

——. "Some Judaeo-Arabic Fragments by Rabbi Abraham He-Hasid, the Jewish Sufi," *Journal of Semitic Studies*, 26, 1981, pp. 47–72.

——. "The Hierarchy of the Saints in Jewish and Islamic Mysticism," *Journal of the Muhyiddin Ibn Arabi Society*, 10, 1991, pp. 12–33.

Fentress, James, and Elizabeth Fentress. "The Hole in the Doughnut," *Past and Present*, 173, 2001, pp. 203–219.

Fischer, Joschka. *Die Rückkehr der Geschichte: die Welt nach dem 11. September und die Erneuerung des Westens*. Cologne, Kiepenheuer & Witsch, 2005.

Fleet, Kate. *European and Islamic Trade in the Early Ottoman State: The Merchants of Genoa and Turkey*. Cambridge, England, Cambridge University Press, 1999.

——. "The Mediterranean," *Journal of Early Modern History*, 6(1), 2002, pp. 63–72.

Fleischer, Cornell. "The Lawgiver as Messiah," *Soliman le Magnifique et son temps*, ed. Gilles Veinstein. Paris, Documentation francaise, 1992, pp. 159–177.

Fleming, K. E. "The Question of Union and the Fall of Constantinople," *Modern Greek Studies Yearbook*, 12–13, 1996–97, pp. 35–48.

Fontenay, Michel. "L'empire ottoman et le risque corsaire au XVIIe siècle," *Revue d'histoire moderne et contemporaine*, 32, 1985, pp. 185–208.

——. "La Place de la course dans l'economie portuaire: l'example de Malte et des Ports Barbaresques," *Annales ESC*, 1988, 6, pp. 1321–1347.

Fowden, Garth. *Empire to Commonwealth: The Consequences of Monotheism in Late Antiquity*. Princeton, N.J., Princeton University Press, 1994.

——. "Varieties of Religious Community," in *Interpreting Late Antiquity. Essays on the Postclassical World*, ed. G. W. Bowersock, Peter Brown, and Oleg Grabar. Cambridge, Mass., Harvard University Press, 2001, pp. 82–106.

Frattarelli Fischer, Lucia. "Alle Radici di Una Identita Composita. La 'Nazione' Greca a Livorno," in *Le Iconostasi di Livorno: Patrimonio iconografico post-bizantino*, ed. Gaetano Passarelli. Livorno, Comune di Livorno, 2001, pp. 49–59.

Frazee, Charles A. *Catholics and Sultans: The Church and the Ottoman Empire, 1453–1923*. London/New York, Cambridge University Press, 1983.

Friedman, Mordechai Akiva. *ha-Rambam, ha-mashiah be-Teman veha-shemad*. Jerusalem, Mekhon Ben-Tsevi le-heker kehilot Yisrael ba-Mizrah, Yad Yitshak Ben-Tsevi veha-Universitah ha-Ivrit bi-Yerushalayim, 2002.

——. *Ribui nashim be-Yisrael: mekorot hadashim mi-Genizat Kahir*. Jerusalem, Mosad Byalik be-shituf im Bet-ha-sefer le-madae ha-Yahadut a. sh. Hayim Rozenberg Universitat Tel-Aviv, 1986.

——. *Jewish Marriage in Palestine: A Cairo Geniza Study*. Tel-Aviv, Jewish Theological Seminary of America, 1980.

Fusaro, Maria, "Les Anglais et les Grecs. Un réseau de coopération commerciale en Méditerranée vénitienne," *Annales*, 58(3), 2003, pp. 605–626.

Galletti, Anne Imelde. "Storie della Sacra Cintola (Schede per un lavoro da fare a Prato)," in *Toscana e Terrasanta nel Medioevo*, ed. Franco Cardini. Florence, Alinea, 1982, pp. 317–338.

Garin, Eugenio. *Lo zodiaco della vita: la polemica sull'astrologia dal Trecento al Cinquecento*, 2nd edn. Rome/Bari, Laterza, 1982.

Geddes, Sharon S. "The Middle English Poem of Floriz and Blauncheflur and the Arabian Nights Tale of 'Ni'amah and Naomi': A Study in Parallels," *Emporia State Research Studies*, 19(1), 1970, pp. 14–24.

Gerber, Jane S. *The Jews of Spain: A History of the Sephardic Experience*. New York, Free Press, 1992.

Al-Ghassani, Mohammad ibn 'Abd al-Wahab. "Rihlat al-Wazir fi Iftikak al-Asir," in *In the Lands of the Christians: Arabic Travel Writing in the Seventeenth Century*, ed. Nabil Matar. New York, Routledge, 2003, pp. 113–196.

Ghosh, Amitav. *In an Antique Land*. New York, Vintage Books, 1994.

Ginzburg, Carlo. *The Cheese and the Worms: The Cosmos of a Sixteenth-Century Miller*. Baltimore, Johns Hopkins University Press, 1992.

Gioja, Melchiorre. *Del merito e delle ricompense: trattato storico e filosofico*. Lugano, Tip. della Svizzera italiana, 1848.

Goitein, Baruch Bendit. *Kesef nivhar*. New York, Be-dafos A. Z. W. Salat, 1945.

Goitein, Shlomo Dov. *A Mediterranean Society: The Jewish Communities of the Arab World as Portrayed in the Documents of the Cairo Geniza*, 6 vols. Berkeley, University of California Press, 1967–93.

——. "A Jewish Addict to Sufism," *Jewish Quarterly Review*, 44, 1953, pp. 37–49.

——. "A New Translation of Maimonides' 'Guide for the Perplexed,'" *Jewish Exponent*, 6 December 1963, p. 54.

——. "Abraham Maimonides and His Pietist Circle," in *Jewish Medieval and Renaissance Studies*, ed. A. Altmann. Cambridge, Mass., Harvard University Press, 1967, pp. 145–164.

——. "Between Hellenism and Renaissance: Islam, the Intermediate Civilization," *Islamic Studies*, 2, 1963, pp. 217–233.

——. "*Bar Talmud* – An Initiation Rite at Sixteen," *Conservative Judaism*, 15(2), 1961, pp. 28–32.

——. "David Hartwig (Zvi) Baneth 1893–1973," in *Studia Orientalia Memoriae D. H. Baneth Dedicata*, ed. Joseph L. Blau. Jerusalem: Magnes Press/Hebrew University, 1979, pp. 1–5.

——. "Evidence on the Muslim Poll Tax from Non-Muslim Sources," *Journal of the Economic and Social History of the Orient*, 6, 1963, pp. 278–279.

——. "Franz Rosenzweig: Jehuda Halevi deutsch," *Der Jude*, 9, 1924, pp. 751–752.

——. *Horaat ha-Ivrit be-Erets-Yisrael*. Tel Aviv, Yavneh, 1945.

——. *Iyunim ba-Mikra: behinato ha-sifrutit veha-hevratit*. Tel Aviv, Yavneh, 1957.

——. *Jews and Arabs: Their Contacts through the Ages*, 3rd edn. New York, Schocken Books, 1974.

——. "Judaeo-Arabic Letters from Spain (Early Twelfth Century)," in *Orientalia Hispanica, sive studia F. M. Pareja octogenario dicata*, ed. J. M. Barral. Leiden, The Netherlands, Brill, 1974.

——. "Le culte du Vendredi musulman: son arrière-plan social et économique," *Revue Annales*, 13, 1958.

——. "M.E.'s [sic] Future in 'Eurafrasia': Third World Power Might Extend from France to Persia," *Jerusalem Post*, 33(8737), 1957, pp. 50–52.

——. "Oriental Studies in Israel," in *Hebrew University Garland; a Silver Jubilee Symposium*, ed. Norman Bentwich. London, Constellation Books, 1952, pp. 96–111.

——. "Political Conflict and the Use of Power in the World of the Geniza," in *Kinship and Consent*, ed. Daniel J. Elazar. Washington, University Press of America, 1983, pp. 169–181.

——. "Religion in Everyday Life as Reflected in the Documents of the Cairo Geniza," in *Religion in a Religious Age*, ed. S. D. Goitein. Cambridge, Mass, Association for Jewish Studies, 1974, pp. 3–17.

——. "S. Y. Agnon: A Personal Account," in *A Memorial Tribute to Dr. Shmuel Yosef Agnon Presented by Dropsie University and the Consulate General of Israel, Sunday, March 29, 1970*. Philadelphia, Dropsie University, 1970, pp. 9–12.

——. "The Biography of Rabbi Judah Ha-Levi in the Light of the Cairo Geniza Documents," *Proceedings of the American Academy for Jewish Research*, 28, 1959, p. 42.

——. "The Concept of Mankind in Islam," in *History and the Idea of Mankind*, ed. W. Warren Wager. Albquerque, University of New Mexico Press, 1971, pp. 72–91.

——. "The Humanistic Aspects of Oriental Studies," *Jerusalem Studies in Arabic and Islam*, 9, 1987, pp. 1–13.

——. "The Jewish Family in the Days of Moses Maimonides," *Conservative Judaism*, 29(1), 1974, pp. 25–35.

——. "The Magical Texts in the Cairo Genizah," in *Genizah Research after Ninety Years, the Case of Judaeo-Arabic: Papers Read at the Third Congress of the Society for Judaeo-Arabic Studies*, ed. Stefan Reif and Joshua Blau. Cambridge, England/New York, Cambridge University Press, 1992, pp. 160–166.

——. "The Mediterranean and Ancient History: In Favour of a Wider Ethnography," in *Rethinking the Mediterranean*, ed. W. V. Harris. Oxford, Oxford University Press, 2005, pp. 38–45.

——. "The Mediterranean Mind in the High Middle Ages (950–1250), as Reflected in the Cairo Geniza Documents," in *Amalfi Nel Medioevo: Convegno Internazionale, 14–16 Giugno 1973*. Salerno, Centro Raffaele Guariglia di studi salernitani, 1977, pp. 179–192.

——. "The Rise of the Near Eastern Bourgeoisie in Early Islamic Times," *Journal of World History*, 32, 1956–57, pp. 583–604.

——. "The School of Oriental Studies: A Memoir," in *Like All the Nations? The Life and Legacy of Judah L. Magnes*, ed. William M. Brinner and Moses Rischin. Albany, State University of New York Press, 1987, pp. 167–175.

——. "The Song of Songs: A Female Composition," in *Feminist Companion to the Song of Songs*, ed. Athalya Brenner. Sheffield, Sheffield Academic Press, 1993, pp. 58–66.

——. "The Unwritten Chapter: Notes towards a Social and Religious History of Geniza Magic," in *Officina magica: Essays on the Practice of Magic in*

Antiquity, ed. Shaul Shaked. Leiden, The Netherlands, Brill, 2005. Translated as "Ha-Perek She-Terem Nikhtav. Haarot Historia Hevratit ve-Datit shel Ha-Magia Ha-Musmachi Genizat Kahir," *Pe'amin*, 85, 2000, pp. 43–61.

——. *Von den Juden Jemens; eine anthologie.* Berlin, Schocken Verlag, 1934.

——. "What Would Jewish and General History Benefit by a Systematic Publication of the Documentary Geniza Papers?" *Proceedings of the American Academy for Jewish Research*, 23, 1954, pp. 29–39.

——. "YHWH the Passionate: The Monotheistic Meaning and Origin of the Name YHWH," *Vetus Testamentum*, 6, 1956, pp. 1–9.

——, and Association for Jewish Studies. *Religion in a Religious Age.* Cambridge, Mass., Association for Jewish Studies, 1974.

——, and Gustave E. von Grunebaum Center for Near Eastern Studies. *A Mediterranean Society: The Jewish Communities of the Arab world as Portrayed in the Documents of the Cairo Geniza, Economic Foundations.* Berkeley/Los Angeles, University of California Press, 1967.

——, Shelomo Morag and Issachar Ben-Ami. *Studies in Geniza and Sepharadi Heritage.* Jerusalem, Magnes Press, 1981.

——, ——, ——, and Norman A. Stillman. *Studies in Judaism and Islam.* Jerusalem, Magnes Press Hebrew University, 1981.

Goodman, Lenn Evan. *Islamic Humanism.* New York, Oxford University Press, 2003.

Gourdin, Philippe. "Les marchands étrangers ont-ils un statut de dhimmi? A propos de quelques statuts de marchands étrangers dans les pays chrétiens et musulmans de Méditerranée occidentale au XIIIe siècle," in *Migrations et diasporas méditerranéennes (Xe–XVIe siècles)*, ed. Michel Balard and Alain Ducellier, Paris, Publications de la Sorbonne, 2002, pp. 435–446.

Greene, M. "Beyond the Northern Invasions: The Mediterranean in the Seventeenth Century," *Past and Present*, 174, February 2002, pp. 40–72.

——. "Resurgent Islam (1500–1700)," in *The Mediterranean in History*, ed. David Abulafia. London, Thames & Hudson, 2003, pp. 219–250.

——. *A Shared World: Christians and Muslims in the Early Modern Mediterranean.* Princeton, N.J., Princeton University Press, 2000.

Grieve, Patricia E. *Floire and Blancheflor and the European Romance.* Cambridge, England/New York, Cambridge University Press, 1997.

Guillot, C., D. Lombard, and R. Ptak. *From the Mediterranean to the China Sea: Miscellaneous Notes.* Wiesbaden, Harrassowitz, 1998.

Gutas, Dmitri. *Greek Thought, Arab Culture: The Graeco-Arabic Translation Movement in Baghdad and Early 'Abbasid Society.* London, Routledge, 1998.

210 *A Faithful Sea*

Hankins, James. "Renaissance Crusaders: Humanist Crusade Literature in the Age of Mehmed II," *Dumbarton Oaks Papers*, 49, 1995, pp. 111–207.

Hanna, Nelly. *Making Big Money in 1600: The Life and Times of Ismail Abu Taqiyya, Egyptian Merchant*. Cairo, American University in Cairo Press, 1998.

Harris, W. V. "The Mediterranean and the Ancient World," in *Rethinking the Mediterranean*, ed. W. V. Harris. Oxford, Oxford University Press, 2005, pp. 1–40.

Hathaway, Jane. *The Politics of Households in Ottoman Egypt: The Rise of the Qazdaglis*. New York, Cambridge University Press, 1997.

Hattox, Ralph S. *Coffee and Coffeehouses: The Origins of a Social Beverage in the Medieval Near East*. Seattle, University of Washington Press, 1988.

Hetherington, Paul. "A Purchase of Byzantine Relics and Reliquaries in Fourteenth-Century Venice," *Arte Venete*, 37, 1983, pp. 9–30.

———. "Byzantine Enamels on a Venetian Book-Cover," *Cahiers archéologiques*, 27, 1978, pp 117–145.

Heuberger, Rachel. *Rabbiner Nehemias Anton Nobel: die jüdische Renaissance in Frankfurt am Main*. Frankfurt am Main, Societäts-Verlag, 2005.

Heyberger, Bernard. *Les chrétiens du Proche-Orient au temps de la réforme catholique: Syrie, Liban, Palestine, XVIIIe siècles*. Rome, Ecole française de Rome, 1994.

Heyd, Uriel, and V. L. Ménage. *Studies in Old Ottoman Criminal Law*. Oxford, Clarendon Press, 1973.

Hitzel, Frederic. "Osman Aga, captif ottoman dans l'empire des Habsbourg a la fin du XVIIe siecle," *Turcica*, 33, 2001, pp. 191–212.

Hodges, Richard, and David Whitehouse. *Mohammed, Charlemagne and the Origins of Europe*. Ithaca, N.Y., Cornell University Press, 1983.

Hodgson, Marshall. *The Venture of Islam: Conscience and History in a World Civilization*, vol. 1, *The Classical Age of Islam*. Chicago, University of Chicago Press, 1974.

Horden, Peregrine, and Nicholas Purcell. *The Corrupting Sea: A Study of Mediterranean History*. Oxford, Blackwell, 2000.

———. "Four Years of Corruption: A Response to Critics," in *Rethinking the Mediterranean*, ed. W. V. Harris. Oxford, Oxford University Press, 2005, pp. 348–376.

Howard, Deborah. *Venice & the East: The Impact of the Islamic World on Venetian Architecture, 1100–1500*. New Haven, Yale University Press, 2000.

Huntington, Samuel P. "The Clash of Civilizations?" *Foreign Affairs*, 72, 1993, pp. 22–49.

———. *The Class of Civilizations and the Remaking of World Order*. New York, Simon & Schuster, 1996.

Ibn Jubayr, Muhammad ibn Ahmad, William Wright, and M. J. de Goeje. *The Travels of Ibn Jubayr.* Leiden, The Netherlands, A. J. Brill, 1907.

Inalcik, Halil. "Imtiyâzât," in *Encyclopaedia of Islam,* 2nd edn. Leiden, The Netherlands, Brill, 1971.

——. *The Ottoman Empire: The Classical Age, 1300–1600.* London, Weidenfeld & Nicolson, 1973.

——. "Jews in the Ottoman Economy and Finances, 1450–1500," in *The Islamic World from Classical to Modern Times: Essays in Honor of Bernard Lewis,* ed. C. E. Bosworth, Charles Issawi, et al. Princeton, N.J., Darwin Press, 1989, pp. 513–550.

——. "Ottoman Galata 1453–1553," in *Premiere Recontre Internationale sur l'Empire ottoman et la Turquie moderne : Institut national des langues et civilisations orientales, Maison des sciences de l'homme, 18-22 janvier 1985,* ed. Edhem Eldem. Istanbul, Editions ISIS, 1991, pp. 17–116.

Israelitische Gemeinde zu Frankfurt am Main. "Vorstand," in *Nachrufe auf Rabbiner N. A. Nobel, geb. 6. November 1871, gest. 24. Januar 1922.* Frankfurt am Main: Vorstand der Israelitischen Gemeinde, 1923.

Jacoby, D. "La population de Constantinople a l'époque Byzantine: un probleme de demographie urbain," *Byzantion,* 31, 1961, pp. 81–109.

Jacov, Marko. *Le missioni cattoliche nei Balcani tra le due grandi guerre: Candia (1645–1669), Vienna e Morea (1683–1699).* Vatican City, Biblioteca apostolica vaticana, 1998.

Jennings, Ronald C. *Christians and Muslims in Ottoman Cyprus and the Mediterranean World, 1571–1640.* New York, New York University Press, 1993.

Johns, Jeremy. *Arabic Administration in Norman Sicily: The Royal Diwan.* Cambridge, England, Cambridge University Press, 2002.

Kafadar, C. "A Death in Venice: Anatolian Muslim Merchants Trading in the Serenissima," *Journal of Turkish Studies,* 10, 1987, pp. 191–218.

Kaklamanes, St., "Markos Defaranas (1503–1575)," *Thesaurismata,* 21, 1991, pp. 210–315.

Kapsali, Elijahu Ben-Älqana, and Aryeh Shmuelevitz. *Seder Eliyahu Zuta: History of the Ottomans and of Venice and that of the Jews in Turkey, Spain and Venice.* Jerusalem, Ben-Zvi Institute of Yad Ben-Zvi, 1977.

Kedar, B. Z. *Crusade and Mission: European Approaches toward the Muslims.* Princeton, N.J., Princeton University Press, 1984.

Keomiwrchean, Eremia, Avedis Krikor Sanjian, and Andreas Tietze. *Eremya Chelebi Kömürjian's Armeno-Turkish Poem "The Jewish Bride."* Wiesbaden, Harrassowitz, 1981.

Kinoshita, Sharon. "In the Beginning Was the Road: Floire et Blancheflor and the Politics of Translation," in *The Medieval Translator,* ed. Rosalynn Voaden, René Tixier, Teresa Sanchez Roura, and Jenny Rebecca Rytting, vol. 8. Turnhout, Belgium, Brepols, 2003, pp. 223–234.

Kraemer, Joel L. *Humanism in the Renaissance of Islam: The Cultural Revival during the Buyid Age*, 2nd edn. Leiden, The Netherlands/New York, Brill, 1992.

Kucher, Michael P. *The Water Supply System of Siena, Italy: The Medieval Roots of the Modern Networked City*. New York, Routledge, 2005.

Kuttner, Stephan. "Raymond of Penyafort as Editor: The 'Decretales' and 'Constitutiones' of Gregory IX," *Bulletin of Medieval Canon Law*, 12, 1982, pp. 65–80.

Laiou, Angeliki. "Italy and the Italians in the Political Geography of the Byzantines (14th Century)," *Dumbarton Oaks Papers*, 49, 1995, pp. 73–98.

Laiou-Thomadakis, Angeliki. "The Byzantine Economy in the Mediterranean Trade System: Thirteenth–Fifteenth Centuries," *Dumbarton Oaks Papers*, 34–35, 1980–81.

Lamm, Julia A. "The Early Philosophical Roots of Schleiermacher's Notion of *Gefühl*, 1788–1794," *Harvard Theological Review*, 87(1), 1994, pp. 67–105.

Lane, Frederic. *Venice: A Maritime Republic*. Baltimore, Johns Hopkins University Press, 1973.

Lea, Henry Charles. *The Inquisition in the Spanish Dependencies: Silicy–Naples–Sardinia–Milan–the Canaries–Mexico–Peru–New Granada*. New York, Macmillan, 1908.

Leon, G. "The Greek Merchant Marine 1453–1850," in *The Greek Merchant Marine*, ed. Stelios Papadopoulos. Athens, National Bank of Greece, 1972, pp. 13–52.

Lévi-Provençal, Évariste. "Une héroine de la resistance musulmane en Sicile au début du XIIIᵉ siècle," *Oriente moderno*, 34, 1954, pp. 283–288.

Levy, Avigdor. *The Sephardim in the Ottoman Empire*. Princeton, N.J., Darwin Press, 1992.

Levy, Rafael, Stefan Reif, and Cambridge University Library. *A Priceless Collection – the Taylor–Schechter Genizah Fragments*. Cambridge, England, Cambridge University Library, 1979.

Lewis, Bernard. *What Went Wrong? Western Impact and Middle East Response*. New York, Oxford University Press, 2002.

——, and Martin S. Kramer. *The Jewish Discovery of Islam: Studies in Honor of Bernard Lewis*. Tel Aviv, Moshe Dayan Center for Middle Eastern and African Studies, Tel Aviv University, 1999.

Libson, Gideon W. "Hidden Worlds and Open Shutters: S. D. Goitein between Judaism and Islam," in *The Jewish Past Revisited: Reflections on Modern Jewish Historians*, ed. David N. Myers and David B. Ruderman. New Haven, Yale University Press, 1998, pp. 163–198.

Longo, Carlo. *Magister Raimundus: atti del Convegno per il IV centenario della canonizzazione di San Raimondo de Penyafort, 1601–2001*. Rome, Istituto storico domenicano, 2002.

Luxenberg, Christoph. *Die syro-aramäische Lesart des Koran: ein Beitrag zur Entschlüsselung der Koransprache.* Berlin, Hans Schiler, 2004.

Maier, Christopher T. "Crusade and Rhetoric against the Muslim Colony of Lucera: Eudes of Châteauroux's *Sermones de Rebellione Sarracenorum Lucherie in Apulia*," *Journal of Medieval History*, 21, 1995, pp. 343–385.

Mallette, Karla. *The Kingdom of Sicily 1100–1250: A Literary History.* Philadelphia, University of Pennsylvania Press, 2005.

Maltezou, Ch. "The Historical and Social Context," in *Literature and Society in Renaissance Crete*, ed. D. Holton. Cambridge, England, Cambridge University Press, 1991.

———. "E Krete ste diarkeia tes periodou tes venetokratias" [Crete during the Period of Venetian Rule], in *Krete: Istoria kai Politismos* [Crete: History and Civilization], ed. N. Panayiotakes. Herakleion, Greece, Vikelaia, 1988, pp. 105–162.

Manousakas, M. I. "E en Veneteia Hellenikes Koinotetas kai oi Metropolitai Filadelphias" [The Greek Community in Venice and the Metropolitans of Philadelphia], *Epeteris Etaireia Byzantinon Spoudon*, 37, 1969–70, pp. 170–210.

———. "Episkopese tes Istorias tes Ellenikes Orthodokses Afelfotetas tes Venetias (1498–1953)" [An Overview of the History of the Greek Fraternity in Venice 1498–1953], *Ta Historika*, 6(11), 1989, pp. 243–264.

———. "Grammata Patriarchon kai Metropoliton tou 16 Aiona ek tou Archeiou tes en Venetia Ellenikes Adelfotetas" [Letters of Patriarchs and of Metropolitans in the Sixteenth Century from the Archives of the Greek Fraternity in Venice], *Thesaurismata*, 5, 1968, pp. 7–22.

Mansfield, M. *The Tale of Queen Rosana: and of Rosana Her Daughter and of the King's Son Aulimento.* London, D. Nutt, 1909.

Mansouri, Tahar. "Vie portuaire à Tunis au bas Moyen Âge (XII–XVe siècle)," *Journal of Oriental and African Studies*, 9, 1998, pp. 39–52.

Mantran, Robert. *Histoire de l'Empire Ottoman.* Paris, Fayard, 1989.

Marchini, Giuseppe. "Vicende di una pala," in *Studies in late Medieval and Renaissance Painting in Honor of Millard Meiss*, edited by Irving Lavin and John Plummer. New York, New York University Press, 1977, pp. 320–324.

Marsili, Luigi Ferdinando, and Bruno Basile. *Ragguaglio della schiavitù.* Rome, Salerno, 1996.

Mas Latrie, L. de. *Traités de paix et de commerce et documents divers concernant las relations des chrétiens avec les Arabes de l'Afrique septentrionale au Moyen âge.* New York, B. Franklin, 1964.

Matar, N. I. *Turks, Moors, and Englishmen in the Age of Discovery.* New York, Columbia University Press, 1999.

Mavroeide, F. *O Hellenismos sto Galata (1453–1600)* [Hellenism in Galata, 1453–1600]. Ioannina, Greece, Panepistemio Ioanninon, 1992.

———. *Symvole sten Historia tes Hellenikes Adelphotetas Venetias sto 16th Aiona* [Contribution to the History of the Greek Fraternity of Venice in the Sixteenth Century]. Athens, Vivliopoleion Note Karavia, 1976.

Meiss, Millard. "Bartolomeo Bulgarini altrimenti detto 'Ugolino Lorenzetti'?" *Rivista dell'arte*, 18, 1936, pp. 113–136.

Mendes-Flohr, Paul. "Fin-de-Siecle Orientalism, the Ostjuden and the Aesthetics of Jewish Affirmation," *Studies in Contemporary Jewry*, 1, 1984, pp. 96–139.

Merton, Robert King. *On the Shoulders of Giants; a Shandean Postscript.* New York, Free Press, 1965.

Messier, Ronald. "The Christian Community of Tunis at the Time of St. Louis' Crusade, A.D. 1270," in *Meeting of Two Worlds: Cultural Exchange between East and West during the Period of the Crusades,* ed. Vladimir Goss. Kalamazoo, Mich., Medieval Institute, 1986, pp. 241–255.

Metcalfe, Alex. *Muslims and Christians in Norman Sicily: Arabic Speakers and the End of Islam.* London, Routledge, 2003.

Metropolitan Museum of Art and John Wyndham Pope-Hennessy. *The Robert Lehman Collection.* New York, Metropolitan Museum of Art, 1987.

Milson, Menahem. "The Beginnings of Arabic and Islamic Studies at the Hebrew University of Jerusalem," *Judaism*, 45, 1996, pp. 169–183.

Momigliano, Arnaldo. *On Pagans, Jews, and Christians.* Wesleyan University Press/University Press of New England, 1987.

Montaigne, Michel de, trans. M. A. Screech. *The Complete Essays.* London/New York: Penguin Books, 1993.

Moore, R. I. *The Formation of a Persecuting Society: Power and Deviance in Western Europe (950–1250).* New York, Blackwell, 1987.

Most, Glenn W. *Doubting Thomas.* Cambridge, Mass., Harvard University Press, 2005.

Müller, Guido. *Weltpolitische Bildung und akademische Reform: Carl Heinrich Beckers Wissenschafts- und Hochschulpolitik 1908–1930.* Cologne, Böhlau, 1991.

Muller, Norman E. "Review," *Journal of the American Institute for Conservation*, 35, 1996, pp. 66–69.

Nelson, Robert S. "The Italian Appreciation and Appropriation of Illuminated Byzantine Manuscripts, ca. 1200–1450," *Dumbarton Oaks Papers*, 49, 1995, pp. 209–235.

Newbigin, Nerida. *Feste d'Oltrarno: Plays in Churches in Fifteenth-Century Florence.* Florence, L. S. Olschki, 1996.

Nirenberg, David. *Communities of Violence: The Persecution of Minorities in Medieval Europe.* Princeton, N.J., Princeton University Press, 1996.

Norman, Diana. *Painting in Late Medieval and Renaissance Siena (1260–1555).* New Haven, Yale University Press, 2003.

———. *Siena and the Virgin: Art and Politics in a Late Medieval City State.* New Haven, Yale University Press, 1999.

Obadiah ben Abraham, Maimonides, and Paul Fenton. *The Treatise of the Pool.* London, Octagon Press, 1981.

Ormsby, Eric. "The Born Schulmeister," *New Criterion,* 22(1), 2003, <http://newcriterion.com/archives/22/09/schulmeister/>.

Os, H. W. van. *Vecchietta and the Sacristy of the Siena Hospital Church: A Study in Renaissance Religious Symbolism.* The Hague: Ministerie van Cultuur Recreatie en Maatschappelijk Werk, 1974.

Osman, Aga. *Prisonnier des infidèles: un soldat ottoman dans l'Empire des Habsbourg,* trans. Frédéric Hitzel. Paris, Sindbad, 1998.

Panopoulou, A. "Oi Technites Naupegeion tou Chandaka kai ton Chanion kata to 16 kai 17 aiona" [The Shipyard Workers of Chandaka and Chania in the Sixteenth and Seventeenth Centuries], *Kretike Estia,* 4(3), 1989–90, pp. 173–194.

Panzac, Daniel. *La caravane maritime: Marins Europeens et Marchands Ottomans en Mediterranee (1680–1830).* Paris, C.R.N.S., 2004.

Parsons, Gerald. *Siena, Civil Religion, and the Sienese.* Aldershot, England/ Burlington, Vt., Ashgate, 2004.

Pashley, Robert, *Travels in Crete,* 2 vols. Athens, Dion N. Karavias, 1989.

Patrineli, Ch. G. "Kretikoi Emboroi ste Moldavia kai ten Polonia kata ton 16 Aiona" [Cretan Merchants in Moldavia and Poland during the Sixteenth Century], in *Pepragmena tou G'Diethnous Krētologikou Synedriou, Rethymnon, 18–23 Septembriou 1971.* Athens, 1973–75, p. 252.

Pedani Fabris, Maria Pia. *Dalla frontiera al confine.* Rome, Herder, 2002.

———. *La dimora della pace: considerazioni sulle capitolazioni tra i paesi islamici e l'Europa.* Venice, Cafoscarina, 1996.

———. *In nome del Gran Signore: inviati ottomani a Venezia dalla caduta di Costantinopoli alla guerra di Candia.* Venice, Deputazione editrice, 1994.

Petrarca, Francesco. *Petrarch's Songbook = Rerum vulgarium fragmenta,* trans. James Wyatt Cook. Binghamton, N.Y., Medieval & Renaissance Texts & Studies, 1995.

Pippidi, A. "Le portrait d'un homme d'affaires Cretois au XVI siecle," in *Pepragmena tou G'Diethnous Krētologikou Synedriou, Rethymnon, 18–23 Septembriou 1971.* Athens, Ministry of Culture, 1973–75, pp. 266–273.

Pirenne, Henri, *Mohammed and Charlemagne,* trans. Bernard Miall. London, Allen & Unwin, 1954.

———. "Mahomet et Charlemagne," *Revue Belge de Philologie et l'Histoire,* 1, 1922, pp. 77–86

Plumides, Giorgio. "Considerazioni sulla popolazione greca a Venezia nella seconda meta del '500," *Studi Veneziani,* 14, 1972, pp. 219–226.

Polites, N. G. *Eklogai apo ta tragoudia tou Hellenikou laou,* 7th edn. Athens, Bagionake, 1978.

Polizzotto, Lorenzo. *Children of the Promise: The Confraternity of the Purification and the Socialization of Youths in Florence, 1427–1785.* Oxford/New York, Oxford University Press, 2004.

Polzer, Joseph. "The 'Master of the Rebel Angels' Reconsidered," *Art Bulletin*, 63, 1981, pp. 563–584.

Pouradier Duteil-Loizidou, Anna. *Consulat de France à Larnaca, 1660–1696. Tome I: documents inédits pour servir à l'histoire de Chypre.* Nicosia: Centre de recherche scientifique, 1991.

Preto, Paolo. *Venezia e i turchi.* Florence: G. C. Sansoni, 1975.

Pulci, Antonia, James Wyatt Cook, and Barbara Collier Cook. *Florentine Drama for Convent and Festival: Seven Sacred Plays, The Other Voice in Early Modern Europe.* Chicago, University of Chicago Press, 1996.

Pullan, Brian S. *The Jews of Europe and the Inquisition of Venice, 1550–1670.* Totowa, N.J., Barnes & Noble, 1983.

Ravid, Benjamin. "A Tale of Three Cities and Their *Raison d'Etat*: Venice, Ancona and Livorno and the Competition for Jewish Merchants in the Sixteenth Century," *Mediterranean Historical Review*, 6(2), 1991, pp. 138–162.

Ravikovitch, Dahlia. "Lying upon the Waters," trans. Chana Bloch and Chana Kronfeld, *New Yorker*, 2(13) and 2(20), 2006, p. 153.

Raymond, André. *Artisans et commerçants au Caire au XVIIIe siècle.* Damascus, Institut français de Damas, 1973.

Raymundus, Xaverius Ochoa, and Aloisius Diez. *Summa de paenitentia.* Rome, Commentarium pro religiosis, 1976.

Reeves, Minou, and P. J. Stewart. *Muhammad in Europe.* Reading, Garnet, 2000.

Reif, Stefan C. *A Jewish Archive from Old Cairo: The History of Cambridge University's Genizah Collection, Culture and Civilisation in the Middle East.* Richmond, England, Curzon, 2000.

Reif, Stefan C., and Shulamit Reif. *The Cambridge Genizah Collections: Their Contents and Significance.* Cambridge, England, Cambridge University Press, 2002.

Reiss, Tom. *The Orientalist: Solving the Mystery of a Strange and a Dangerous Life.* Prince Frederick, Md., R.B. Large Print, 2005.

Ricci, Giovanni. *Ossessione turca: in una retrovia cristiana dell'Europa moderna.* Bologna, Il mulino, 2002.

Riising, Anne. "The Fate of Henri Pirenne's Theses on the Consequences of the Islamic Expansion," *Classica et Medievalia*, 13, 1952, pp. 87–130.

Robbert, Louise B. "Rialto Businessmen and Constantinople," *Dumbarton Oaks Papers*, 49, 1995, pp. 43–58.

Rostagno, Lucia. "Apostasia all'Islam e Santo Ufficio in un Processo dell'Inquisizione Veneziana," *Il Veltro*, 23(2–4), 1979, pp. 293–314.

——. *Mi faccio Turco: esperienze ed immagini dell'islam nell'Italia moderna.* Rome, Istituto per l'Oriente C. A. Nallino, 1983.

Rycaut, Paul. *The Present State of the Ottoman Empire.* London, J. Starkey & H. Brome, 1668.

Said, Edward. "The Clash of Definitions: On Samuel Huntington," *Reflections on Exile and Other Essays.* Cambridge, Mass., Harvard University Press, 2000, pp. 569–592.

——. *Orientalism.* New York, Pantheon, 1978.

Salzmann, Ariel. "Notes from Rome: Islam, Italy's Internal Frontier," in *Views from the Edge: Essays in Honor of Richard W. Bulliet,* ed. Neguin Yavari, Lawrence G. Potter, and Jean-Marc Ran Oppenheim. New York, Columbia University Press/Middle East Institute, 2004, pp. 240–254.

——. *Vita e Avventure di un Rinnegato.* Venice, Centro Internazionale della Grafica, 1992.

Sanfilippo, Matteo. "La Congregazione de Propaganda Fide e la dominazione turca sul Mediterraneo centro-orientale nel XVII secolo," in *I Turchi, il Mediterraneo e l'Europa,* ed. Giovanna Motta. Milan, FrancoAngeli, 1998, pp. 197–211.

Sanudo, Mario. *I Diarii.* Venice, F. Visentini, 1897–1903.

Schaeder, Hans Heinrich. "Die islamische Lehre vom Vollkommenen Menschen, ihre Herkunft und ihre dichterische Gestaltung," *Zeitschrift der Deutschen Morgenländischen Gesellschaft,* 79, 1925, pp. 192–268.

Scholem, Gershom Gerhard, Richard Sieburth, and Steven M. Wasserstrom. *The Fullness of Time: Poems.* Jerusalem, Ibis, 2003.

Scholem, Gershom. "'The Master of Mysticism.' Review of *From Berlin to Jerusalem: Memories of My Youth,* translated by Harry Zohn (Schocken)," *New York Review of Books,* 27(20), 1980.

Schorsh, Ismar. "The Myth of Sephardic Supremacy," *Leo Baeck Institute Yearbook,* 34, 1989, pp. 47–66.

Schulte, Christoph. *Deutschtum und Judentum: ein Disput unter Juden aus Deutschland.* Stuttgart, Reclam, 1993.

Schunk-Heller, Sabine. *Die Darstellung des ungläubigen Thomas in der italienischen Kunst bis um 1500 unter Berücksichtigung der lukanischen Ostentatio vulnerum.* Munich, Scaneg, 1995.

Schwoebel, Robert H. "Coexistence, Conversion, and the Crusade against the Turks," *Studies in the Renaissance,* 12, 1965, pp. 164–187.

Setton, Kenneth Meyer. *The Papacy and the Levant, (1204–1571),* vol. 2, *The Fifteenth Century.* Philadelphia, American Philosophical Society, 1978.

——. *Venice, Austria, and the Turks in the Seventeenth Century.* Philadelphia, American Philosophical Society, 1991.

Sfyroeras, V. *Ta Hellenika Plyromata tou Tourkikou Stolou.* Athens, 1968.

Shatzmiller, Joseph. "Travelling in the Mediterranean in 1563: The Testimony of Eliahu of Pesaro," in *The Mediterranean and the Jews:*

Banking, Finance and International Trade (XVI–XVII Centuries), ed. Ariel Toaff and Simon Schwartzfuchs. Ramat Gan, Israel, Bar Ilan University Press, 1989, pp. 237–248.

Shear, Adam. "Judah Halevi's *Kuzari* in the Haskalah: The Reinterpretation and Re-imagining of a Medieval Work," in *Renewing the Past, Reconfiguring Jewish Culture from al-Andalus to the Haskalah*, ed. Ross Brann and Adam Sutcliffe. University Park, University of Pennsylvania Press, 2004, pp. 71–93.

Şişman, Cengiz. "Sabetayciliğin Osmanli ve Türkiye Serüveni," *Tarih ve Toplum*, 223, 2002, pp. 4–6.

Skaug, Erling S. *Punch Marks from Giotto to Fra Angelico: Attribution, Chronology, and Workshop Relationships in Tuscan Panel Painting: With Particular Consideration to Florence, c.1330–1430*. Oslo, I.I.C. Nordic Group the Norwegian Section, 1994.

Soykut, Mustafa. *Image of the "Turk" in Italy: A History of the "Other" in Early Modern Europe, 1453–1683*. Berlin, K. Schwarz, 2001.

Spanakes, St. "Relazione de sr. Isepo Civran tornato di Prov. R. Gen.l di Candia 1639," *Kretika Chronika*, 21, 1969, pp. 365–458.

——. "Relazione del Nobil Huomo Zuanne Mocenigo ritornato provveditore generale del regno di Candia presentata nell'eccellentissimo consillio 17 Aprile 1589," in *Mnemeia tes Kretikes Istorias* [Monuments of Cretan history] (Herakleion, Greece), 1, 1940, pp. 1–169.

——. "Relazione Pietro Giustiniano capitan generale de Resmo 1630," in *Mnemeia tes Kretikes Istorias* [Monuments of Cretan History] (Herakleion, Greece), 5, 1969, pp. 1–252.

——. "1610 a 9 Genaro, Relation de s. Doflin Venier ritornato di duca di Candia," *Kretika Chronika*, 4, 1950, pp. 313–352.

Spencer, John R. "Spatial Imagery of the Annunciation in Fifteenth Century Florence," *Art Bulletin*, 37(4), 1955, pp. 273–280.

Steiner, Arthur. "History of the Jews in Kojetin (Kojetein) in Brno (Brunn), 1929," <http://members.tripod.com/~A30s/gold1a.html>.

Steinhoff, Judith. "Artistic Working Relationships after the Black Death," *Journal for the Society for Renaissance Studies*, 14, 2000, pp. 1–45.

Steinhoff-Morrison, Judith. "Bartolomeo Bulgarini and Sienese Painting of the Mid-Fourteenth Century," Ph.D. diss., Princeton University, 1990.

Stoianovich, Traian. "The Conquering Balkan Orthodox Merchant," *Journal of Economic History*, 20, 1960, pp. 234–313.

Strehlke, Carl Brandon. "Review," *Burlington Magazine*, 137, 1995, pp. 753–754.

Subrahmanyam, Sanjay. *Explorations in Connected History: From Tagus to the Ganges*. Oxford, Oxford University Press, 2005.

Taylor, Julie. *Muslims in Medieval Italy: The Colony at Lucera*. Lanham, Md., Lexington Books, 2003.

Thiriet, F. *La romaine venitienne au Moyen Age.* Paris, De Boccard, 1959.

Tolan, John Victor. *Saracens: Islam in the Medieval European Imagination.* New York, Columbia University Press, 2002.

Tsirpanles, Zacharias N. *Anekdota engrapha ek ton Archeion tou Vatikanou (1625–1667), Pegai kai meletai tes Kypriakes historias; 4.* Leukosia, Cyprus Research Centre, 1973.

Valensi, Lucette. "Inter-communal Relations and Changes in Religious Affiliation in the Middle East (Seventeenth to Nineteenth Centuries)," *Comparative Study of Society and History,* 39, 1997, pp. 251–269.

Vatin, Jean-Claude. "Le Voyage: Elements pour Une Taxonomie," in *La Fuite en Egypte: Supplément aux Voyages Européens en Orient,* ed. Jean-Claude Vatin. Cairo, C.E.D.E.J., 1989, pp. 9–50.

Vaughan, Dorothy Margaret. *Europe and the Turk: A Pattern of Alliances, 1350–1700.* Liverpool, Liverpool University Press, 1954.

Vercellin, Giorgio, and Biblioteca nazionale marciana. *Venezia e l'origine della stampa in caratteri arabi.* Padova, Il poligrafo, 2001.

Viallon, Marie F. *Venise et la porte Ottomane (1453–1566): un siècle de relations vénéto-ottomanes, de la prise de Constantinople à la mort de Soliman.* Paris, Economica, 1995.

Vlassopoulos, N. St. *Ionioi Emboroi kai Karavokyrides ste Mesogeio 16os–18os Aionas* [Ionian Merchants and Shipowners in the Mediterranean 16th–18th Centuries]. Athens, Finatec-Multimedia, 2001.

Wasserstrom, Steven M. *Between Muslim and Jew: The Problem of Symbiosis under Early Islam.* Princeton, N.J., Princeton University Press, 1995.

——. "Hans Jonas in Marburg, 1928," in *Judaism and the Phenomenon of Life: The Legacy of Hans Jonas,* ed. Hava Samuelson and Christian Wiese. Leiden, The Netherlands: E. J. Brill, forthcoming.

——. "Jewish–Muslim Relations in the Context of Andalusian Emigration," *Christians, Muslims and Jews in Medieval and Early Modern Spain,* ed. Mark D. Meyerson and Edward D. English. Notre Dame, Ind., University of Notre Dame Press, 1999, pp. 69–91.

——. "Recent Works on the 'Creative Symbiosis' of Judaism and Islam," *Religious Studies Review,* 16, 1990, pp. 42–47.

——. *Religion after Religion: Gershom Scholem, Mircea Eliade, and Henry Corbin at Eranos.* Princeton, N.J., Princeton University Press, 1999.

Winroth, Anders. *The Making of Gratian's Decretum.* Cambridge, England, Cambridge University Press, 2000.

Yapp, M. E. "Europe in the Turkish Mirror," *Past and Present,* 137, 1992, pp. 134–155

Yehoshua, Abraham B. *A Journey to the End of the Millenium.* New York, Doubleday, 1999.

Yerushalmi, Yosef Hayim. Zakhor, *Jewish History and Jewish Memory, the Samuel and Althea Stroum Lectures in Jewish Studies.* New York, Schocken Books/Pantheon Books, 1989.

Zammit Ciantar, Joe. *A Benedictine's Notes on Seventeenth-Century Malta.* Hal Tarxien, Malta, Gutenberg Press, 1998.

INDEX